TOMMY'S WORLD

With charm, warmth and humour, Billy Hopkins tells the story of his beloved dad...

Tommy Hopkins' early years aren't very promising. Born at the end of the nineteenth century in a slum district of Manchester, he's blessed with loving parents, but they don't have two ha'pennies to rub together. At school, he and his friends plot money-making schemes and play lots of football, while learning enough to keep the teachers off their backs. Then, leaving the playground behind, Tommy finds employment in Manchester's Smithfield market, where he works his way up to become a porter, and where, amongst the young women who catch his eye, is Kate Lally – who may just be the love of his life.

TOMMY'S WORLD

TOMMY'S WORLD

by

Billy Hopkins

Magna Large Print Books
Long Preston, North Yorkshire,
BD23 4ND, England.

British Library Cataloguing in Publication Data.

Hopkins, Billy
    Tommy's world.

        A catalogue record of this book is
        available from the British Library

        ISBN   978-0-7505-3390-4

First published in Great Britain in 2009 by
Headline Publishing Group

Copyright © 2009 Wilfred Hopkins

Cover illustration © Rod Ashford

The right of Wilfred Hopkins to be identified as the author of this work
has been asserted by him in accordance with the Copyright, Designs
and Patents Act, 1988

Published in Large Print 2011 by arrangement with
Headline Publishing Group Ltd.

Magna Large Print is an imprint of Library Magna Books Ltd.

Printed and bound in Great Britain by
T.J. (International) Ltd., Cornwall, PL28 8RW

I dedicate this book to
the memory of my father,
Tommy Hopkins (1886-1973)

Acknowledgements

Though this is the seventh book that I have written, it is really part of one story in seven episodes: *Tommy's World, Kate's Story, Our Kid, High Hopes, Going Places, Anything Goes* and *Whatever Next!* This is probably the best order in which to read them but not absolutely essential since each book should stand in its own right.

There are many people whom I should like to thank for their help in reading and making valuable comments on early drafts. My own children, especially Catherine, Peter and Paul and, as always, special thanks must go to my wife Clare. I am indebted, too, to Steve Lovering, Peter Rawcliffe and Manchester author Bill Keeth for their invaluable help in research and tracking down various references.

In the publishing world, I wish to express my gratitude to all those who have made my books possible. At Blake Friedmann Literary Agency: to Isobel Dixon and support staff. At Headline Book Publishing: to Fiction Publishing Director, Marion Donaldson; Fiction Managing Editor, Nicky Jeanes; copy editor, Jane Heller; and to all backroom staff involved in proof-reading, cover design, promotion and sales.

Finally my thanks go out to all those people

who have read my books, visited my website (*www.billysbooks.info*) and given me encouragement and support with their many letters and emails (*billy@billysbooks.info*). These are very much appreciated.

Foreword

When my dad was just over eighty years of age, I used to go with him to his local pub, the New Broom, on the Langley Estate, Middleton. There, over a pint, he would tell me about some of his experiences of living and working in Manchester around the beginning of the last century. I was unable to tape-record his story as I did with my mother's tale a few years later, but I did jot down a few notes from memory. The present book told in Tommy's voice is based on these notes.

The book is a mixture of fact and fiction. While the basic facts of his life are true, I cannot vouch for the accuracy of some of his stories nor of the actual words used in dialogues that took place. In addition, some of the characters in the book are composites of people described by him, and names, with the exception of close relatives, have been changed to protect their privacy and that of their families and descendants. The names of streets and places, however, are authentic, being those that appeared on nineteenth-century maps of Manchester, although many street names have since changed.

At the present time (2009) we are being warned that we must expect to go through a tough period of belt-tightening because of a severe economic recession. In addition, we are faced with threats to our health and well-being from terrorists, crime, bugs and I don't know what else. But in writing this story, I was given a sharp reminder of the extreme hardships of poverty and deprivation that our predecessors had to endure just over a century ago, and I could not help reflecting that we are still having it easy by comparison.

I hope you derive some pleasure from reading the book because our great-grandparents always enjoyed a ready sense of humour no matter what, and Tommy's life story may help us to see our own trials and tribulations in perspective. If the story conveys to you a fraction of the hard times that our forefathers underwent, then I feel my labours have not been in vain.

Billy Hopkins
July 2009

Give me a sense of humour O Lord,
Give me the grace to see a joke,
To get some happiness from life,
And pass it on to other folk.

Prayer in Chester Cathedral

Part I

Chapter One

Life, they say, is a lottery. Being conceived, born, and then living to tell the tale are remarkable feats in themselves for anyone, anywhere, at any time. But to achieve these things at the end of the nineteenth century in a slum district of Manchester is nothing less than miraculous.

Although I must have been present at my own birth, I don't remember too much about it and certainly can't remember any of the details. So, in telling you about these events, I've had to rely on other evidence, such as official documents and what other people have said. For instance, my birth certificate tells me that I was born on Monday, 4 October 1886 in St Michael's Ward at 147 Teignmouth Street, Collyhurst, one of the poorest inner-city suburbs. A Monday child, you notice. How did that rhyme go again?

Monday's child is fair of face,
Tuesday's child is full of grace,
Wednesday's child is full of woe,
Thursday's child has far to go.
Friday's child is loving and giving,
Saturday's child works hard for a living,
And the child that is born on the Sabbath Day,
Is bonny and blithe and good and gay.

Later on, when I got to see my face in the mirror,

I saw how daft the rhyme was 'cos I had a face like one of those gargoyles on St Chad's Church. And when you've heard my story, you'll think maybe I was born two days too early and that a Wednesday predicting a life full of woe might have been a more fitting day for me to come into this world. Anyroad, people said I was lucky to be here at all 'cos my mother had had two miscarriages before me and it was only after consulting Dr Becker, our local doctor, and following his medical advice (which my dad had to pawn his Sunday suit to pay for) that I managed to stay alive in the womb until it was time to pop my head out. Getting myself born and then surviving were probably the two greatest achievements of my life 'cos most of the babies born around that time in our part of the world never got past the first hurdle. A magazine that I was reading in the barber's the other day said that out of every ten working-class preg-nancies, only half the kids made it to their first birthday. And after that, there were lots of nasty diseases lurking about the place ready to kill off the newborn infants. Like measles, diphtheria, scarlet fever, and whooping cough to name but a few. No wonder people said I was lucky to be here at all.

I was an only child and 'only' children are sup-posed to be spoiled. No hope of that happening to me, seeing how my mam and dad didn't have two ha'pennies to rub together even though my dad had quite a good job and our home, as I remember it, was one filled with love, affection and laughter. All the same, I think they worried about me all the time because my birth had been that dodgy, they were afraid they might lose me at any time. Maybe they had good reason to be worried and, when you've heard what happened to young Herbert Lamb, my best pal, you'll understand why.

The Lamb family were considered to be a bit above the rest of us in the social scale 'cos they lived in an end terrace house in Paley Street, the one next to ours. I was about two years old at this time and so was Herbert. He was a snub-nosed likeable little kid, with curly fair hair and as bright as a button, curious about everything that came into his hands. Though not all that well-off, his mam and dad were always buying toys for him to play with, including a miniature Punch and Judy show, a wooden engine with carriages, a Noah's Ark with little animals, and glove puppets. They had avoided a fort and lead toy soldiers in case Herbert was tempted to put them in his mouth and swallow them.

'Everything he gets his hands on,' Annie Lamb said to my mam one day, 'he has to find out what it's made of, what it can do, what it tastes like and whether it's nice to eat. We have to watch him like a hawk.'

I loved it when Mam took me round to their house to play because Herbert not only had the sort of toys I could only dream about but also a sandpit in the back yard which his dad had built by lugging home three or four bags of sand from the building site where he was a bricklayer.

One of the biggest problems we had in those days in Collyhurst was dealing with the various kinds of vermin that plagued the area. Every home was tormented by common house pests like

21

mice, rats, fleas, lice, cockroaches and bedbugs, and it was a never-ending struggle to keep them at bay. Each family had its own favourite solution for dealing with the pests. Some favoured traps, others put down poisons or disinfectants and, in extreme cases, smoke bombs. My own mam and dad preferred traps to poisons in case I ever tried to sample any of the latter if left lying around. The best answer, Mam maintained, was strict hygiene in all washing of floors and bedlinen, though in extreme cases it could be necessary to bring in outside help from the health authorities.

Needless to say, Herbert and I were not a bit bothered by all the fuss our parents made about these things and were only too happy to play in the mud with whatever materials came to hand.

The Lambs were particularly bothered by bedbugs and they tried everything in their power to get rid of them but to no avail. One morning they found Herbert covered in bites – minor swellings in the skin which began to itch the little lad like mad.

'I'm at my wits' end as to what to do next,' Annie Lamb told Mam. 'We've managed to get rid of the mice, the rats and the cockroaches but the bedbugs seem to be getting worse. Their eggs are in the cracks in the furniture, the mattresses, and even behind the wallpaper. It's so hard to kill them as they hide during the day and only come out at night.'

Mam advised washing all bedlinen in strong disinfectant.

'I've tried all that,' said Annie Lamb. 'I'm at the end of my tether with the bloody things.'

Some time later, their old granny visiting the Lambs advised using carbolic acid placed in a saucer and then put under the wardrobe in their bedroom.

'The fumes from the acid will rise up and kill all the bugs behind the wallpaper,' the old granny explained.

'I do hope so. I'll try anything,' replied Annie. 'We can't go on living with these bloody bugs. They're making our lives a misery.'

They adopted the advice and placed the saucer with the acid under the wardrobe right at the back. It worked and the number of bug bites began to diminish. Then one terrible day, disaster struck.

One morning when Annie Lamb was busy in the cellar doing the laundry, Herbert wandered off and began exploring. He climbed the stairs into the bedroom. Then somehow or other and in some way never fully understood or explained, he managed to reach under the wardrobe and pull out the saucer. Thinking the coloured liquid was some kind of mineral drink like Tizer, my best pal, Herbert, drank the acid. In the cellar, his mam heard the agonized screams and rushed up to him. It's hard to imagine the horror of the scene. Alerted by the screams and the pandemonium, neighbours rushed into the house to help but no one knew what to do. Should they force Herbert to drink water, milk, make him vomit, or what? There was no time to weigh up alternatives; no time to go for a doctor or the police in the hope they would organize a wheeled litter trolley to take him to hospital. Joe Murray, an unemployed man who lived a couple of doors down, took matters in hand by picking up the lifeless body of Herbert and running the three miles to Ancoats Hospital with him in his arms. But it was too late. Herbert was already dead when he got him there. Poor Herbert died a terrible death and for weeks afterwards the district was in shock. As for me, I missed him terribly. My chief sorrow was that not only had I lost my best playmate but also his wonderful toys because after the funeral, his parents gave them to the hospital. That was my first experience of tragedy, of losing someone close to me and, even at that tender age, I realized in some vague way that it was best not to expect things, whether people or toys, to last for ever because they could easily be snatched away without any warning. I played on my own for a while but, as you will hear, I made other friends a bit later, this time with two little girls who lived further down our street.

But given the terrible tragedy of poor Herbert, was it any wonder that my own mam and dad were so anxious that a similar accident might happen to me?

I was given my name by Mam and Dad of course and so I had no choice in the matter. But, thank God, they didn't name me Marmaduke or Lucifer or anything like that. Or, worse, a name that could be a boy's *or* a girl's name, such as Pat or Evelyn. Imagine the trouble I'd have had at school with those names.

But why Thomas? Maybe it was because that was my dad's name. He was a real doubting

Thomas, always starting his sentences with things like, 'It's unbelievable!' or 'I can't believe what's just happened...' He told me that my grandad was just the same and that's where he'd picked up this habit. But I think it's more probable that he was given the name 'cos that was his own dad's name and it was passed down the line to me. So now you know how I got my handle. Thomas the Third. Sometimes there was a mix-up with me having the same name as my dad. For example, if Mam called, 'Come here, Thomas. I want to show you something,' both of us would pipe up with, 'Which one do you mean? Little Thomas or Big Thomas?' So they decided to shorten my name to Tom, but that had such weird notions attached to it, for instance peeping Tom, or 'Tom, Tom the piper's son who stole a pig and away did run'. Later my name was changed again to Tommy 'cos in their opinion it was more lovey-dovey, though I thought it was namby-pamby. Most kids around that time had their names changed like this. So Sam became Sammy; Jim, Jimmy; Alf, Alfie.

There were other reasons that I hated the name Tommy. For a start it made me sound like somebody's stomach or a piece of bread, a toffee or even a Red Indian's tomahawk. And later when I went to school, the other kids made fun of me by calling me Tom-tom as if I was an African drum. And whenever I did or said something wrong, the teacher was bound to say, 'Tommy-rot,' and everyone had a good laugh at me. At first, that is. Until I learned to look after myself and give as much as I got. It could have been worse, I suppose. Imagine having a name like Richard shortened to Dick or

William shortened to Willie. You can be sure I'd have had problems with those names at school. Why, I'd have been thumped black and blue preserving my honour.

And while on the subject of names, in our family we were each rationed to just one apiece and one only. Dad was simply Thomas and, on my mother's side, her whole family had just the one Christian name each: Grandad Mitchell was Owen, Grandma was Bridget, and their kids were Patrick, Dorothy, James and Mary, my mother.

Toffs and famous people seem to need two or more, like William Ewart Gladstone, David Lloyd George – or fancy being stuck with a handle like Herbert Beerbohm Tree. As for Churchill, he had not only Winston but about another twenty, while Queen Victoria needed about fifty.

Chapter Two

The house we lived in was a back-to-back, two-up and two-down, though strictly speaking it should have been two-up and three-down 'cos we had a cellar, made obvious to everybody by the coalhole with the iron lid on the pavement outside our front door. For miles and miles, the houses were identical, row after row of streets blackened by the soot and grime that belched from the hundreds of factories in the district. Some of the street names give an idea of the industries that were carried on around us: Iron Street, Zinc

Street, Copper Street, Pump Street, Foundry Street. For the most part the people of the district were respectable working-class folk who worked hard for a living, though the area also had its share of lowlife – thieves, jailbirds, drunkards and loose women.

Inside our house, the two upstairs rooms were our bedrooms while downstairs we had a kitchen-cum-dining room, and a best room or parlour for special occasions like Christmas or a birthday and for entertaining important visitors, like a priest or a doctor. In our parlour there was a horsehair sofa and a big mahogany dresser with statues of the Sacred Heart and Our Lady. The wooden floorboards were covered with a cheap oilcloth but there was a bright coloured peg rug on the hearth. The only luxuries I can remember were the two pictures which Mam had picked up at our church's jumble sale and which now hung proudly on our walls: Rubens' 'Daniel in the Den of Lions' and Sir Joshua Reynolds' 'Moses in the Bulrushes'. Upstairs there was my cot, a couple of beds, a wardrobe and a dressing table bought second-hand when Mam and Dad first married.

At the back was a small yard with a tin bath (much used by Dad) hanging on a big nail on the wall. And that was it. No lavatory of our own and no running water. The privies in the back entry were shared by the block and, even though there was a big reservoir at Longendale, there were only three standpipes for the whole street of forty-eight houses. All this meant queues at most times of the day for the privies and for water. For light, we still used oil lamps as the gas pipes being installed by the new gasworks had not yet reached our street.

In the living room, there was no kitchen as such but in the corner of the room there was a slop-stone for washing the pots, the pans and ourselves. Cooking was done on a big iron range which had an oven for roasting and baking while the black-leaded fireplace had a hob for boiling kettles and heating up pans of water. There was a brass fender and fire irons on the hearth and a fireguard to stop me from falling into the fire. Above it all was the mantelpiece with the tasselled pelmet and the big black chiming clock which had been a wedding present from Mam's parents. We didn't have much in the way of furniture. Taking up most of the space in the dining room was a big pine table and four wooden hardback chairs. At Christmas and at Easter, the table was decorated in a magnificent plush velvet maroon table cover. I recall how my heart was filled with a simple joy on seeing that cover brought out and unwrapped from its tissue paper packing 'cos it signalled the coming of the holidays when Dad didn't have to go to work for a couple of days and we might have trips out. That plush velvet table-cloth never failed to conjure up memories of those happy occasions for me.

Christmas was of course the most special of these. I listened avidly to the stories of baby Jesus and his birth in the stable at Bethlehem. A visit to the crib at St Chad's was for me one of the high-lights of the season because the church went to a great deal of trouble to create an authentic scene of the stable, complete with the ox, the ass, the statues of St Joseph, Our Lady and the little baby

28

in the cradle. Even the bright star in the East and the three wise men standing at the entrance to the stable were on display. At Mass, the choir sang all the best known carols of the day: 'Silent Night', 'The First Noel', 'Good King Wenceslas', 'O Little Town'.

Never to be forgotten was the story of Father Christmas and his journey with his reindeers from the North Pole. It was a magic wonderland and I believed every word they told me about him. One Christmas, it must have been 1890 because I was about four years old, I dutifully hung up one of Dad's big socks at the end of the bed and, lo and behold, next morning I found inside it an apple, a tangerine, and a bar of Fry's chocolate, while at the foot of the bed was something I'd specially asked for: a Noah's Ark with lots of wooden animals just like the ones that Herbert Lamb used to have before his accident.

We went to nine o'clock Mass at St Chad's and I can remember still how impatient and fidgety I was during the service. How I longed to get back home to play with my new toy! Mam spent the rest of the day preparing the dinner while Dad simply put his feet up in front of the fire and smoked a cigar. The rich smell of Havana tobacco lingers in my nostrils still! Dad's greatest joy of the day was not having to get up early to go to that factory of his.

On Boxing Day we joined Mam's family, the Mitchells, for dinner and party games, like blind man's buff, pass the parcel, pin the tail on the donkey, guess who (when the blindfolded victim tried to identify a person by feeling his face),

29

consequences and reading out the silly sentences which built up as a folded piece of paper was passed around. I was too young to join in most of them but I can still remember how the two lads of the family, Patrick and Jamesey, were always acting the fool and never took any of the rules seriously. Mam and her younger twenty-two-year-old sister, Dorothy, sang a harmonized version of 'Angels We Have Heard on High', with the rest of the family letting rip on the 'Gloria!' It gave me a warm feeling inside to see my mother and my aunt so friendly and performing together. We finished the visit with communal singing – Grandad Owen had a fine Irish tenor voice – and finally with more Christmas carols. Happy days!

Before the age of two and a half, life consisted simply of the basic bodily functions: sleeping, eating and evacuation, summed up by some wit or other in a humorous definition: 'A baby,' he said, 'is an alimentary tract with a loud squawk at one end and no respectability at the other.' In those early days, my social life was no more than one big confusion of faces, figures and noises with a stream of gigantic monsters picking me up and making funny cooing sounds over me. After the age of about two and a half or three, however, things began to make a little more sense and I started to remember things, often quite vividly. As a party piece to entertain relatives and visitors, I was taught to stand on a chair and to recite like a trained monkey: 'My name is Tommy Hopkins and I live at number one four seven Teignmouth Street.' For this I was given a toffee or, if I was lucky, a chocolate biscuit.

The centre of the world whirling about me was Mam, always present, always ready to minister to my every need. Never far from my immediate gaze, she was the most important person in my universe; nobody else mattered. If ever she wasn't around, I was in a state of constant anxiety in case something had happened to her and she wouldn't be coming back. And since I'd had such a dodgy entry into this world, she in turn pampered me in case I might be somehow suddenly snatched away from her. So, in a way, I suppose I *was* spoiled. Before her marriage she had been a bracemaker at Blair's corset factory on Ancoats Lane but, on marrying, she had given up work on Dad's insistence. Like him, she was very proud of her work and liked to boast about it when she got the chance.

'Those body braces and corsets I worked on at Blair's were made with real leather and made to last. None of your elastic rubbish.'

Just the same, Dad didn't want her to continue there. 'No wife of mine is going to go out to work,' he used to say. 'A woman's place is in the home and I'll not have my missus working, as long as I have a pair of hands to work with and can look after my family. I'll not have her going off to labour in some bloody factory for slave wages. No, her place is here at home where she doesn't have to work so hard and can take things easy doing homely things like shopping, cooking, baking, washing, ironing, and looking after young Tommy.'

I wasn't sure whether Dad was being funny or

31

not until Mam dug him playfully in the ribs and laughed.

I loved the way her bright blue Irish eyes seemed to dance when she laughed like this and, when she did, I used to think how lucky I was to have such a nice-looking mother with her auburn hair and beautiful rosy complexion.

'If that's what you call taking things easy,' she'd reply, 'I think I'll go back to the corset factory. Now that was easy compared to looking after this house and little Tommy here.'

It was true what Mam was saying because she was run off her feet most of the day doing all the things Dad had dismissed as 'not having to work so hard'. Houses in the area were sometimes described as 'slums' but if that was supposed to mean grimy and uncared-for, it was entirely the wrong word. Like many other housewives in the district, Mam believed in keeping the house spotless and couldn't abide muck of any kind. In the summer there were lots of flies and other insects to deal with and she was constantly replacing the sticky fly-paper which hung from the ceiling and which seemed to get full in a matter of hours. Perhaps I had a cruel streak even then but I can remember how I loved to hear the crackling sound of the dead flies burning when she threw the old fly-paper into the fire. Mam fought an endless battle against the dirt, the dust and the soot thrown up by the numerous factory chimneys and the thousands of household fires. Her days were taken up completely doing all the 'easy' things Dad had listed. At night when the day's labouring was over, she liked nothing better than to sit down in her rocking chair and rest her weary bones.

Her day began at half past five when the district knocker-up rapped on our window with his long pole and shouted up, 'Come on, 'Opkins lot, let's be having you outa them there beds. Time to go to work.' Mam would get up, light the fire and brew a pot of tea for Dad who had to be at work by six o'clock. While all this was going on, I used to lie there in my cot listening to the clickety-clack of clogs along the pavements as workers made their way to their places of work – the mills, the factories and the foundries. When Dad had gone, she went out to a standpipe in the street and filled buckets and pans with water for the day.

Out of all her chores, the worst was definitely the one involving the cleaning of our privy in the back alley. There were four adjoining privies divided into four closets for our block of sixteen houses which could have housed up to a hundred people or more. Our closet was meant for numbers 143, 145, 147 and 149 and the big key for it was kept behind a loose brick in the wall. The people living in these four houses were responsible for keeping their own privy clean. The emptying of the privies was left to the night soil men who came along the alleyway with their cart in the early hours of Thursday. What a stench! There was no escaping it even if you closed all the doors and windows tight. The fumes were enough to suffocate you.

The routine for using and cleaning the privy sounds reasonable enough until you look at the people we had to share it with – our nearest neighbours, that is. The end house, number 149, was occupied by the Gannon family, downright villains and a bunch of criminal layabouts if ever there was one, with the family living in the four rooms and God knows how many resident lodgers in the cellar. Most of the time they seemed to be drunk or drugged on laudanum which was so cheap and easy to buy from Wiseman's, the local chemist's shop, on Rochdale Road. Their house was in terrible condition with its broken boarded-up windows, leaking roof, and doors falling off the hinges. Neither the Gannons nor the landlord bothered to repair anything. Everyone in the street knew about the family and they were regarded as the lowest of the low. Old man Gannon was in and out of prison for drunkenness and violence, and as for the mother, she was in the habit of fighting, usually other women, after the boozers closed on a Friday night. One night it took three policemen to get the cuffs on her before they carted her off to Willert Street police station on a wheelbarrow.

'Take your bleeding hands off me,' she screeched, 'or I'll have the bleeding law on you.'

When it was explained to her that they were the law, she went quiet.

Mam and Dad tried to protect me from hearing this swearing.

'Such bad language,' Mam said. 'The worst in the street. We don't want our lad picking it up. Take him indoors, Thomas.'

The Gannons had two grown-up sons, Jed and Jake, and the family made their living by stealing and flogging their ill-gotten gains in pubs like the

34

Brown Cow and the Bull's Head in Woodward Street. When not selling their loot, the family earned extra lolly by chopping firewood in the back yard and hawking the bundles round the nearby streets. God knows where they got the wood from and no one dared to ask. But when it came to swilling out the privy, there was no way any of them would be taking their turn. They just emptied their chamber pots in the back alley.

No one in the street trusted them; they'd have stolen the shirt off your back given the chance.

'It's got so I can't hang the washing out in the back yard in case their lads nip over the wall and nick it when I'm not looking,' Mam said.

At number 143 lived Mr and Mrs Sugarman but there was no chance of either of them doing a stint. Mr Sugarman had once been a tailor but now they were over eighty years old and down on their luck. The missus could hardly walk, let alone get down on her knees to scrub out the privy. Mam often did their shopping for them when they could not get out themselves and they were always glad of help and a bit of conversation as no one else seemed to visit them. That left Mr and Mrs Buckley at 145. A friendly and respectable family who tried to hold up their heads and keep their dignity, no easy task in Collyhurst. Sid Buckley worked long hours at the Irkdale iron factory and so we didn't see much of him but Bella Buckley and my mam got on well together and between them they kept the privy clean by washing it out each day. Except for the Gannons, neighbours on the street got on well together too. On warm summer evenings, people used to sit out on chairs or stools and call out to each other, exchanging views and opinions on various happenings.

'Has your 'Arry found a job yet?' 'How's your Andy goin' on in the army?' 'Our Vera's never been the same since she came out of Ancoats after that last operation.'

Further up the street at the gable end lived Mr and Mrs O'Gara with their two daughters, Alice and Josie. Mr O'Gara was a train driver with the Lancashire and Yorkshire Railway and was something of a mystery, like Mr Buckley, as we hardly caught sight of him. Alice and her younger sister often came to play down our end of the street and they were forever fussing and bossing me about as if I were one of their dolls whenever my mam left me outside the front door in my bassinet. The two girls went to St Oswald's Anglican School on Rochdale Road. Sitting there in my chariot, I used to watch the women donkey-stoning their steps and window sills, then mopping and scouring the flags outside the front doors. And there was always a procession of visitors to the street: the milkman who used to wiggle my cheeks and say, 'Chubby cheeks,' before ladling out his milk from his big churn; the rent man who forever had problems catching the Gannons in; the tallyman who collected families' weekly payments for things bought on the never-never; the insurance man who came on a big sit-up-and-beg bike; the knife grinder; the gypsies with their paper flowers; and finally the rag-and-bone man who sounded like his own donkey in agony when he bawled out, 'Rag bone!', a piercing cry that could be heard several streets away. I liked him, though, because he usually handed me a paper windmill on a stick even when we had no old clothes or bits of iron to give him.

Chapter Three

During the week we didn't see much of my dad as he was out at work most of the day. He had a good job as a mechanic at William Berry's blacking factory and even though it was only a cock's stride away in Fitzgeorge Street on Barney's waste ground, he didn't get back home until around six or seven o'clock at night. He worked half a day on Saturdays. In the district we were regarded as being quite well-off 'cos Dad was in regular work in a skilled occupation and earned what was seen as a good wage. He was paid eighteen shillings for a seventy-hour week and people said he was one of the lucky ones to have a job at all as many men in the district had to scrape a living the best way they could on next to nothing.

'The money doesn't go far,' Mam said. 'The rent's four-and-six, food's eight, soap and washing materials and all that stuff, two. Then after the clothing-club man and the insurance man have taken their cut, there's not much left, I can tell you.'

When Dad got home after work, Mam always had a mug of hot, sweet tea ready for him to help him recover and relax after his long day at the factory. He was always as black as the ace of spades after working on the boot polish machines. His overalls were saturated in soot and, despite wearing a cap all day, so was his hair; the stuff got right down into the pores of his skin. As he supped his tea avidly, I used to study his black face with the two white eyes peering out at me. It meant he had to have a thorough wash-down standing in the tin bath in the cellar warmed by the fire under the boiler which Mam had to heat up for him every night. While he was relaxing with his mug of tea, Mam and me used to take our 'wash-downs' first. Then Dad would use the same water immediately after us as we couldn't afford to boil up a second lot. Mam and I would go back upstairs to let Dad clean up in privacy. For me it was also a case of nit-hunting every night when, after washing my hair with Lifebuoy Disinfectant Soap, she would go on a safari hunt searching for the pests, calling out, 'Got one!' when one was trapped in the fine-tooth comb. She would kill it with the back of her thumbnail.

Dad was very proud of his work and was for-ever boasting about the company. He always treated me like a grown-up, explaining things to me, and I loved him for it. He'd say, 'William Berry, manufacturer of waterproof blacking. Best boot polish in the world by appointment to her Imperial Majesty Queen Victoria. And did you know that the great writer Charles Dickens once worked in a blacking factory as a youngster?'

'What do you make blacking out of, Dad?' I asked.

'We make it out of chimney soot, son, and a few other things mixed in.'

Mam smiled. 'Don't tell the lad fibs, Thomas.'

'No, it's true, Mary. We do use soot. It's called lampblack and we use lots and lots of the stuff. That's why Berry's works is on Barney's waste ground – so as to be near the brick kilns where we get tons of soot from the chimneys.'

My dad seemed to have a thing about boots and shoes. Not only did he mend his and mine on his last in the cellar, he often told us funny stories about things that happened in the blacking trade.

'Yesterday, a young lad started work with us and all the workers kept patting him on his face and nose like this.' He grinned, showing me how it was done. 'Then they would say, "Welcome to Berry's, lad," leaving little black spots on the youngster's face – the boy didn't know about them until he looked in the mirror.'

Then he hugged and kissed me goodnight. I can still remember how his moustache tickled. It was only after he'd gone downstairs and Mam showed me *my* face in the mirror that I saw how he'd tricked me and left black smudges on my nose too. I used to tell him that his moustache made him look like a buffalo. 'Oh, is that so?' he used to answer, tickling and making me giggle helplessly.

Sometimes he brought home samples from work and showed me how to polish shoes properly – his own were always gleaming so bright you could see your face in them.

'You can always tell a man's character by the state of his shoes,' he used to say. 'Show me a man who doesn't take care of his footwear and

39

I'll show you a man with no pride and no principles. Shiny shoes show that a man cares about his appearance. Now, as for polishing your shoes: before you begin, check that your boots are clean and dry,' he said, picking up my little boots to demonstrate. 'Then brush on the blacking evenly with the small brush and make sure you cover everything including the tongue, and even the eyelet holes. Next, take the bigger brush and polish everything with gusto like this,' he said, suiting the action to the words. 'Lastly, apply the finishing touch with a clean flannelette cloth and start buffing for all you're worth, making it crack like a whip. If you want an extra shine, you can rub the polish in gently with a little spit and you'll end up with a mirror-like, high-gloss finish that any sergeant major in the land would be proud of.'

This spit-and-polish method was something I remembered and practised for the rest of my days.

Chapter Four

Monday in our house, and most other working-class homes in the district, meant washing day, with Mam and me spending the whole morning in the cellar where the boiler gave off so much steam that you could hardly see your hand in front of you. There seemed to be a lot of scrubbing with Lifebuoy soap on a washboard and the use of Robin's starch on Dad's collars as he liked them to be stiff and white. After that, it was time to put the clothes through the mangle before hanging them up in the yard or, in bad weather, on the rope pulley in the kitchen. I spent my time balancing on the six-legged washing dolly and trying to walk like a wooden man, though half the time I fell off and landed on my backside. The washday chores usually stretched into a second day when Mam tackled the ironing, which involved heating up a couple of big irons on the kitchen range and then running them over the clothes to smooth out the creases.

When the washing was done, Mam was glad to get out of the steam and so, after a dinner of lentil soup made from the Sunday stock, she used to put on her shawl if the weather was nice and take me shopping on Rochdale Road. Our first call was the Co-op for a few groceries, then to the UCP shop to buy some tripe for Dad's tea. I never knew what they saw in it 'cos I once tasted the stuff and it was like eating rubber with vinegar on it. On the way back, we would stop at St Oswald's Grove where there was a cow and a donkey grazing in the field. I was completely bedazzled by the sight of these two strange creatures. In the case of the donkey, it was love at first sight. We gazed into each other's eyes and he looked so sad, there was an immediate bond between us right from the word go.

'One day, Mam,' I said, 'I'll have my own donkey. You'll see.'

'That'll be the day.' She laughed. 'We'd have to be rich toffs for you to have your own donkey.'

Every Monday after the laundry chore, I looked forward to our walk and in August we were even able to pick a few blackberries along the way which Mam baked into a pie. One day, however, we came back home to something of a disaster. Dad's best white Sunday shirt was missing from the clothes line and, what was worse, the tin bath was gone from the nail on the wall.

Mam was very upset. She sat down at the table, put her head in her hands and began to cry 'cos the missing things were precious in our house.

'I don't know what your father will say,' she wept. 'Who could have taken them? And why? Your dad'll be furious.'

She was right about Dad. He hit the roof when he got the news.

'No need to ask who's pinched the things,' he fumed. 'It's the bloody Gannons next door. They've climbed over the backyard wall and helped themselves. Well, they'll not get away with it.'

He stormed out of the house and banged on the door of number 149. There was the sound of bolts being drawn and, after five or six minutes, the door was opened by the eldest son Jed. And to rub salt into the wound, he was wearing Dad's white shirt, though by this time it was looking a little grubby.

'Where did you get that shirt?' Dad demanded. 'And where's our bloody tin bath?'

'What? This shirt what I'm wearin'?' Jed snapped. 'What's it got to do with you where I got my bloody shirt, I'd like to know. An' I know nowt about no bloody tin bath.'

'That's my shirt you've got on,' Dad roared. 'You took that from our washing line this afternoon while Mrs Hopkins was out walking with our Tommy.'

Dad was a terrifying figure as he stood there, still black from his work, looking like something out of hell and in his present vicious mood like Old Nick himself.

'I didn't take your bloody shirt,' Jed replied. 'I bought this from Beaty Brothers on Deansgate for five bob. An' what do I want with a bloody rusty old bath?'

'That is *my* shirt,' barked Dad, glowering with rage.

By this time, the rest of the Gannon family had gathered behind Jed in support.

'Prove it,' snarled old Mr Gannon from behind Jed.

'Yeah, prove it,' screeched Mrs Gannon. 'An' if you can't, piss off.'

'We'll soon see about that,' Dad said coldly as he strode away. 'I'll have the law on you.'

'That frightens me to death,' Jed sneered. 'Fetch the coppers. They all know me, they're mates of mine.'

'It's no use,' Dad said to Mam when he got back. 'I'd bring a policeman round to claim the shirt but without proof I don't stand a chance of getting it back.'

'I think I know a way of proving it's your shirt,' Mam replied mysteriously. 'Go and fetch the policeman and we'll face the Gannon lot with the proof.'

Dad listened to Mam's explanation and a broad

grin spread across his face.

'That ought to do it,' he said.

He walked across to nearby Willert Street police station and it wasn't long before he was back with a beefy, red-faced constable, Fergus O'Leary by name. Dad and he went round to the Gannons' and thumped on their door. It was Jed who came to the door again, still insolent, still wearing the shirt.

'Right,' said the policeman. 'Mr Hopkins here says you've stolen his shirt and you are now wearing it.'

'Yeah, but he can't prove it,' Jed sneered. 'Where's his receipt?'

'I think I *can* prove it,' Dad said, now much calmer. 'My missus replaced the two lowest buttons on the shirt last week and as she had no white cotton she had to use green.'

'That's good enough for me,' the copper said. 'Let's be having the shirt off you so we can check the buttons.'

Scowling, Jed pulled the shirt off for examination. And there it was! Green cotton on the two buttons.

'Right, me lad,' said the officer. 'That's proof enough for me. I'm giving this shirt back to the gentleman. Think yourself lucky I'm not going to arrest you on this occasion. But any more hanky-panky and you'll be banged up good and proper before you can say Jack Robinson.'

Dad got his shirt back but there was no sign of the bath and he had to buy a new one from Barmy Mick on Salford's Flat Iron Market. The new bath was kept in the cellar forever afterwards.

'Make sure this shirt gets a double or even a treble wash, Mary,' Dad said grimly as he handed the shirt over to Mam.

A few days later, Mam learned that the Buckleys next door had had items stolen from the clothes line. Together they decided to mark the clothes by stitching the family initials on to the articles.

There was a sequel to the sorry tale some months later. The ragbone man had received some old clothes and a few bits and pieces from Mam and he had given me the usual windmill on a stick to add to my collection.

'Ta very much, Mrs Hopkins,' he said as he piled the stuff on to his barrow 'I don't suppose you have any more things like that tin bath I bought from you a couple of months ago? Oh, wait a minute. Sorry, it wasn't you; it was the Gannons what sold me that bath. My mistake.'

There was nothing to be done about the bath as by then the matter was ancient history but from that day forward, Mam and Dad kept their belongings under lock and key and made sure they had receipts for everything they bought. As for the Gannons, they had learned one important lesson, namely that the Hopkins family was not one to be messed with.

Chapter Five

Mam and I enjoyed our trips to St Oswald's Grove so much that we usually took a few carrot tops for the donkey, but I left it to Mam to feed them to him as I didn't fancy getting my hand too close to his mouth. During the school holidays, Alice and Josie from further up the street asked to accompany us as they knew the Grove well. On one never-to-be-forgotten occasion, we had arrived at St Oswald's Grove and I was, as ever, talking to my friend the donkey, when a tall, well-dressed gentleman wearing a clerical collar approached us.

'Good afternoon,' he said.

'Good afternoon, Father,' Mam answered respectfully. 'Nice weather we're having.'

'Yes, indeed,' the man said, 'but as I'm not a Catholic priest, no need to address me as "Father". I am James Welbeck and I'm the rector of St Oswald's Church across the road.'

Then he looked more closely at the two girls. He smiled. 'I seem to know your faces,' he said.

'Yes, sir. I'm Alice Buckley and this is my sister Josie and we go to St Oswald's School.'

'Of course. Now I remember you. You're in Miss Cardew's class and your little sister is in Miss Fletcher's. Clever little girls by all accounts.'

Alice flushed with pleasure. 'Thank you, Mr Welbeck, for the both of us.'

Then, turning his attention to me, he said, 'I see you're interested in our donkey. His name is Brownie and he takes me in my trap into Manchester when I need to go on business. He's a friendly fellow, is our Brownie. How would you like a ride on him?'

Would I!

'Yes, please, sir. Very much.'

'No sooner said than done,' he replied. Then he lifted me on to Brownie's back and leading him by the bridle began walking us round the Grove. I was in seventh heaven or whatever the expression is. I would rather have had that ride on the donkey's back than a million pounds. That day I knew what real joy was and for the rest of the week I could talk of nothing else and was forever pestering Mam to take me on the walk again.

'Do you think I've got nothing else to do but take you to see your donkey?' she said to me one day. 'I've got to rinse through some of your father's overalls and I just don't have the time at the moment.'

Alice happened to be in hearing distance.

'Why not let Josie and me take him?' she suggested.

'Please, please, Mam. Let me go. I'll be all right with them,' I pleaded.

'Well, er, I don't know...' Mam demurred.

'We'd love to take Tommy,' Josie added. 'No need to worry, Mrs Hopkins. We'll take good care of him. Honest. Our Alice is nine and I'm seven.'

'And *I'm* nearly four, Mam,' I chipped in. 'I wanna go with Alice and Josie. Please, please let me...'

'I'm not sure,' Mam murmured. 'Tommy's a little gypsy and likes to go a-wandering. So if I say yes, you'll both have to keep your eye on him.'

'We will. We will,' said Alice.

Mam was still dithering when Mrs O'Gara, who could never resist a bit of chit-chat, came out and joined in the debate.

'Listen, our Alice and Josie,' she said. 'If Mrs Hopkins lets you go, you just make sure you watch out for him. And no going off visiting your friends across Rochdale Road, or else you'll feel the back of my hand. Crossing that busy road is too dangerous with a little boy to look after, what with all them horse and carts, pony and traps, horsetrams which go at such speed, not to mention the occasional runaway horse! So think on, madam.'

'Don't worry about it, Mam. We wouldn't think of crossing Rochdale Road with Tommy. We'll go straight there and straight back.'

Mrs O'Gara then assured my mam that her daughters could be trusted.

'Its a nice summer afternoon, Mrs Hopkins,' she said, 'and I'm sure the three of them will enjoy a nice walk to the Grove. Alice and Josie are both quite sensible.'

That clinched it and Mam decided to let us go.

With lots of warnings about not letting me out of their sight for a single second still ringing in our ears, we set off for the Grove.

'You behave yourself, Tommy,' Mam called out as she watched us go. 'Now Alice and Josie, you take good care of him and watch him like a hawk.'

'We will. We will, Mrs Hopkins. We'll be back in about half an hour. We'll just say hello to Brownie, feed him these bits of carrot and then come right back.'

As soon as we turned the corner into Hannah Street, Alice said, 'Can't you walk any faster than that, Tommy? Come on, hurry up!'

'I'm not as big as you two,' I protested.

'Give the little lad a chance,' said Josie, taking my side. 'After all, he's just a toddler. You're doing your best, aren't you, Tommy?'

'Doesn't matter,' Alice snapped, putting her hand on the small of my back and driving me along. 'Come on, we haven't got all day.'

Josie took my hand and said, 'I'll stay with you, Tommy, if Alice goes too fast and gets ahead of us.'

I liked Josie more than Alice as she was always kinder than her big sister who was impatient and bossy.

We reached the Grove much quicker than I usually did with Mam. My legs were aching as they'd walked so quickly and I'd had to trot to keep level with them. By this time, I'd become much braver at feeding Brownie and I held out the carrot top which the donkey gently took from my hand.

'Right, that's enough of that,' said Alice, taking my hand roughly. 'Now we're going to our friend's house. We want to swap some comics.'

'Can't we stay a bit longer?' I said. 'Mam always gives me a chance to talk to Brownie. I don't wanna go yet. And that nice man might come again and give me a ride on Brownie's back.'

'Surely we can give Tommy a bit longer,' pleaded Josie. 'We've only just got here.'

'Look, Josie,' said Alice, 'we have to get a move on if we're going to have time to swap comics and get back without Mrs Hopkins and our mam losing their tempers.' Then addressing me, Alice continued, 'You're not with your mam now, Tommy. You're with us and you'll do just as you're told.'

She yanked me away from the Grove and pushed me along by the shoulders as if I were a pram.

She dragged me across Rochdale Road over the tram lines and down two or three narrow streets. Eventually we reached a house in Eliza Ann Street where Alice knocked on the door which was opened by a fat, spotty-faced girl.

'Hello, Ada,' said Alice. 'We've come to swap comics with you like we agreed at school. We've got last week's *Girl's Own Paper* and *Nuggets*.'

'That's great. I've got *Comic Cuts* and *Chips*. Come in and we'll do a swap.'

Alice then turned to me. 'Wait there, Tommy. Sit on the doorstep and I'll leave the door open. Don't move an inch. We'll only be a minute.'

'I'll stay with him to keep him company,' Josie said. 'You never know who might be walking down this street while we're inside.'

'Don't be so daft,' Alice answered. 'He'll be all right. We won't be that long.'

Josie still wasn't happy about the arrangement. 'No, I think I should stay with him,' she protested.

'You're just a big softie,' Alice snapped. 'He won't come to any harm sitting there for a few minutes. Besides, we can see him through the window.'

I was beginning to dislike Alice more and more but warming to Josie who was acting as my protector. But that was that. I was left sitting there on the cold step for what seemed like forever though it couldn't have been more than ten minutes.

When they reappeared, Alice grabbed my hand.

'Right, let's go,' she announced. 'We'll have to step on it because Mam will belt us on the legs if we keep this little nuisance out too long.'

'Don't be so hard on the little lad,' Josie said. 'He wanted to stay a bit longer with the donkey and we dragged him away.'

'Too bad,' Alice replied. Then turning to me, she said, 'Don't you dare tell anyone that we came to our friend's house to swap comics. Remember, it's our secret and if you tell on us, you'll get a taste of this.' She brandished her fist and, for a minute, she looked just like her mother. Still gripping my hand tightly, she yanked me along through the same streets until we were back in Teignmouth Street. My mam was in the yard hanging out the clothes when we reached home.

The door was ajar and Alice opened it fully, calling down the lobby, 'We're back, Mrs Hopkins. All safe and sound. I hope we weren't too long.'

'You were a bit longer than I expected,' Mam said, coming to the door, 'but anyroad, you're back and that's all that matters.'

'We'll go back home now, Mrs Hopkins,' Alice said sweetly. 'We want to read our comics but if you need us again, you only have to say.'

As Mam was going back to her chores, Alice showed me her fist and hissed, 'Don't forget, Tommy, what we said. It's our little secret. So no

51

telling tales.'

'You've been a very good boy,' Josie said. 'Wait there and I'll bring you a chocolate biscuit for being so good.'

A minute later she was back with the promised reward.

When they'd gone, Mam turned towards me. 'Stay from under my feet for a minute or two, Tommy, there's a good lad. Just sit there on the front step while I finish hanging up your dad's overalls and then I'll come and join you. We'll both have a nice cup of tea in the fresh air.'

I sat there for a while with Josie's biscuit in my hand but I wasn't happy. I felt disappointed and that somehow I'd been short-changed, robbed of my time with Brownie. Alice had pushed me there and pulled me back without giving me a chance to talk properly to my donkey friend. I'd been hoping, too, that I might get the chance for another ride.

But then, I thought, why do I have to wait for someone to take me to Brownie's field? I've been there three times and so I know where it is. I know what I'll do. I'll walk there by myself without Alice prodding me in the back. I'll be able to talk to my donkey properly and, not only that, the nice vicar man might come again and give me a ride on its back. There's lots of other kids playing in the street as it doesn't get dark until much later, so there's plenty of time for me to get there and back quickly.

I got off the step and began heading in what I thought was the direction of the Grove.

Chapter Six

From Teignmouth Street I turned left as I remembered I'd done with Mam and the girls. Then I was stuck. Was it left or right? I decided on right but I didn't recognize any of the places I passed. I came to the big wide road with the horse trams and the pony and traps running up and down it. Should I cross it or not? I couldn't remember. Maybe the Grove was over there on the opposite side. But how did I get across? I'd just have to take a chance. I darted across and reached the other pavement though it wasn't easy as the trams seemed to be going so fast and they clanged at me angrily. Don't ask me how but by some miracle I did it without getting run over. Now where did I go?

I walked and walked, down street after street, but all the houses looked the same – black bricks, grey roofs, dirty windows. I passed a big black cat which hissed at me, then a dog which barked angrily at me and attacked my ankles. I thought it was going to bite me and I started to cry. Where was the Grove? Where was Brownie? Where was our house? Where was my mam? Then I saw a big oil-cloth factory with long rolls of lino standing up in the yard but I couldn't see any people to ask the way. Next I came to a big waste ground called Barney's and as I started to cross, it began to rain. Soon I was soaked through to the skin but couldn't see any place to shelter. All around

53

me were clay pits and I slipped a few times in the greasy ground and my shorts became caked with mud. I began to shiver with cold; I was filled with panic and didn't know where to go or what to do next. I began to wail, all thoughts of Brownie and the nice vicar forgotten.

'Please, Mam. Please, Dad. Where are you? Please come and get me!'

Then on the other side of the waste ground I saw what looked like a big brick shed and I stumbled through slushy streams towards it to get out of the wet. It was warm inside and so I sat on some bricks still whimpering, 'Mam! Dad! Where are you?'

'What's the matter, son?' a man's voice boomed from the dark interior. 'Are you lost?' For a minute, I thought it was God speaking to me.

I looked round in shock 'cos I hadn't seen anybody when I'd come in. My eyes became accustomed to the gloom and there behind some bricks right at the back of the kiln I made out the figures of a couple of tramps also taking shelter. They both came a little nearer to take a closer look at me and I saw they both had dirty faces, stubbly chins and the clothes they wore were no more than filthy rags. They stank like the night-soil men but there was also another peculiar sweet smell about them, one that I'd never met before.

'Please, mister,' I said to one. 'Can you help me? I can't find Brownie.'

'Brownie? Who the bloody hell's Brownie?' the tall one of the pair asked.

'It's a donkey in a field,' I mumbled. 'And I've

given him the carrot tops and now I want to go home.'

'I think the little bugger's lost all right, Sid,' said the shorter of the tramps. 'Where do you live, son?'

Now I was on familiar ground and, like a parrot, I mumbled my party piece. 'My name is Tommy Hopkins and I live at one four seven Teignmouth Street.' There was no chocolate biscuit on this occasion.

'Tame-mouse Street?' said Sid, the tall one. 'I don't know that one.'

'Not Tame-mouse! Teignmouth!' I blubbered.

'Then, by God, you're a long way from home for such a little fellah,' he replied. 'How are you going to get back?'

'I don't know,' I whinged.

'I think you should ask a policeman to take you home,' the little bloke said. Turning to his companion, he added, 'Maybe we should take him to Willert Street, Sid.'

'No fear, not me,' said Sid. 'You won't catch me going into Willert Street station. The cops'll nab us soon as look at us.'

'We could just leave him at the door and then do a runner.'

And that's what they did. They took me as far as the station and pointed out the door.

'You go straight in there, son, and tell them who you are,' Sid told me. 'Just give them your little speech. What was it again?'

'My name is Tommy Hopkins and I live at one four seven Teignmouth Street,' I repeated for his benefit and entertainment.

I walked into the station. I must have been a bedraggled, sorry-looking sight but sheer joy ran through my veins when I saw who the policeman behind the desk was. No other than big Constable Fergus O'Leary, the officer who had sorted out Dad's shirt, and I knew I was all right. He gave me a milky tea with lots of sugar in it and a big slice of bread with lashings of best butter.

'Your mam's already been here to report you as missing,' he told me. 'Now, young fellah, we'd better get you home. You look as if you've been swimming in the River Irk. Your mam and dad are in for a shock when they clap eyes on you.'

The copper was right. They fell on me when they saw me with the policeman at the door. I had been away for nearly three hours, half the street had been out looking for me and there'd even been talk by the more panic-stricken neighbours about dragging the river. It was straight into a warm bath in the cellar and, as a special reward for being so brave, I was given a big mug of Fry's cocoa and a butty of raspberry jam, my favourite. I was also given a good telling-off by Mam.

'You've been very naughty, Tommy! Don't you ever go wandering off like that again! We thought you were drowned or murdered. I must have prayed to St Anthony, St Jude and every other saint in heaven to bring you back and my prayers have been answered.'

That night as Mam was putting me to bed, we said special prayers of thanksgiving for me being saved. Maybe those two tramps in the brick kiln had been St Anthony and St Jude. If so, they were both in need of a good wash and brush-up.

After our prayers, Mam began tucking me in and I said, 'I know a big secret.'

'And what's that, Tommy?'

'Alice and Josie took me across Rochdale Road to swap comics with their friend, Ada, in Eliza Ann Street.'

My tale-telling landed the two sisters in big trouble for being disobedient and they were both given a good leg-slapping by their mam. Served them both right, especially Alice, the bully, but then they couldn't really expect a four year old to keep a secret for long, could they? I always felt, though, that Josie had been treated unfairly as she'd opposed her big sister from the beginning but had lost the argument.

A few weeks later it had all been forgotten and the girls forgiven but they were not allowed to take me walking away from the street ever again.

Chapter Seven

On the pavement along our street, while bigger boys played cops and robbers, girls hopscotch, or rope-skipping, my favourite pastime was sailing matchsticks and paper boats along the gutter after heavy rain, or using empty blacking tins to make mud pies from the slush that built up round the grid.

One day, about a month after my incident with the two sisters, they called round with their friend Ada and asked if they could play with me again.

As a small 'un, I was a useful prop in their games. I was the baby when they played House, the customer when it came to a game of Shop, the bad boy in the pretend School.

'Very well,' my mam said, 'as long as you don't leave the street. We don't want him lost again.'

'I've been given a nurse's outfit for my birthday,' Alice explained, 'and we're going to play at Hospital outside our house.'

'Very well,' Mam answered. 'But think on. You're not to leave the street.'

'We won't, Mrs Hopkins. Honest to God. We've set up the hospital right outside our front door.'

The hospital was an old blanket, spread out on the pavement. Naturally I was to be the patient, Alice the doctor, and Josie and Ada the operation nurses. I was given a walking stick and told to limp into the hospital, at the same time moaning as if in pain. I thought I played my part very convincingly, though at that point I didn't really know what was supposed to be wrong with me. Perhaps at that early age I had ambitions to become an actor.

'This is the little boy who has been knocked down by a runaway horse,' Josie said. 'He was crossing Rochdale Road and wasn't looking where he was going. It's a good job it wasn't a tram.'

'Tut! Tut! These kids! Will they never learn?' exclaimed Doctor Alice. 'Lay him down here on the bed and let's have a look at him.'

She looked very professional in her medical uniform which consisted of a surgeon's hat, an imitation stethoscope, and an armband bearing the Red Cross symbol. She had a range of little bottles containing her medicines and ointments.

Helped by Josie and Ada, I was put down on the blanket and told to stretch out. Still howling, I allowed them to put me on my back, which left me exposed to their tender mercies.

'First, let's see if there's anything broken,' Alice said.

She began examining the top of my head.

'Nothing wrong here, no cuts or bruises. But it looks as if he's had a bad cut on the cheek; it'll need five stitches. Are you feeling all right, little boy?'

'Yes, doctor,' I replied, 'but I have a pain in my chest and one in my leg.'

'We must take a look at them,' she replied, placing a hand on my chest and tapping her fingers as she had seen a doctor doing last time she'd been ill. 'Now, cough for me, there's a good lad.'

I did as I was asked.

'I don't like the sound of that cough,' she said. 'He may need an operation on his lungs. Now let's see about that pain in your leg, son. Where exactly does it hurt, my little love?'

'On my knee,' I answered plaintively, warming to my role.

Alice examined my kneecaps by exerting pressure with her two thumbs.

'Ah, yes, I can see the trouble now. Nurse, pass me the knee ointment and disinfectant.'

There was a bit of an argument between the nurses as to who would have the responsibility of passing the medicaments to the doctor. Eventually, Ada won the day over the ointment by giving Josie a push that sent her flying.

'I'm senior nurse in this hospital,' she snapped,

59

snatching it from her. Josie had to settle for the disinfectant.

The ointment was soft soap and the disinfectant a cup of sarsaparilla. Alice applied them gently to the wound.

'There,' she said, 'that should fix it. I think a bandage round your knee will do the trick. Nurse, the bandage! Quick!'

Josie tore a strip off an old sheet and Alice skilfully wrapped it round my knee, securing it with a large safety pin.

'Now let's have a look at the rest of you,' she said, all concerned. 'Tell me where it hurts.'

She examined my ankles, my shins, then the calves of my legs. Finally she put her hand up my trouser leg and took a firm hold of my willy and squeezed it.

'I've found a little lump here,' she announced to her assistants. 'I think it needs an operation to remove it.'

I may have been only a four-year-old toddler but I knew it was wrong for her to do that. Operate, I mean! I stood up. I'd had enough of this game and I tore the bandage off my knee.

'I'm going home,' I said, 'and I'm going to tell my mam what you did.'

'It was only pretend,' Alice protested. 'No need to tell your mam.'

Nevertheless, I did.

'That's it,' Mam said when she heard the story. 'She's had her last chance. You mustn't play with them again 'cos they're naughty.'

As things turned out, I didn't get the chance to

play with them again 'cos a few weeks after the 'hospital' incident, something happened that ended any further games with the two sisters.

Mrs O'Gara had slipped out to the corner shop, leaving the two girls playing with their doll's house in front of the fire in the living room. As they were setting out the miniature tea set, a tiny cup had fallen on the hearth behind the fireguard. Alice removed the guard and Josie went behind to retrieve it. The fire caught her dress and in seconds she was in flames. She ran out of the house shrieking in agony but the wind whipped round her and fanned the flames. Her mother, still in the shop, heard Josie's tormented screams and rushed out to find her daughter burning in agony. Mrs O'Gara's shrill, panic-stricken shrieks for help roused the rest of the street. Neighbours came running out of their houses and there was turmoil, with distraught women screaming in shocked confusion. As with young Herbert Lamb, no one seemed to know what to do next. Though there were a few litter trolleys available, they were always too slow to attend an emergency as it meant someone would have to run to the police, the fire station or the hospital itself to alert the ambulance service. By the time the trolley was wheeled to the scene, it was usually too late. Assisted by one or two neighbours, Mrs O'Gara improvised her own 'ambulance' by wrapping Josie up in blankets and rushing her to hospital in an open pram. As in Herbert's case, it was too late and Josie died later that afternoon in the Ancoats burns unit.

After Josie's death, the mothers and fathers in

the district, including, my own, carried out stringent checks on their fireguards, even screwing them to the wall. Children were given severe warnings about not moving or interfering in any way with the arrangement.

The whole district turned out to mourn the little girl's tragic death. I couldn't have been more than four and a half but I remembered the black horses and the carriage for the rest of my life. Josie had a white coffin and the horses wore beautiful white plumes on their halters. She was buried in a pauper's grave as the O'Garas did not have any insurance money for a plot or a headstone. It was the second death of someone I'd really liked. What made me feel really guilty, though, was the thought that I wouldn't have minded so much had it been Alice instead of young Josie who, after all, had been kind to me and had given me a chocolate biscuit.

Chapter Eight

I always thought my dad was the greatest. He could do anything. When I grew up, I wanted to be a blacking maker like him. During the week, when he came home from work, he looked like a coal miner coming off his shift. He was always so tired after a thirteen-hour day in the blacking factory that he just wanted to get his bath, have his dinner, and settle before the fire with the *Manchester Evening News*. Then it was off to bed for all of us as we had to be up early next morning. But Dad always found time to tuck me in at night and he never failed to sing a few nursery rhymes or tell me a fairy story. He knew all the rhymes in alphabetical order and, starting with A, he opened with, 'All around the mulberry bush the monkey chased the weasel. The monkey thought 'twas all in fun – Pop! goes the weasel.'

He could go right through to Y with 'Young Lambs to Sell' but he could never think of one beginning with Z. I think he knew every fairy tale written by the Grimm Brothers and he told me a different one every night: 'Rumpelstiltskin', 'Snow White', 'Cinderella', 'Hansel and Gretel'. But my favourite was always the one about the brave little tailor who tricked the giant by pretending to be so strong that he could squeeze a stone until water ran out of it although it was really a piece of cheese.

On Friday nights, you could hear Dad coming down the street on his way home a hundred yards away for he was invariably whistling a happy tune, usually 'Waltzing Matilda'. As he came through the door, he was full of smiles and jokes and for the rest of the evening he laughingly told us about some of the funny things that had happened at work during the week. And he never failed to bring Mam a bunch of flowers to celebrate getting his week's wages. In addition, he always bought something special for tea such as Eccles cakes or a packet of Peek Frean's 'Tiffin' biscuits. He never missed our Friday-night treat of chocolate: a bar of Fry's 'Five Boys' for me and a bar of Cadbury's Dairy Milk for Mam 'cos she was fond of a bit of chocolate as well.

Dad may have come home on week nights with his overalls black with soot but at weekends it was a different kettle of fish and he wasn't the same man. His time off was so precious to him that he didn't want to waste a single second.

Some Saturday afternoons, he played football for Berry's Blacking second team where he was centre forward. Sometimes he took me with him to watch and I'll never forget seeing him running out dressed in the company's football gear of black shirt with the Berry's Blacking logo on the front and knickerbocker shorts. On one occasion he scored the winning goal against the Police Reserve Eleven at the Willert Street recreation ground. When everyone started cheering, I wanted to go round the crowd there and tell them, 'That was my dad who just scored that goal!'

After the local match, Dad usually went for a drink with his fellow work and team mates to the nearby Berry social club while I hung around kicking a football with a few lads until Dad came out. He was not a big drinker and I think he was too tired when he came home from work to be bothered going out, preferring to spend his time relaxing at home. Some weekends, though, he brought a couple of bottles of stout home and he and Mam enjoyed a quiet drink.

On the occasional Saturday when he wasn't playing, we took horse trams to football matches on Newton Heath, especially if Berry's first team was playing. My dad was usually a quiet bloke but I'd never seen him get so excited as he did at a match between Berry's and the Monsall dye works; it was as if he'd gone completely off his head.

'That was a good shot, Dad,' I shouted on one occasion, remarking on a fine effort by the Berry's centre forward.

I was a bit put out when I saw that he'd become so absorbed in the match he'd forgotten all about me. Not a bit like the dad I knew at home as he had now become a screaming lunatic, watching this hard-fought battle between the two rival teams. He was yelling his head off, telling the ref what he thought of him for making the wrong decisions, which, in his opinion, was most of the time.

'Get a pair of specs, ref,' or, 'Get back to the blind school, ref,' he would bawl.

The best football matches I ever saw were between the railway clubs. Once or twice we watched Newton Heath Lancashire and Yorkshire Railway (LYR) Club, known as the Heathens, which later became Manchester United. Best players on that team were Bobby Donaldson, Harry Stafford and Alf Farman.

When there was no football on, we visited relatives. Dad's own father was dead but his mother, Gran'ma Edna, was alive and kicking and residing still at 26 Ludgate Hill in Ancoats, the house where he'd been born. She was always attired from head to foot in black, like Queen Victoria in mourning for her Prince Albert. Come to think of it, most of the old women of the time seemed to be permanently sharing the Queen's sorrow because they were dressed in similar fashion. I don't think Gran'ma Edna liked children 'cos on the few occasions we went to visit, I can't remember her ever speaking to me except to tell me 'to sit up straight' and 'not to make a nuisance of myself'.

'Children should be seen and not heard,' she told Dad.

That put me in my place all right. So I just sat there like a dummy until it was time to go home.

But I really liked visiting my mam's family, the Mitchells, who lived in Church Court off Old Mount Street. They were a happy lot, always laughing, joking, pulling each others' legs.

'Top o' the mornin' to you, young Thomas,' Grandad Owen used to say. 'I hope that mother of yours has been taking good care of you.'

At that point in time, I was his only grandchild and he used to spoil me a little by slipping a penny into my hand, at the same whispering confidentially, 'Get yourself some sweets, son, but don't let on to your grandma or she'll skin me alive.'

Sweets! For me that could mean only one thing. A sherbet dab! This came in a triangular paper packet with a little lollipop sticking out of it. First, you sucked the lollipop until it was nice and sticky and then you dipped it into the sherbet powder. The taste that followed was like a little explosion in the mouth of the most wonderful flavour you can imagine.

I realized even at that tender age that the real boss of the family was Grandma Bridget who had more to say for herself than her husband. At the table she would order the family about with, 'Sit up straight! Don't slouch! Elbows off the table!

Don't slurp your soup! Don't talk with your mouth full!' The family jumped to attention when she gave her commands even though they were quite grown up. Patrick, the eldest, was thirty; Mary, my mam, twenty-eight; Dorothy, engaged to Brodie Langley, a market worker, was twenty-two; while Jamesey, the youngest, was twenty. Jamesey was my favourite 'cos he showed me lots of card tricks and gave me rides on his back, galloping madly up Ludgate Hill and back down again along Sharp Street. Jamesey was always trying card tricks out on me.

'Pick a card but don't let me see it,' he'd say.

Then after a lot of mumbo-jumbo, he'd announce, 'Ten o' spades.' Always right but he refused to tell me how he did it. He got on well with my dad 'cos they both fancied themselves as conjurors and magicians and I suppose they swapped tricks.

Dad too was forever trying out his conjuring tricks on me. He could juggle three balls in the air but never did manage four. When he did try, the fourth ball came down and clumped him on the head and everyone laughed. And that made him angry. Another trick was to hold out a ping-pong ball and pretend to swallow it, then make it appear from my ear.

'Don't you ever try to do this trick, Tommy,' he would say,' 'cos if you swallow it, you'll have to go to Ancoats Hospital to have your tummy cut open to get it out.'

I cannot ever remember a time when I was bored or had nothing to do. For the evenings we had indoor games like draughts, snakes and ladders, ludo, rings, bagatelle. The one we got most fun out of was Blow Tennis when Dad would play against Mam and me. We always lost, of course, as he had more puff and he didn't mind cheating. Any kind of football was a game he obviously took seriously.

Outside on the pavement in front of the house, Alice and her friend Ada from Eliza Ann Street joined us in our games of quoits or hopscotch using the flags chalked out in numbered squares and a tin cocoa lid. It was great fun but I wasn't very good at jumping and so one day Dad decided to teach me. He stood me on the window sill, brushing aside Mam's complaint that she'd only just donkey-stoned it.

'Right, Tommy,' he said. 'Let's see you jump. Come on, I'll catch you.'

I didn't fancy it as it was about three feet off the ground but, trusting Dad, I leaped. He was there ready to catch me. 'Well done, Tommy. Brave little lad. Again,' he said. This time I did not hesitate and Dad caught me again. We did it several times more and I was ready to do it all day long but Dad got fed up after the umpteenth time.

'Right,' he said, 'you're a splendid jumper. Now you'll be able to play hopscotch with your girl friends.' He went indoors to read his paper.

But I had enjoyed the thrill of jumping off the window sill so much I reckoned I didn't need him any more. After all, hadn't he said, 'Brave little lad'?

I clambered up on to the sill and looked down. It seemed a lot higher than I'd imagined but I'll show him, I thought. I leaped off into space. I hit the flags hard, and then in a sequence I couldn't stop, I hurtled forward and bashed the side of my face against the edge of the upturned tin lid which the girls had left on the pavement. The sharp tin tore into my cheek, leaving an ugly gash below my right eye. Blood gushed from the wound.

'Mam! Dad! Come quick! I'm bleeding!' I yelled.

Dad reached me first and cradled me in his arms. Mam was next with a towel dabbing the cut.

'It's all right, Tommy,' she said. 'You're going to be all right, you'll see.'

'Sorry, Dad. I shouldn't have tried it without you.'

'Don't worry about that now, Tommy,' he said. 'That window sill was pretty high. Much too high for your little legs.' Then turning to Mam, he said, 'That cut looks nasty. I think he needs to go to hospital.'

'I'll be all right, Dad,' I pleaded. 'No need for hospital.'

I'd heard the horror stories from my female playmates about some of the unspeakable things the nurses did to you at Ancoats, like drugging you with those coloured liquids they stored in the jars on the shelves and then selling you to the gypsies.

'No, son. I think that cut needs attention. Your mam can stay home while I rush you there. We shouldn't be long, we'll be back in a jiffy.'

Dad picked me up like I was a feather, cradling me gently in the crook of his right arm and holding the towel to my head with his left. Briskly he strode the three miles to Ancoats in Mill Street.

The hospital was a frightening place with its strong, overpowering smells of chloroform, iodine, disinfectants, and its oddly-shaped glass jars containing all kinds of coloured medicines, designed no doubt to deliver maximum pain and stings when applied to children's cuts and bruises. The nurses seemed to be about seven feet tall in their big starched headdresses and their blue striped uniforms.

In the accident room, we found ourselves behind an old woman who had fallen downstairs and a youth who had come off his bike and broken his arm. After a half-hour wait, an Amazonian nurse came into the room and called in a severe, disapproving tone of voice, 'Thomas Hopkins.' Dad carried me forward and, like a bird caught in a trap, I watched every movement of the nurses and orderlies hurrying to and fro around me, wondering what awful things they were planning for me.

The weary-looking doctor on duty took one look at my injury and announced in a matter-of-fact voice, 'Needs three or four stitches.' My heart did a double somersault when I heard this.

The nurse by his side dabbed iodine on the cut, which stung like mad. Tears sprang to my eyes but I was determined not to cry out. Dad held my hand tightly while the doctor put in four stitches. 'Be a brave soldier,' Dad said, sounding as worried as I was. 'I'm here by your side to look after you.' All very well for Dad to say that, I thought, but I was the one being stitched up. It took all my determination not to yell out as the needle was inserted, for it was the worst pain I'd ever felt in my whole life – all four years of it. But somehow or other I got through it. When it was over, the doctor said, 'Well done, my lad. You deserve a medal for your bravery.' I didn't get the Victoria Cross or anything like that but Dad did buy me a lollipop as he tenderly carried me home.

On Sundays, we went to nine o'clock Mass at St Chad's Church on Cheetham Hill Road. It was a good walk from our house in Teignmouth Street and so Dad had to carry me part of the way. We were a proud little family dressed in our Sunday best and many fellow parishioners greeted us in recognition with, 'Good morning, Mr and Mrs Hopkins, lovely day,' as we made our way to the church along Lord Street, Mam linking Dad and at the same time holding her missal in her free hand. As befitted a visit to church, she was dressed modestly but tastefully in her finest navy-blue coat, a pair of white gloves, while over her head and shoulders she draped a lovely black lace mantilla, one of her proudest possessions. When I saw my mother all dressed up like this, I couldn't help thinking how beautiful she was and how lucky I was that she was my mother.

Not to be outdone in the matter of dress, Dad was every bit the gentleman, moustache neatly trimmed, wearing his black suit complete with waistcoat and the obligatory hunter watch and chain (I loved his habit of whirling it round on its chain to make it land in his waistcoat pocket); on his head as a complete change from his weekday cloth cap he sported a bowler hat of finest felt material. The nine o'clock Mass was said by the parish priest Father Sheehan who had officiated at their wedding in 1883. I loved these Sunday mornings as I was so proud to be out with my mam and dad on such a public occasion. I loved, too, the ceremony of the Mass, the communal recitation of the prayers, the sound of the Latin words, though I hadn't a clue what they meant, the sweet smell of incense as the altar boy swung the thurible like a pendulum. I wasn't very keen on the sermons, though, 'cos, like the Latin, they were well above my head but then I don't think my mam understood them either.

On the way home, Dad asked, 'What did you think then of Father Sheehan's sermon, Mary?'

'I didn't understand most of it,' she said, 'but it sounded good and I like the way he waved his arms and waggled his hands. He's obviously learned to declaim like one of those politicians. And when he pointed his finger at us all and said, "Be on your guard lest the devil seek ye out," I'm sure he was pointing at me.'

'Don't think so,' Dad grinned, 'because I'm sure it was me he had singled out.'

After a traditional breakfast of bacon and egg, we took off our best outfits and, dressed in casual clothes, had an outing to some place of interest. Like Queen's Park where, in fine weather, we'd sit around the bandstand listening to military marches or Gilbert and Sullivan songs. Dad and I often played roly-poly down a steep grass verge or had a kick-about on the grass with him dribbling rings around me with a rubber ball.

Sometimes, if the weather was really sunny, Dad

simply stretched out on the grass and went to sleep. Understandable after his week's hard grind in the blacking factory.

When it was raining, we went into the museum but I always found that boring – a lot of statues, bones, and old coins – and then into the art gallery with lots of pictures of stuck-up posh people in their wigs, big hats and old-fashioned clothes. Some of the pictures were rude because the men and women had no clothes on and my mam and dad hurried me away before I could get a proper look. Nude pictures or not, I couldn't wait to get out in the air again regardless of the rain. Once or twice, if the weather was particularly nice, we caught the horse tram to a park with a name that sounded like a swear word – Boggart Hole Clough – a local beauty spot where we listened to the band, sometimes the same band we'd heard at Queen's Park. The Clough had permanent benches which were most welcome after the long walk from the gates on Rochdale Road.

One week, Dad showed me how to make a kite using coloured tissue paper and thin sticks of wood by assembling and sticking them together with an adhesive made up of flour and water. Every week night after work, we went into the cellar and he taught me how to cut up the paper and slice parings of wood.

'Make sure you cut the wood carefully with a sharp knife but watch out you cut the slices out of the *wood* and not your fingers or you'll find yourself back in Ancoats.'

The result of our labours was a beautiful kite over two feet long with a colourful tail of ribbon

73

and screwed-up tissue papers trailing behind it. The tail was longer than the kite itself.

'Will it fly, Dad? Will it fly?' I asked excitedly.

'If we get a strong puff of wind, it will, Tommy. We can only hope and pray.'

The following Sunday we went to Boggart Hole Clough to try out our handiwork. Our prayers were answered 'cos there was a strong breeze blowing. Success! The kite flew a treat at this park because not only was there a good blow, there were lots of hills and dales. Holding the cross piece with the kite flapping in his hands as if eager to show off its capabilities, Dad ran up one of the hills like a gazelle, with me at the bottom holding the winding stick. At the top he tied his spotted handkerchief to the tail and waited for the right moment. Then he shouted down to me, 'Now, Tommy!' and let the kite go. A gust picked it up immediately and it soared high into the blue. It was a funny feeling holding on to the kite as it pulled away from me, almost like a tug of war with some invisible opponent who was trying to wrench it out of my hands.

Dad dashed down to me to give me instructions.

'Pull on it, Tommy lad. That's it! Tighten the string! Now release it a bit! Give it its head! Now make it taut!'

He was like a little boy again, holding on to the stick with me and yanking the kite in the wind. The picture of him that Sunday was one that became forever etched on my mind.

Of our Sunday park trips, I loved going to this particular one best until Dad told me one day that

'Boggart' meant 'Bogey' or 'ghost'. And there were stories about people being haunted by bogeymen while walking around the park. I went off the place after that.

The excursion that stood out from the rest was the day of my fourth birthday, 4 October 1890. It was a Saturday, and Dad, having managed to get off work a bit earlier than usual, had arranged a visit to Manchester's Belle Vue Zoological Gardens. With a mountain of ham sandwiches that Mam had made up plus a couple of bottles of Tizer, we took the tram to Hyde Road. For me Belle Vue was a dreamland; it had just about everything – a park, a brass band, a boating lake and, wonder of wonders, a collection of exotic animals that I'd seen only in picture books: giraffes, kangaroos, lions, bears, monkeys, and a chimpanzee that not only wore a man's jacket and hat but smoked a clay pipe as well. But the most impressive animal in the menagerie was the huge elephant which lumbered about the grounds led by its keeper Lorenzo Lawrence. When Dad booked a place on the children's ride for me, my day was complete. At first I was a bit nervous about climbing on to the seat when the elephant knelt down but, seeing that the other kids didn't look worried, I clambered aboard and enjoyed viewing the world from my lofty throne. We rounded off the day with a boat ride on the lake, with Dad doing the rowing while Mam and me lay back like toffs trailing our hands through the water. What a day! The happiest of my life and one I never forgot.

Chapter Nine

It was a Friday night about three months before my fifth birthday. It was half past six and Mam and I were waiting for Dad to come home from work and I was listening out for his familiar whistle, the sign that he was in a happy mood. It was pay night and, as I said earlier, he never failed to bring home something nice for us. He'd recently had a raise in pay to one pound a week and so it might be something extra special. What would it be? Perhaps a magazine like *Woman: For Up-to-date Womankind* for Mam and a comic like *The Wonder* for me. Maybe a packet of chocolate biscuits or Parkinson's butterscotch, Mam's favourite. Furthermore, I was really looking forward to this weekend 'cos he'd promised to take us to Heaton Park on Sunday afternoon to listen to the Black Dyke Mills band over in Manchester on a visit from Yorkshire.

Then I heard his footsteps and I perked up in anticipation. But there was something wrong. There was no whistle and his steps seemed slower and heavier than usual. He came through the door, soot-black as he did every night but now there was a weariness about him that I'd never seen before. Mam saw it too.

'Thomas,' she said anxiously. 'How are you feeling?'

'Not so good, Mary. I've had a bad headache

76

ever since I went to work this morning. Can't seem to shake it off. Also I seem to have a very stiff neck. I put it down to standing in the same position most of the day.'

'Well, sit yourself down and let's have those shoes off you. There's fresh tea in the pot – only just brewed as we waited for you. I'll bring you a cup right away. That should buck you up. Tommy and I have had our baths and there's hot water waiting for you in the cellar.'

'Thanks, Mary. You're a good wife. I was going to bring you and Tommy a special something tonight to celebrate my wage increase but somehow I felt I had to get back home as soon as I could.'

'I've got some tripe and onions for your tea,' Mam continued, trying to cheer Dad up. 'I know how much you like it.'

'Right,' he said. 'I'll have a good scrub-down and then after tea I think it best if I get straight into bed.'

I felt a twinge of disappointment when I heard this news. No comic. No sweets. Maybe no outing to Heaton Park on Sunday. But then, I said to myself, Dad isn't feeling so good and it's selfish of me to be thinking about sweets and comics.

My hopes bucked up a little when I heard him say, 'I should be all right tomorrow, God willing. I'll go into work for the morning shift and as for the afternoon ... well, we'll see.'

After his wash-down, Dad tried to eat his dinner but could manage only half of it. He wasn't interested in reading the *Evening News* but went straight to bed. Mam looked really worried.

'Try not to make any noise, Tommy,' she whispered. 'A good night's sleep is what your dad needs.'

Next morning, however, Dad was no better. He looked pale and had a high temperature, as could be seen by the beads of sweat on his forehead. The dark fringes of soot residue around his eyelids gave him a haunted look.

Now he couldn't move his neck at all and trying to crane forward to reach his tea resulted in terrible pain. There was no chance that he would be able to go into work that morning. Mam sent a message to the works through a fellow worker, Alf Critchley, who lived in the next street.

For the rest of the weekend, Dad's condition got steadily worse. Mam closed the curtains as he couldn't stand the sunlight streaming through the window. The slightest noise upset him. When the ragbone man came along shouting out his usual call, 'Raag boh-ohn!' Dad became very angry.

'For God's sake, tell that bloody man to go to the next street,' he snapped, 'or we'll set the law on him.'

On Sunday, Mam and I went to Mass alone, leaving Dad asleep at home. As we walked up Lord Street, neighbours inquired after him. 'Where's Mr Hopkins this morning?' or 'Where's the master today? Hope he's not ill.'

At Mass, Mam and I offered up our prayers for Dad and, after the service, Mam went into the vestry to see Father about a Mass for him. When we got home, we found Dad feverish and shivering. He seemed to be babbling to himself about something at work but we didn't understand him. Mam was lost and didn't know what to do. She piled the blankets on him in an effort to stop the trembling but she didn't know if that was the right thing to do.

'Tomorrow,' she said, 'I'll ask Dr Becker to call.' I knew then that things were really serious, for a house call by the doctor cost half a crown, an eighth of Dad's wages.

The doctor came in late afternoon all businesslike and carrying his black bag.

'Now, Mrs Hopkins,' he said. 'What seems to be the matter?'

'It's my husband, Thomas. He came home from work on Friday night not feeling well. Splitting headache, can't move his neck, and he has a high fever. He can't stand bright light or any kind of noise.'

'I see. I see,' Dr Becker purred, not showing any kind of reaction. 'Well, let's have a look at the patient.'

Mam and he went into the bedroom and I was told to wait downstairs. I thought that wasn't fair because I wanted to know what was wrong with Dad as much as they did.

The doctor carried out a strange test, or so Mam informed me later. Dad was told to lie on his back, bend his right knee, try to turn it sideways and then stretch it right out. Dad yelled out in pain and he could only stretch his leg halfway. Dr Becker said nothing.

When they came downstairs again, the doctor again said nothing but he looked gloomy.

'If it is what I think it is, it could be serious. There's a lot of it about at the present time, I'm

79

afraid. There's nothing can be done at present. The illness must be left to take its course.'

'Nothing to be done!' Mam exclaimed. 'Surely there's something I can do? Is there no medicine I can give him? What shall I do about the fever? As for food, he can't keep anything down.' Mam sounded helpless and desperate.

'For the fever, cold compresses. Not too many blankets but keep him warm and comfortable. You may find that he's not interested in food but if you can feed him a little soup, that might help. Keep the curtains closed and...' then looking directly at me, 'make sure he has peace and quiet. I'll call back on Friday afternoon to see how he is getting on.'

But Dr Becker's second visit was not needed because Dad died on Thursday afternoon at three o'clock. He heaved a deep sigh and fell into a sleep from which he never woke up – except maybe on Judgement Day. He was twenty-eight years of age. On the death certificate, the cause was given as cerebral spinal meningitis. We didn't understand what that was and neither did any of our relatives, though a few neighbours said they knew of someone else who had suffered from it. We didn't know how he'd managed to catch it either. Was it something he ate? Something to do with his work? Had he picked up an infection? Had he been working too hard? Nobody seemed to know.

Mam and I were heartbroken and remained in a state of shock all weekend. It had all happened so quickly. Last Friday he had gone to work normally, come home not feeling too well and within

the week he was dead. Mam was completely bewildered and lost as to what to do next; the enormity of her loss had not fully registered in her
mind. Mrs Buckley from next door and Mam's
sister, Dorothy, came to the rescue and helped lay
out the body. Mam's brothers, Patrick and
Jamesey, called and took over the numerous procedures necessary when someone in a household
dies, like registering the death, contacting the
Royal London, Dad's insurance company, and
the Co-op undertakers. As was the custom, the
coffin was placed on trestles in front of the window in the parlour and there was a stream of
visitors to view the body: first Dad's mother,
Gran'ma Edna; then members of Mam's family,
the Mitchells – father, mother, Dorothy's husband, Brodie, and many cousins I'd never set eyes
on before.

'Doesn't he look peaceful?' many visitors
remarked.

'You're going to have to be a brave little lad from
now on,' my uncle-in-law, Brodie, said, pushing a
shilling into my hand. 'You'll be the man of the
house and you'll have to take care of your mother.'

A kind man, I thought to myself. I'm glad
Aunty Dorothy married him in the end.

'The undertakers have fixed him up well,' said
one or two. 'He looks so smart lying there, it's
hard to believe he's really dead.'

Jamesey and I went in to see him together. Dad
had on a black cassock and the white shirt that
had caused the big row with the Gannons. He
had a strange smile on his face as if he thought
dying was some kind of joke. I wouldn't have

been surprised if he had sat up and said, 'Now for my next trick...'

'Why is he smiling like that?' I asked Jamesey.

'I think it's put there by the undertakers to make him look happy,' he answered.

'Or maybe he doesn't realize he's dead,' I said.

'Or perhaps he's happy 'cos he's in heaven,' said Jamesey.

Lastly came a few neighbours, like the Buckleys who had organized a street wreath, the O'Garas, fresh from their own bereavement, and many of Dad's workmates. All offered sympathy.

'Sid and me,' Mrs Buckley said, 'haven't been able to eat a thing since we heard about Thomas passing away. So unexpected.'

'We at Berry's blacking works are so sorry for your loss,' said Joe Greenhalgh, the manager. 'Thomas was one of our most skilful and hardest workers. We've had a collection for you and we hope it is of some help to you at this difficult time.'

But Mam was inconsolable and beside herself with grief. She simply stared into the fire, shaking her head from side to side, unable to take in the fact that her husband, who'd been her best friend, had passed away. Many of the visitors pushed coins into my hand saying things like, 'Poor kid,' as if in some way money would make up for the loss of my father.

The funeral was held at St Chad's and the Requiem Mass was said by Father Sheehan, the priest who had married him in 1883, assisted by another priest, Father Gadd. There was a good crowd present – neighbours and his workmates plus Joe Greenhalgh.

Burial took place at Moston Cemetery and, as the coffin was gently lowered into the grave, the priest pronounced the words, 'In sure and certain hope of the resurrection to eternal life through our Lord Jesus Christ, we commend to Almighty God our brother Thomas Hopkins and we commit his body to the ground; earth to earth, ashes to ashes, dust to dust. The Lord bless him and keep him, the Lord make his face to shine upon him and be gracious unto him and give him peace. Amen.

'Requiem aeternam dona ei, Domine, et lux perpetua luceat ei. Requiescat in pace. Amen.

'Eternal rest give unto him, O Lord, and let perpetual light shine upon him. May he rest in peace. Amen.'

The men looked solemn and the women wept but not Mam, for she still couldn't believe that it was her husband Thomas lying in that box. Then it was back to Collyhurst and a little reception in the upstairs room over a pub called the Mitchell Arms in Every Street. Everyone sat around saying what a great man Dad had been, husband, father, footballer, blacking maker. There was even a feeble attempt at humour.

'We're so famous,' joked Mam's brother, Patrick, 'that they named this pub after us.'

'Or maybe it's because you drink so much,' replied Jamesey, 'they thought they may as well name the pub after you.'

But no one seemed to find it funny.

Up to this point, Mam had been so busy since Dad's death, what with dealing with official regulations, insurance, funeral arrangements, entertaining the many visitors, she'd not had time to think. It was only when she and I got back home and were alone in the empty house that reality and the magnitude of our loss truly struck home. Dad had been our linchpin, the centre of our universe, the core round which our lives had revolved and been organized. Now he was gone. Mam wept copiously as she clung to me.

'What are we going to do now, Tommy? What are we going to do? It's as if I've lost part of me. He was my reason for living and now he's not here. Who can I run to when I need help and advice? How are we going to manage?'

The loss, the pain began to register deeply with me too. No more kite-flying, no more excursions to the parks or to Belle Vue, no more visits to football matches, no more card or conjuring tricks, no more of his jokes or his stories. It seemed as if the joy had gone out of our lives. The good times were over.

Chapter Ten

It was Jamesey, Mam's brother, who brought us down to earth and made Mam think about what her next move might be. He came round a couple of days after the funeral and sat down at the table and, holding a mug of tea between his hands, made Mam face up to the practical issues of survival.

'First, Mary,' he asked, 'what about money? How are you fixed?'

'We have no savings,' she said, 'and the insurance was just about enough to bury him but we can get by for a couple of weeks on what's left. Then Berry's blacking works have been kind enough to help out by paying me four weeks of Thomas's wages, so we should be able to survive for a few weeks at least.'

'And after that?' he asked. 'What then?'

'We'll have to cut back on what we spend, I suppose. The weekly rent of five shillings is a bit high and so I think we'll have to flit to somewhere cheaper. Then I could always go back to work as seamstress at Blair's corset factory if they'll have me.'

Jamesey and Mam talked for the rest of the morning and got through several pots of tea in the process. At the end they'd decided that Mam would see if she could go back to work and we'd move to cheaper accommodation. And the best news of all, which made my heart leap for joy, was that Jamesey said he'd come to live with us and look after Mam and me. It wasn't like having Dad back of course but considering all the terrible things that had been happening to us, it was like a light suddenly shining out of the darkness.

There remained the problem of what to do with me. I was nearly five and perhaps I could be sent to school at St William's Elementary Infants Department. Mam said she'd go to see Sister Gabriel, the headmistress, as soon as she could. But if Mam got the job at Blair's, she couldn't be home until gone six thirty, and since Jamesey was also working – a bricklayer with a full-time job – I'd be left with nowhere to go 'cos the infants school finished at half past three. I couldn't be left to wander the streets for three hours or so. But who could watch over me during these three hours?

Gran'ma Edna on my father's side couldn't take on such a job as she was knocking on seventy and she didn't like kids anyway; she felt they were 'noisy little buggers and nothing but trouble'. Then there was Grandad Owen and Grandma Bridget on my mother's side but they were both working during the day; he worked long hours on a building site in town while she was a costermonger with her own barrow on Shudehill. They certainly didn't have time to take on the job of looking after a young 'un like me during the day. Their son Patrick, also in the building trade, was away working in other towns most of the time and so he couldn't help. That left Dorothy and her husband Brodie who both worked with donkey and cart as carriers in Smithfield Market. Brodie's father, Zeb – short for Zebediah, or so they told me – lived with them and, though he was old, he could stand in for them when they weren't there. I was told I had to call him Gran'pa Zeb (though he wasn't really my gran'pa) to distinguish him from my other grandad, Owen.

As I listened to Jamesey and Mam discussing these plans, my heart sank into my boots and I was filled with trepidation wondering what was to become of me. Oh, Dad, I said to myself over and over again, why did you have to die and leave us in this terrible situation?

Three weeks later, it had all been decided and our lives were turned upside down when Mam and Jamesey found furnished rooms at 83 North Kent Street, Collyhurst. It was a sad day when we left Teignmouth Street. The place held so many happy memories for us. Mam and Dad had moved in there immediately after their wedding and I had been born there. And there were so many associations with Dad: his coming home every night black with soot, his wash-downs in the cellar, his jokes, his constant attempts at conjuring and the board games we played. Every room had some connection and reminded us of him. For me, it was the games in the street, the outings to the football matches, the parks and to Belle Vue. Even the unpleasant things brought back fond memories of him: his row with the Gannons over the stolen shirt; me getting lost after visiting Brownie, the donkey; my accident jumping off the window sill and the tender way he'd carried me in his arms to the hospital. We would miss our neighbours too: the Sugarmans and the occasional chat Mam used to have with them; we would miss especially the Buckleys next door, for Mam and Bella had struck up a warm friendship. Strange to say, we'd even perhaps miss the Gannons whose scandalous behaviour regularly provided Mam and Mrs Buckley with juicy topics for gossip.

As there was little room in the new accommodation, Mam had to sell various items of surplus furniture, like the big wardrobe and the mahogany dresser, all of great sentimental value since she and Dad had bought them in their courtship days. Saddest of all was having to sell Dad's possessions like his hunter fob watch and chain, his suit and finally his boots to which he had given such loving attention. Going through his things in the wardrobe, Mam recalled how proud he'd been when wearing the derby to Mass on Sunday mornings and her eyes filmed over again. Fighting back the tears, she emptied the contents of the drawers and found more poignant reminders: his ties and starched collars, his cufflinks and his shirt studs. After all these things had gone, Mam simply sat at the table, put her head in her hands and cried her eyes out because these little mementos brought home to her in a way that nothing else could that Dad had gone, really gone, and was not coming back.

Our new accommodation was something of a comedown in the world, consisting as it did of a parlour and living room-cum-kitchen with access to the cellar. Mam and I would sleep in the big bed in the parlour while Jamesey would sleep in the living room. This did not present a problem as he usually went to bed last and was the first to get up for an early start. The laundry cellar and the privy were shared with Mr and Mrs Kaminsky who lived upstairs with their three babies, who never seemed to stop whingeing. Despite that, we got on well with the family though initially there was a dispute about who owned the lobby from the front door area to the stairs. They claimed that, since these areas belonged to us, it was our responsibility to mop them out and keep them clean. Jamesey solved the problem by telling them that if that was the case, he was sorry but he'd no choice but to deny them access. That was the end of the disagreement and the Kaminskys took their turn in the washing-out chore. After that, we became very friendly with the family and helped each other out in various ways. At weekends we sometimes minded their babies while they went out shopping; in turn, they were happy to tackle some of the chores like washing and donkey-stoning the front-door steps and window sill, or getting an item from the stores if Mam had forgotten something.

The walls of our rooms were dripping with damp and there was a terrible stench from the drains, which explains maybe why our rent was only half a crown a week and even that seemed an overcharge. The water and lavatory arrangements were much the same as at Teignmouth Street, with the communal water tap outside and one privy between four houses – seven families, in-cluding us, using the one toilet. It required careful timing to avoid clashing with our fellow users. Peak periods were best avoided, with night-time and wet weather easing the congestion somewhat.

The final touches to our new lives were agreed and put in place. I was to start at St William's Elementary (Infants) in Simpson Street at the beginning of the new term beginning on Mon-day, 2 September 1891. After school at half past three, I was to go straight to Aunty Dorothy's house which was opposite St Michael's Flags at the bottom end of Angel Meadow – so named as it led to St Michael and All Angels Church – where I would be in the care of my aunty if she was back from working in Smithfield Market. If she wasn't there, I was to be looked after by her father-in-law, old Zeb, who scared me half to death for he had a wooden left leg and a glass eye. He'd lost both these body parts in America when fighting for the Yankees in their war with the South. Like Gran'ma Edna, he was impatient and didn't like children; 'bloody pests and nuisances,' he called us.

I heard him say to my aunty one day when we were visiting him to make final arrangements, 'I don't see any bloody reason why he should come to us. Let him go to your mother's, she's only in the next street.'

'You know very well that she's too busy working on her barrow,' Dorothy retorted. 'She just doesn't have the time.'

'And neither do I! Besides, I'm too old and infirm to be looking after a kid,' he whined.

'Tommy is coming for *me* to look after, not you,' she replied.

But the old cripple went on muttering in protest. 'But I'll have the little bugger here pestering me after school until you get home after supping in the Turk's Head.'

I just hoped and prayed he would never be left in charge of me for too long because he was well known in the family for his nasty temper.

When I told Jamesey about my fears, he simply laughed it off. 'Don't be scared of old Zeb. He's got a chip on his shoulder because of his war injuries. He's very self-conscious about them and doesn't like to be seen in public 'cos kids mock him and call after him "Peg Leg Pete" or "Long John Silver". Anyroad, you've only to run and he'll never catch you.'

'That's not true, Jamesey. You'd be surprised at the speed he can move at. You should see him hobble along.'

'Maybe so. Anyroad, when he lost his leg in the American War, he applied for compensation but was turned down as the government said he hadn't a leg to stand on.'

Mam thought it was funny but I didn't get it.

'Where was old Zeb wounded, Jamesey?' I asked.

'At the Battle of Gettysburg in eighteen sixty-three, or so he claims. He also gets a small pension from the American Government. The lucky old bastard.'

I was in a deep sleep and having a strange dream. I was lost wandering round the streets of Collyhurst again when Dad, with soot-blackened face and wearing ragged clothes, found me and put me astride a donkey to take me back home. I had reached Teignmouth Street when I heard Mam's voice calling.

'Come on, Tommy. Today's your big day. Your first day at school.'

I opened my eyes and came to, suddenly remembering where I was and what day it was. I'd spent the past week worried out of my mind about this particular day, afraid of what was going to happen to me and what those nuns that looked like the penguins I'd seen in my picture books were going to do to me. We'd paid a brief visit to the school earlier that month, and Mam had arranged matters and talked with Sister Gabriel about me as if I were deaf and dumb or wasn't there.

On this fateful morning, I got out of bed, and went into the next room where Mam gave me a good swill at the slop stone before taking my best short trousers off the brass knob on the bedpost, then putting on my white shirt and jersey. Last of all came my new stockings and boots which had a shine worthy of my dad and, what's more, a pair of new black laces to finish them off. I knew I was lucky to have all these clothes as many of the other kids in the streets around us were in rags. How long, I thought, would it be before I was the same, now we didn't have Dad's wages?

'We can't have you going in your old clothes on your first day,' she said.

I wish she'd stop saying 'on your first day', I thought. Each time she says it, my stomach turns over.

On the table she had a plate of porridge ready for me but before that she made me take my morning dose of Scott's Emulsion which she and Dad always swore by.

'That'll keep the bugs at bay,' she said. 'Now, eat your porridge, son. It'll stick to your ribs on a cold morning like this.'

It was no use. I swallowed the emulsion but couldn't eat anything else, I was that nervous.

'Where's Jamesey?' I asked because he usually gave me courage when I was faced with a trial.

'He's been gone to work over an hour ago. And now we must be off as well. You don't want to be late on your first morning, do you? What'll the good nuns think?'

I didn't care what the good nuns thought. I just knew that I didn't want to go to that terrifying place called St William's.

'Here, have a little drink of tea and a piece of toast with best butter,' she said, trying to encourage me.

She poured the tea into a saucer. I drank the tea thirstily and nibbled at the toast. Then it was time to go. It was a good fifteen minutes' walk to Gould Street where she was to leave me. We crossed over the Rochdale Road tramways, keeping a careful eye on the traffic as well as the thick horse droppings deposited in the road. It wouldn't do to get muck on my new boots.

At the corner of Gould Street, she kissed me, saying, 'Now, Tommy, you run straight to school and go into the yard there, that's a good boy. You're going to love this school, I'm sure. The sisters are such lovely people and so kind, you'll see.'

At the corner of New Mount Street, she pointed out the Pot o' Beer pub at the corner.

'At dinnertime, I'll meet you outside this pub at half past twelve and from there we can go and have a bit of dinner in the dining rooms, a few shops along Rochdale Road. I can get out of work for only half an hour, so be sure to wait for me there. If I'm a bit late, don't worry. I'll be there as soon as I can.'

The school yard was only a short distance from where Mam had left me and I reached it sooner than I really wanted to. There were a lot of other kids – boys as well as girls – streaming into the yard. Some were with their mothers, some were whingeing, some resisting and pleading to go home, some – like me – had resigned themselves to their fate. One or two snotty-nosed kids were barefoot and in threadbare clothes – girls in ragged dresses and boys in patched-up trousers. A few were dressed up – me included, I suppose – in their Sunday best.

A tall nun with a kind face came forward and, after checking that there were no stragglers and that the parents had departed, shut and locked the big iron gate behind us, enclosing us in the school quadrangle. Then she began swinging a big handbell trying to get some order out of the mass of kids who were milling around her higgledy-piggledy. She was so vigorous in her bell-ringing that one or two kids were almost poleaxed in the downward swing.

'Come along, children,' she called. 'Form a line.'

Most of the kids didn't have a clue as to what she meant by a 'line' and she had to take quite a few by the shoulders and push them into position. When all was to her satisfaction, a small bespectacled nun glided into the yard; I say 'glided' because, as far as I could see, she had no legs and must have been on roller skates.

She called out in a sharp voice that could be heard right round the yard and maybe several streets away. Such a shrill voice from such a small body.

'Everyone stand still, arms by your sides and listen. I don't want to see a single one of you move an inch.'

The two dozen kids froze in their tracks. 'I am

Sister Gabriel and I am the headmistress of St William's School. You are the new admission class and this is your teacher, Sister Philomena. You will do everything she tells you. Thank you, Sister, I'll now leave them to you.' She turned on her heel and went inside.

From the start I liked the look of Sister Philomena with her rosy cheeks and her friendly smiling face. She almost made the nun's habit look attractive and fashionable. If she hadn't been a nun, I'd have said she was pretty. She marched us into our new classroom and told us to stand against the wall. We looked wonderingly round the room where we were to spend the next year. There was a cheerful fire at the front of the room, a welcome sight on that rather cold September morning.

All round the walls were lots of pictures, pride of place being given to one of Queen Victoria, the rest of saints and other holy people, mainly men with long beards and holding shepherd's crooks. On the front wall was a large crucifix looking down on the rows of double-seater desks below. Also pinned round the walls were pictures illustrating the twenty-six letters of the alphabet. A for Apple, B for Ball, C for Cat and so on to Z for Zebra.

'Now, children,' Sister Philomena said, clapping her hands, 'I know many of you were hoping to go to St Patrick's School in Livesey Street but they were full and so you've had to come here instead. We'll do our best to make your time here a happy time. Now, I'm going to allocate you to your desks. Boys will sit next to boys and girls next to girls.'

This took about twenty minutes as the sister had to take us by the hand and lead us to our places – girls at the front and boys at the back. All very haphazard and I found myself next to a fair-haired lad with a freckled face, bright blue eyes and an impish grin. He made the mistake of sitting down immediately.

'Stand up, that boy! Stand up at once!' the nun shouted angrily. 'How dare you sit down without my permission.'

The lad jumped up like a jack-in-the-box.

'Now you may *all* sit down,' she said. 'The first rule you must learn is that you don't do anything in this classroom unless I have told you first. You don't speak or call out without my permission. And you call me "Sister". What do you call me?'

'We call you Sister, Sister!' we chorused.

Next, she commanded us to introduce ourselves to the rest of the class.

'Stand up when I tell you and say your name in a loud, clear voice. Then all the rest of you will answer in a similar voice, "How do you do?"'

I felt a right fool saying it but thought it best to stay on the side of this strange woman in black on my first day.

Many of the kids, especially the girls, were too shy to speak up and it was hard to hear what they'd said. One of the shoeless, ragged lads announced himself as 'Kenny Bogg', which I remember thinking was a most peculiar name 'cos it reminded me of the rude word for lavatory. People in Collyhurst used to say 'I'm off to the bog-house' and everyone knew they meant the privy.

Two little girls sitting next to each other – one dark-haired with a shy smile and long pigtails which hung down her back, the other hazel-eyed with fluffy fair hair and a turned-up nose – said their names so that everyone could hear. Angela Rocca and Doris Doonican. Even at that young age, I could weigh up girls. Doris, the fair-haired one, was quite pretty though a bit tubby but Angela was a raven-haired, black-eyed beauty and I took a fancy to her right away even though, in those far-off days, boys were expected to hate girls. The biggest insult to a boy was to be told to stop being such a softie and to 'go and play with the girls'.

'I am Tommy Hopkins,' I announced when it came to my turn, going into my act.

'How do you do?' the rest of the class chorused.

'I am Jimmy Dixon from St Pat's parish,' my desk neighbour told us.

'Now we shall practise some of my rules,' Sister announced. 'First, fold your arms.'

Most of us, including me, didn't know what she meant. How do you fold your arms, they're not made of paper? I thought. The sister showed us how and we all imitated her.

'Next, when I want everyone to be quiet, I shall say, "Fingers on lips!" Do it now!'

We spent the next hour learning to obey these commands and others which she put into a song which we learned to sing together:

This is the way we wash our hands,
  wash our hands, wash our hands...

This is the way we wash our face, wash our face,
   wash our face...
This is the way we fold our arms, fold our arms,
   fold our arms...
This is the way we put fingers on lips,
   fingers on lips, fingers on lips...

We had some difficulty fitting the last line into
the tune but we managed it in the end.

First lesson was religion. Sister asked us about
our prayers and if we knew how to make the sign
of the cross. For a fair number, this was all new
and so we had to practise that too. 'In the name
of the Father and the Son, and the Holy Ghost,
Amen,' suiting the actions to the words. We spent
the next half-hour until break saying and learning the Hail Mary which I already knew from
going to church with Mam and Dad.

It was here that I got into trouble and received
my first punishment. Jimmy Dixon, my neighbour, turned out to be a bit of a comedian and
when we began reciting the Hail Mary, he began
the prayer with, 'Hello, Mary, Funny Face.'

I started giggling.

The sister became red-faced with anger.

'Come out here, that boy who is laughing. You
are a very naughty boy,' she barked. 'You must
not laugh during prayers – ever! It is a very bad
sin. Now kneel down at the front of the class. You
will stay there until playtime.'

Not a good start to my educational career and
it was no use trying to explain or blame my
partner. I'd been found guilty without a trial and
it was pointless challenging the decision.

'When we say our prayers, children,' Sister continued, pointing to the crucifix suspended on the front wall, 'think of Jesus on the cross, looking down upon us with his bleeding hands and bleeding feet, suffering for our sins.'

I wondered if I'd heard her right. Did she just say 'bleeding hands and bleeding feet'? When drunken Mrs Gannon in Teignmouth Street had shouted this word before being carted off by the police, Mam had said it was the worst example of swearing in the whole of Collyhurst and that was saying something. 'Bleeding' was even more serious than 'bloody', it seemed. I dismissed the matter from my mind. I must have misheard her. Nuns don't swear, do they? Must wash the wax out of my ears, I told myself.

Sister next told us about the catechism and how we would learn to answer questions.

'Here is the first one,' she said by way of illustration. 'I ask you, "Who made you?" and you answer, "God made me." Try it now. Who made you?' she demanded of the boy with the patched-up spectacles sitting at the front.

'God made me, Sister,' he repeated dutifully.

'No, not made your sister, you stupid boy. What is your name?'

'Duggie Dimson, Sister.'

'Very well, Duggie Dimson. Just answer "God made me". Now, the next. "Why did God make you?" You must answer, "God made me to know Him, love Him, serve Him in this world and be happy with Him forever in the next".'

It took a considerable time for us to get that into our thick heads but we managed it in the end by saying it over and over again, about two thousand times. It looked as if learning in this class was to be mainly recitation and I liked it.

After religion, it was break time and I was allowed to go back to my place.

'Ah, it's half-time,' I said to Jimmy Dixon, thinking of the football matches I'd been to with Dad. We were taken out to the school yard and shown where the lavatories were. One side for the boys, the other for the girls. Then we were allowed to go. About time, I thought, as I'd been bursting all morning and had been afraid to ask in case it was against the rules. Many boys were rude and had competitions as to who could pee highest. One buck-toothed boy called Gordon Bennett said he thought it was very rude and he was going to tell Sister about it after playtime.

'You do,' said the tallest boy in the class showing his fist, 'and you'll get a taste of this.'

That seemed to work, for Gordon looked cowed. Kenny Bogg – most appropriately perhaps – had first go and sent a jet high up the wall. Duggie Dimson, the dopey-looking lad with the renovated spectacles balanced precariously on the end of his nose, was next to try. The fact that one of his lenses had been replaced with a circular piece of cardboard didn't help his aim and as a result his effort was judged pathetic. A lad with a cowlick hairstyle who'd told us his name was Charlie Madden then pushed the others aside and said 'Watch this!' and produced a stream which went nearly to the top of the urinal stone. Obviously an expert and the outright winner, we thought – until, that is, the big, tow-haired kid who'd given his name as Alfie Rigby elbowed his way through and said, 'That's nothing! Our cat can do better than that. Now lemme see any of you beat this, if you can!' And he proceeded to create a fountain that would have rivalled the one in Queen's Park. After this demonstration of prowess, Alfie Rigby made an announcement. 'I can lick anyone here at peeing *and* fighting. So I'm the cock of this class. Anyone want to fight me for it?'

Since no one could beat his effort and since he was also the biggest, chunkiest lad in the class, no one challenged his claim and so, by default, he became the cock of the class. While I thought this peeing competition was very funny, I was too shy to join in and so I opted out. Not only that, I could see I didn't stand a chance against these experts who'd obviously had lots of practice or maybe had unusual bladders.

After playtime, it was sums. We began with simple learning and counting up to twenty and then moved on to adding up, '2 and 1 make 3; 2 and 2 make 4', working our way up to more advanced sums like '2 and 8 make 10', at the same time counting up on our fingers. Sister demonstrated all this at the front of the class with a large abacus. Then she gave out slates to each child, also a sharpened slate pencil. There was a horrible squeaking of slate on slate, the kind of grating noise that goes through you, as kids experimented with the new tools. Sister went berserk.

'You must not write on your slates until I tell you,' she shouted. 'Everyone put your pencils down. Before you write anything, you must learn to clean your slate.' She gave out a few damp cloths. There weren't enough to go round, so many of the enthusiastic learners used their sleeves or spat on the slates and cleaned them with their hands.

The sister wrote a few simple sums on the big blackboard at the front: $2 + 2 = 4$; $2 + 3 = 5$; $2 + 4 = 6$.

We were told to copy these on to our slates as practice in the way we set out sums. For ten minutes, there was the hum of busy activity and the squeaking of slates. For some, it was the first time in their lives that they'd been required to write anything. It was not an easy task and they twisted this way and that in their desks, while some stuck out their tongues and narrowed their eyes, the better to concentrate.

We spent the rest of that first morning writing out different sums to get used to copying out the stuff from the big blackboard. We rounded off the lessons by reciting the two-times table. 'Once two is two; two twos are four,' and so on right up to 'two twelves are twenty-four.' Saying it like this gave weaker pupils, like Duggie Dimson, a chance to remember it even if they didn't entirely understand what they were saying.

We had all taken in a lot of information for our first session at school. I loved it all for I found I had a pretty good memory. An enjoyable morning then, except maybe being made to kneel down on the hard wooden floor for half an hour, but I knew from that first day that I was going to like going to school.

At the end of the lessons, Sister asked us about our dinner and if we had brought any with us. Many of the better-off kids, and I suppose that included me, said their mothers were coming for them; others had brought food with them such as bread and jam or cold toast left over from their breakfast. The barefooted ones seemed to have nothing and Sister told them to report after prayers to Sister Gabriel who would find them something and maybe try to get them clogs as well, provided they kept up good attendance.

Before noon, we were taken into the hall to join Infants Class 2, who were a year ahead of us. There, accompanied by a lot of other nuns I'd not seen before and all dressed in mourning clothes like the women at my dad's funeral, we recited the Angelus.

The Angel of the Lord declared unto Mary.
And she conceived of the Holy Ghost.
Behold the handmaid of the Lord
May it be done unto me according to
　Thy word.

My class did not know this prayer, of course, but the rest of the school did. Uh-oh, I thought, another new prayer for us to learn. I hoped there was enough room in my head for all this new material.

At twelve o'clock the hooters in the district went off, signalling to one and all that it was dinnertime. I rushed up the brew to the top of Gould Street to meet Mam and tell her all the exciting things that had been happening. I was worried about finding the pub again and so I asked a man who was passing by if he knew where the Pot o' Beer pub was.

'Ah, I think you mean this one,' he said, pointing out the pub at the corner of the street. 'It's called the Harp and Shamrock round here.'

I had to wait for fifteen minutes outside the pub before Mam arrived. At last she came with a big smile on her face. From there we went to the dining rooms she'd mentioned where we got a pot of tea and a meat and potato pie with a few chips.

'Well, Tommy,' she said. 'How did you like it, your first day at school?'

I talked nonstop about all the morning's happenings while Mam just smiled with a wistful look on her face.

'Loved it, Mam,' I gushed, pouring out my news. 'I was made to kneel at the front of the class for laughing during the Hail Mary, and we're learning the catechism all about who made us and why, and how to do sums. I can say the two times table and Sister Philomena said "bleeding hands and bleeding feet", I've made a new pal called Jimmy Dixon and a big lad named Alfie Rigby is cock of the class.'

Mam laughed. 'My! A lot *has* been happening to you in one morning. And I am quite sure the nun was not swearing like you think. She'd be talking about Christ being crucified. And what does that mean, "cock of the class"? I hope you haven't been fighting.'

'No, Mam. Cock of the class means that Alfie Rigby can beat anyone in the class at peeing and fighting and he can boss the rest of us about and tell us which games we'll have at playtime.'

How that half an hour flew by! Then it was back to work for her and back to the schoolyard for me till Sister opened the place up at half past one.

In the afternoon, we were introduced to the alphabet letters on the wall. I knew them all from the time my dad had sung the nursery rhymes starting with 'A dillar, A dollar, A ten o'clock scholar' and so I was soon able to say the letters as the nun went round the room saying them.

'A is for Apple, B for Ball, C for Cat, D for Dog...'

We must have gone over them about twenty times till everyone knew them by heart. As a final test, Sister called on individual children to go out to the various letters and say what they were. G is for Girl; S is for Sun; T is for Tram; Z is for Zebra. Then we spent the rest of the lesson copying out the letters on to our slates. Though I didn't know it at the time, copying from the blackboard was to be the mainstay of my education for the rest of my time at school.

After all this mental activity, it was time for another break in the yard where everyone could go wild and let off steam. The noise was deafening as we boys got rid of our endless energy in wrestling, running, riding piggyback in games of war on horseback, trying to unseat each other; the girls preferred more ladylike activities such as skipping to rhymes like:

Two little dicky birds, sitting on a wall;
One named Peter, the other named Paul.
Fly away, Peter! Fly away, Paul!
Come back, Peter! Come back, Paul!

Oddly enough, Doris Doonican preferred playing with the boys in their rougher horseplay games where she could give as much as she got. She was certainly big enough to hold her own.

'Why don't you go and play with the other girls?' I asked.

'Their games are too sissy,' she replied, tossing her head.

'She's a tomboy,' Jimmy Dixon said to me.

I was a bit annoyed when he said that.

'How do you mean?' I asked. 'She's not mine. I hope you're not saying she's my girlfriend or anything like that.'

'No, no.' He laughed. 'Nothing like that. It means she likes doing boys' things and playing boys' games. That's all. Understandable, I suppose, in Doris's case, because she has four big older brothers at St Pat's and she's more used to their rough and tumble than playing with dolls.'

'Then keep her well away from me, whatever you do.'

After the break, it was story time until three o'clock. Sister Philomena proved to be an excellent story-teller; the only trouble was that her tales always had a lesson or a moral to be learned, like 'The Boy Who Cried Wolf' – everyone knows the sorry tale of how he lied time after time and how, in the end, the wolf devoured his sheep. There was 'The Boy Who Wouldn't Eat His Soup'

('He's like a little bit of thread, And on the fifth day, he was – dead'). Then there was the tale of Harriet and the Matches:

> So she was burnt, with all her clothes
> And arms, and hands, and nose.
> Till she had nothing more to lose
> Except her little scarlet shoes;
> And nothing else but these were found
> Among her ashes on the ground.

Around that time, just after my dad died, I'd developed the habit of sucking my thumb, though it must be said, only when I was worried. So the rhyme of 'Little Suck-a-Thumb' seemed to be aimed at me and the one or two others in the class who had also acquired the habit. I could remember the verse years later even when I became a man. It went:

> One day Mamma said: Thomas dear
> I must go out and leave you here
> But mind now Thomas what I say,
> Don't suck your thumb while I'm away.
> The great tall tailor always comes
> To little boys who suck their thumbs.
> And fore they know what he's about,
> He takes his great sharp scissors out
> And cuts their thumbs clean off – and then,
> You know, they never grow again.

From the sound of it, it looked like a pretty dangerous habit to have and soon afterwards I gave it up.

Chapter Eleven

At three thirty, we were let out and this was the part of the day I wasn't looking forward to. I didn't mind so much being left with Aunty Dorothy even though her house always seemed to smell a little like the pub doorways I used to pass along the road. No, it was that nasty, bad-tempered, one-eyed, one-legged Zeb who had me quaking in my boots.

From Simpson Street, I began the walk down Angel Meadow. What a name to give to one of the dingiest slum districts in the whole of Manchester! As I passed along, I couldn't help casting a few hasty glances to either side. The street was dirty and muddy, and as I turned into the so-called meadow, I was hit by the stench of sewage and unwashed humanity and I passed a few drunken bodies slumped on the pavement. A more wretched place I'd never seen. The houses along the route were in a much worse state than any to be seen up at our end of Collyhurst. I was able to look down through the barred windows into cellar after cellar where I could see wretches wallowing on filthy rags or mattresses filled with shavings or straw. Lurking in doorways were villainous-looking men on the lookout no doubt for easy pickings like me.

At last I reached Aunty Dorothy's house which was in a little better condition since it had three steps raising it up from street level. Nervously I reached up and rapped on the door using the rusty iron knocker. There was no mistaking who would be opening the door for I could hear the distinctive limp (whump–bedhump! whump–bedhump!) gait of Gran'pa Zeb Langley. It took some considerable time for him to draw the many bolts on the door but then there he was scowling down on me with his one good eye. He poked his crutch at me, almost knocking me back down the steps.

'Well, whaddya want?' he snapped. He obviously didn't recognize me or he was deliberately being his nasty self.

'It's me, Gran'pa. Tommy. I was told I had to come here after school.'

'Well, your Aunty Dorothy ain't home from the market yet. So you'll have to sit there on the step till she is.'

I didn't fancy sitting there one bit, not for three hours I didn't, especially as there were some ugly-looking characters hanging about in that vile street and I was still wearing my best clothes. But what choice did I have? The front door was slammed shut in my face, so there was nothing to be done but to settle there and wait. I plonked myself down on the top step and prepared to sit it out. It wasn't long before I attracted attention. An old hag of a woman in filthy rags approached me.

'Excuse me, young sir,' she croaked, 'but could you spare a copper for an old woman to buy a crust?'

'Sorry,' I mumbled, pulling out the lining of my pockets to show I was broke. 'I don't have anything. I'm skint.'

'Then may God strike you down, you little bas-tard,' she screeched as she ambled off.

Five minutes later, a man, not unlike the tramps who'd found me on Barney's when I'd been lost a couple of years back, approached me. Dirty old overcoat, shoes coming apart, bloodshot eyes, stubble-chinned, he stood there weighing up both me and my clothes.

'Them's a good pair o' boots you have on, young master. What size are they?'

'I don't really know. My dad got 'em for me.'

'Now I have a young son like you at home; he's about the same size. Just take off your boots for a minute, son, so's I can see the size. Then maybe I'll buy them off you.'

But I hadn't been born yesterday. Didn't I know the antics of the Gannon family in Teign-mouth Street? This man wasn't in their class.

'Very well,' I replied, knocking loudly on the door. 'I'll just ask my dad who's an Irish navvy to see if it's all right.'

The beggar hurried off up Angel Meadow mut-tering curses and imploring the devil and his angels to send all manner of diseases down on my head.

Gran'pa Zeb was standing at the door once more.

'What the bloody hell do you want now? I told you to wait on the step till your aunty comes. What's up with you?'

'If you don't let me in, Gran'pa, there's people out here who'll have the shirt off my back and the boots off my feet.'

'Well, I suppose you'd better come in then. You're a bloody nuisance and if Dorothy thinks I'm going to be a nanny and look after you every day, she's got another think coming.'

I went inside and found the house an untidy mess. The walls and ceiling of the room were black with age and soot. The floor was filthy; breakfast pots still in the slop stone, a fire that had burned to a low glow in the grate, clothes strewn about the place. In the middle of the room was a deal table upon which stood a candle stuck in a beer bottle, a basin of milk sops, a bottle of gin and a half-filled glass.

Oh, God, I thought, is this where I am to spend two or three hours every day after school? I hoped Aunty Dorothy wouldn't be too long in rescuing me from her despicable father-in-law or that Mam wouldn't be late in coming to rescue me at half past six as I could see that this old man and me weren't, to put it mildly, going to get along.

'Right,' the old man barked. 'If you've got to come in, you're not going to sit around on your arse. You can do some work. When I was a kid your age, we didn't have no school. We had to work in the mines or the cotton mills. And that's what you should be doing, working to help your mother pay the rent and put food on the table, not wasting your bloody time at this here school of yours. Book work never did nobody any good.

'Anyroad, while you're here, you can make yourself useful. While I'm finishing off my tea, you can get some coal in the scuttle and get the fire going again,' he said, spooning dollops of pobs into his mouth. 'After that, you can sweep the yard, then wash the breakfast pots what your aunty and uncle, the cheeky buggers, left for me to wash this morning when they rushed out to the market.'

'Where's the coal, Gran'pa?'

'Down the steps, in the cellar! In the coal-hole! Where the hell do you think, you daft little bugger!'

I took the scuttle down into the cellar and half filled it. It was a heavy thing for me to lug up the stairs but I managed it by lifting it one step at a time. I put a few lumps on to the dying fire, hoping it might spring into life.

'I've never swept anything before, Gran'pa,' I explained, in an attempt to cover my shortcomings, 'and I've never washed pots at home. I'm not allowed in case I break something.'

'Then you can bloody well start learning. You've been getting away with it but not any more. Start sweeping the yard and see to it that there's no slacking, I'll be keeping an eye on you.'

He removed his glass eye from its socket and placed it on the window sill overlooking the yard.

'See this?'

'Yes, Gran'pa.'

'Well, it can see you as well. I'll be watching you through that. Any lazing about and I'll know'

I began sweeping with a broom that I could hardly lift and with a long handle I could only grip halfway. I did the best I could and after half an hour called out, 'Finished, Gran'pa!'

He came out and put his eye back and inspected my work with his good eye. 'Not very good,' he

112

said, 'but I suppose it'll have to do. Now into the scullery to wash the pots.'

'They're very greasy, Gran'pa. Any hot water?'

'Hot water! Hot water! I'll give you hot water. Do you think we're made of money? Go out to the tap in the back street and fill that pan. That'll have to do.'

I did as I was told to the best of my ability and came back with a pan half filled which was the most I could carry. I stood on a chair to wash the crockery at the slop stone but there was so much fat and grease on the dishes I knew I wasn't making a very good job of it. I lifted a plate to swill it and it slipped from my hand and smashed into smithereens on the stone scullery floor.

'Sorry, Gran'pa. It just slid out of my hand, it were that slippy.'

He went berserk. 'Sorry! Sorry! You stupid little bastard,' he roared. 'Why don't you be careful what you're doing! You've broken one of our best plates. Your Aunty Dorothy will go mad when she sees that. You deserve to be thrashed for that.'

His good eye bulged and he scowled as he limped into the scullery with a rush and gave me a stinging slap across the face which made my head spin. Then he removed the thick belt from around his waist and began belting me around the legs, leaving red welts where the leather struck.

'That'll teach you to be more careful next time,' he fumed.

'I want my Mam,' I whinged, 'and I'm going to tell her what you've done when she gets here.'

'See if I bloody well care,' he rasped.

113

At half past five, Aunty Dorothy and Uncle Brodie came home. They looked the worse for wear and it was obvious from their beery breath and funny, slurred speech that they had been on the booze. She looked at me whimpering in the corner.

'What's been going on?' she asked.

'This little clumsy bugger has gone and broke one of your best plates, that's what's been going on,' Gran'pa said.

'I'm sure ish wash an accident, and little Tommy didn't mean it,' Brodie lisped through his drunken haze. 'Don't be too hard on the little mite, Da.'

'I hope you've not been belting him or anything, you old goat,' Dorothy said angrily, noticing the redness on my legs. 'Our Mary'll be livid. I pity you if you have 'cos she'll have your guts. All hell will be let loose, you'll see. She's very touchy about anyone hitting her son.'

'I hardly touched the lad though he deserved a good hiding,' Gran'pa retorted, now sounding less sure of himself. 'He's got to learn to take more care of other people's things next time. Anyroad, I only gave him a little slap on his legs. "Spare the rod and spoil the child" is what my old dad used to say and the occasional belt did me no harm. This kid doesn't know he's born. He should have seen what I suffered in the war. Then he'd know what a good hiding was.'

'Did you give the little lad a cup of tea or summat to eat?' she asked. 'He's not had nothing to eat since dinnertime.'

'I didn't. It's not my job to be feeding the little swine. Anyroad, you know I can't get about so

114

easy on this crutch.'

'You don't even try, you old cripple,' she barked. 'Anyroad, I'll make a pot of tea for all of us while I'm about it.'

Just gone half past six, Mam came to collect me.

'I won't take my coat off as I want to get this little lad home for his tea,' she said. 'I'll bet he's hungry by now.'

She put on my coat, took my hand and we were through the door so quickly that it was obvious that she was in a hurry to get home as she'd had a long day at the corset factory. We hadn't gone far when she noticed my limp.

'What's the matter, Tommy? Why can't you walk properly?'

She stooped to examine my legs and saw the red welts.

'What's this? What's been happening, Tommy?'

It all came out in a flood of tears.

'Gran'pa Zeb slapped my face and strapped me round the legs with his belt for breaking a plate.'

'He did what! Belted you for breaking a plate! How did you do that?'

'It were an accident, Mam. It slipped outa my hand when I were washing the breakfast pots.'

'Slipped outa your hand! Washing the breakfast pots! What the hell has been going on while I've been at work? The bloody old villain! He'll not get away with this. Not as long as I'm alive, he won't. Come on, Tommy. We're going right back. I'll give the old devil a piece of mind he'll not forget.'

'No, Mam. Please. Let's forget it and go home,' I pleaded. 'It'll only cause trouble.'

'There'll be trouble all right, Tommy. Come on. We're going back.'

And go back we did. Mam thumped on the door which was opened by mild-mannered hiccoughing Brodie. Mam barged past him into the house.

'Where's that old bugger with the crutch?' she exploded. 'I'll crutch him all right! I'll ram it down his bloody throat.'

'What's the matter, Mary?' Dorothy protested, playing the innocent.

'I'll tell you what's the matter, our Dorothy. It's that bloody glass-eyed father-in-law of yours. That's what's the matter! He's been belting our Tommy across the legs. Look at the marks he's left.'

She went into the scullery where the old man sat squinting at the paper, pretending to read it.

'Listen to me, you!' Mam bellowed. 'You bloody old villain, you. What do you mean belting our Tommy? Just look at the poor lad's legs! He came here while I'm at work and this is what happens to him. But if you touch him again with that belt you'll have me to answer to and I won't be responsible for my actions. I'll take the law into my own hands. If he does something wrong, I'll be the one to chastize him, not you! Do you understand me, you bloody old rogue?'

Gran'pa Zeb sat cowed and rattled by the onslaught.

'Do you understand?' Mam bawled at him.

'Yes, I understand,' he mumbled.

'And another thing. I don't mind if you give him one or two things to do but I'll not have him running around like one of your slaves. Tommy washing dishes! He's only five. As for breaking dishes, any more of your bullying and there'll be another plate smashed. This time over your head. Come on, Tommy. We're going home.'

The old cripple could do nothing but nod meekly. A different character to the one I'd had bawling at me only a couple of hours earlier.

On the way out, Mam spoke to Dorothy and Brodie.

'Sorry about the trouble and the shouting. Hope that's the end of it but I want you to know how grateful I am to both of you for taking Tommy in. We couldn't manage without you.'

The two sisters embraced on the doorstep.

'You're welcome, Mary,' Dorothy said. 'We know what a rotten time you've been going through and we're glad to help. Don't worry about old Peg Leg Pete in there. The only things he's interested in are gin, pobs and fags.'

'What are those? Pobs?' I asked.

'They're crusts of bread soaked in hot milk and sugar,' Mam explained. 'People eat them when they're toothless and gummy.'

'Anyroad,' Dorothy continued, 'we'll see to it that there's no more trouble. Now you get home and give the lad his tea. You must be fair wore out having to work so hard and then having to come back to sort out the old man there. Somehow I think there won't be any more problems with him. That blistering telling-off you've just given him should keep him quiet.'

Dorothy was right and there was no more trouble with the old man for some time to come.

Chapter Twelve

At school, my education continued unabated. We were introduced to, not the three Rs, but the four Rs – Reading, wRriting, aRithmetic and Religion.

The day always began with morning prayers followed by the calling of the register and there were usually a number of absentees, chiefly of those poor ragged kids who'd arrived on the first day minus shoes. Once or twice mothers and fathers came up to the school and demanded with threats that their kids be allowed to return home where they were needed for various jobs like looking after younger brothers and sisters, or helping in the family business such as chopping and bundling firewood.

After roll call, the first lesson of the day was always religion. A great deal of time was devoted to this subject which in the admission class meant first of all learning the main prayers, leading up to longer and harder prayers. We began by learning a few catechism answers like:

What is prayer?

Prayer is the raising up of the mind and heart to God.

How do we raise up our mind and heart to God?

We raise up our mind and heart to God by thinking of God; by adoring, praising, and thanking Him; and by begging of Him all blessings for soul and body.

We went on from there to learn the main prayers: the Lord's Prayer, the Hail Mary, the Hail Holy Queen.

We were also told stories about the life of Jesus and characters from the Bible, all of which we loved as there were so many miracles and other magic tricks. We were taught about the way Jesus was born in a stable at Bethlehem and at Christmas we acted it out as a play. We heard how Jesus became lost once (just like me in Collyhurst, I thought) and was later found in the synagogue talking to the clever rabbis who were amazed by his learning (with me it had been the tramps in the brick kiln and then the coppers in Willert Street station but I don't think any of them thought too much of my knowledge). We were told about the miracles Jesus had worked like curing the sick and the blind, raising Lazarus from the dead, how he had walked on water and how he once fed five thousand people with a few loaves and a few fishes. We were horrified by the cruelty of his scourging at the pillar, his death and crucifixion at Calvary and we were incensed by the treachery of Judas.

'I wish my dad could've got hold of him!' exclaimed Charlie Madden fiercely. 'He'd have slapped his face and then chopped his head off.'

Sister also told us many stories from the Bible: Adam and Eve in the Garden of Eden and how the first man was tempted by his wife and ate the forbidden fruit. We had problems, though, understanding why we had to pay the price of Adam's disobedience.

'That's not fair,' argued Alfie Rigby, getting all worked up about the matter. 'It's like me in our house. Sometimes when my brother spills something or steals money out of me mam's purse, I get the blame and then my dad belts me when he comes in from work. So why should I get punished 'cos this fellah Adam ate an apple? Doesn't seem right to me.'

Some of the other Bible stories, like Jonah and the whale, puzzled us. 'How did he manage to live in the belly of a big fish without food or drink?' Then there was King Solomon with all those wives and said to be the wisest man who ever lived in history.

'How did Solomon become the wisest man of all times?' Sister asked after telling us how God had granted his wish.

'Because he had so many women to advise him,' said Angela Rocca.

One or two biblical incidents horrified us, like the way God told Abraham to kill his son.

'Did Isaac know his dad was going to kill him?' asked Jimmy Dixon aghast.

'No,' said Sister, 'but Isaac must have wondered why there was no lamb to be sacrificed.'

'I think that was very cruel of God to tell Abraham to kill his own son like that,' I said indignantly.

'God was testing Abraham,' Sister answered. 'As Abraham was taking out his knife, his hands were trembling. He was about to sacrifice his son when he heard the voice of God saying, "Abraham, stop! Do not hurt your son".'

'Doesn't matter,' I persisted. 'God was wrong.

120

It wasn't a game and somebody might've got hurt. Abraham was an old man and he might not have heard God in time and then Isaac would have been stabbed to death. So God was wrong.'

For answering back and challenging divine authority, I spent the rest of that lesson kneeling at the front. It was becoming my established position in religious lessons.

The story we loved above all others though was that of David and Goliath and the way the young lad knocked down a nine-foot giant by throwing a stone. Idealists among my readers may think that our admiration of David was perhaps an early sign of the development of a British sense of fair play and support for the underdog. You'd be wrong, however, for our hero worship of David stemmed not from any sense of justice but from our amazement at his stone-throwing ability, a skill we spent much of our time practising and trying to perfect.

In our other lessons, we learned the alphabet and the rudiments of reading and writing, plus basic arithmetic. The nuns were keen on recitation of material over and over again until the information was firmly implanted in our thick skulls. They didn't believe in wasting time and we learned and memorised something new every day. In reading, we were trained to spell out the words phonetically one sound at a time from the wall chart displayed on the blackboard, like 'c–a-t, m–a-t, d–o–g, l–o–g', and we were soon stringing simple words together like, 'The cat sat on the mat, the dog sat on the log'. They didn't always make much sense. One page on a chart read, 'Ben has a nag and a gig. The nag is fat and big. Now the gig has a fat pig in it. The fat pig can dig.'

We couldn't make any sense of it as most of us had never seen a gig and certainly had never seen a fat pig digging. No matter. Anyone passing our classroom would have heard us chanting our hearts out on spelling single-syllable words from A to Z: 'a – p – e spells APE; z – o – o spells ZOO'.

Any child letting his attention wander by watching a fly buzzing on the windowpane or by simply staring into space was made to continue the chanting from a kneeling position at the front of the class, Sister's favoured punishment position. Poor learners with memory problems were easily identified by their red kneecaps and their knee scabs.

One day Sister decided to vary her approach.

'All round the walls, children,' she said, 'you can see all the words we have learned so far. Let's read them all out together.'

'Yes, Sister,' we responded obediently. We began chanting out the words which were written and illustrated on slates around the room: nun, jug, sun, gun, can, pan, pig, hen, doll, and so on until we had completed the full circle.

'Now as a change,' Sister continued, 'I want each of you to make up your own sentences from these words and write them on your slates.'

For a good twenty minutes, there was the sound of children sucking on their slate pencils as they tried to make sense out of the one-syllable words.

'Very well, children,' Sister said at last. 'Let's hear your efforts. First, Charlie.'

'My dad sat on the cat,' Charlie said proudly.

'Now my dad needs a fag.'

'Yes, very well,' Sister said doubtfully. 'Now, Alfie.'

'The dog bit my dad. My dad hit the dog. My dad is a fat pig. Now my dad needs a nap.'

'Another one about a dad,' Sister sighed. 'I'm not sure your fathers would be too pleased if they heard what you've written about them. Anyway, let's hear one or two from the girls.'

'My mam goes on the tram to the shop to buy ham,' offered Doris.

'Sal has a big doll,' this from the lovely Angela. I knew I was in love with her when I heard her gentle voice speak these words.

'Well done, you two,' Sister said. 'Now the turn of Jimmy and Tommy.'

'We've written our sentences together to make a story,' Jimmy explained.

'Very well. Sounds interesting,' Sister commented. 'Read out what you've written.'

'The nun has a bun,' said Jimmy. 'Dan wants the bun.'

'Dan has a gun,' I said, adding my contribution. 'Dan shoots the nun.'

'Now the cops are after Dan,' Jimmy continued.

'Run, Dan, run,' I said, rounding off the story.

To our surprise, Sister Philomena was laughing and she went on giggling for the rest of that morning.

In arithmetic we had learned to do simple adding and taking away sums copied on to our slates. After playtime each day, the sing-song voices of the infant admission class reciting the tables rang

123

round the school. Then followed quick mental questions on what we'd learned.

'Two add three! Come on! Quickly! Quickly!'

'Eight and seven make...? Come on! Come on!'

'Fifteen take away six? Yes, yes, come along! Come along!'

We found this part the hardest since the numbers were all mixed up and taken out of order, so we had to think fast to avoid the 'kneel-at-the-front' torture. Poor Duggie Dimson was left floundering and gave up trying to give the right answer and almost volunteered himself to kneel at the front to escape the merciless inquisition. As for the rest of us, none of us understood how the solutions were arrived at but, by golly, we had to think fast and come up with the answers. Or else.

At the end of our first year, that would be 1892 and I'd be going on six, we were told that we would be tested to see how much we had learned in our first year at the school.

'If you pass the tests,' Sister told us, 'you will go up into Sister Monica's class for the next two years until you are ready to go to the big school, St Chad's. If you don't pass, you'll stay in the infants class for another year or as long as it takes till you do pass.'

I was worried stiff as I didn't fancy another spell or two among the babies. I found out that I wasn't the only one who was nervous.

'My mam and dad'll go mad if I don't pass,' Jimmy said, 'but if I do, they're going to take me to town to buy me a present.'

Lucky him, I thought. At least he's got a dad to go mad.

'My mam might belt me if I don't pass,' said Kenny Bogg. 'But if I don't tell her, she won't know, will she?'

The tough kids, like Charlie and Alfie, said their mams and dads couldn't care less. Duggie said he didn't have a cat in hell's chance of passing the test.

Unlike the other kids, I didn't have to worry about a dad and what he might say but at least I had one parent who really did care. My mam had simply said, 'Just do your best. That's all we can ask.'

I hoped the girls would get through, especially Angela and Doris. Their chances were good as they had strong parental support, their fathers had good jobs and were anxious to see their daughters get on. Angela's father was an ice-cream seller by trade (lucky Angela, I thought) and Doris's father had his own retail fruit stall on Smithfield Market.

The day of the test came round and, to my surprise, I found the test nowhere as hard as I'd feared. It was dead easy as all it involved was reading out a few sentences with mainly single-syllable words like, 'John and Mary live in a house with their mam and dad. They have a big dog called Spot. They play with the dog in the garden.'

The rest of the tests were things like writing out your name and copying easy sentences from the blackboard; doing simple sums adding and taking away; answering a few questions about the Bible and knowing our prayers which we'd recited about two million times. Finally we had to recite any poem we'd learned at school. My favourite verse became my party piece and my mam was always asking me to recite it if she wanted to show me off to visitors. I remember it now even seventy-odd years later. It goes like this:

If all the seas were one sea,
What a great sea that would be!
If all the trees were one tree,
What a great tree that would be!
And if all the axes were one axe,
What a great axe that would be!
And if all the men were one man,
What a great man that would be!
And if the great man took the great axe,
And chopped down the great tree,
And it fell into the great sea,
What a splish-splash that would be!

Nearly all of us passed, including the two girls I fancied and the cheeky kids like Charlie, Alfie and, surprise, surprise, even Duggie. And of course Gordon Bennett, teacher's pet.

Many of the ragged, shoeless kids didn't make it. They failed not because they lacked footwear but because many of them had poor attendance records. Their parents kept coming up to the school to take them away to do jobs at home, much to the despair of the School Board man.

One of these poor kids was Kenny Bogg. When I found that he lived in Back Hannah Street just round the corner from us, we became good friends.

I thought us Hopkins were poor but we didn't

compare with the Boggs family in that respect. He had come to school in ragged clothes and without shoes on his feet and had had to rely on the charity of the sisters for a pair of clogs. Like me he'd lost his father through illness – TB, he told me – and so we got on well together because we had this loss in common. There were five kids altogether in his family: two younger brothers and two younger sisters. He invited me home one day; I found it a real eye-opener and I began to think that perhaps we weren't so badly off after all.

Kenny's family lived in two furnished rooms; the three boys slept in one bed in the back room and the mother and two girls in the living room/kitchen. The mother was ill in bed, coughing her heart out and puffing on a fag. A bare-arsed baby was crawling about the floor from room to room, a toddler sucking a dummy and still in nappies gawped at me as if I was some curiosity, while the remaining two were busy bouncing a ball in the back yard even though it was drizzling.

'Pease pudding hot, pease pudding cold, pease pudding in a pot, nine days old,' they recited in time to the bouncing ball. Interesting that they're reciting a rhyme about food, I thought. Wishful thinking maybe.

The living room/kitchen was a complete mess with kids' clothes and bedding strewn about the place. On the table could be seen a cracked jug containing milk and four jam jars which obviously served the family as cups. The only cutlery I could see was a knife, three soiled forks and three or four spoons of different sizes. The stink of urine and shit almost knocked me off my feet.

'Is it OK if I cut a piece of bread and jam for myself and my pal, Mam?' Kenny called.

'Who's your pal, Kenny?' his mam croaked from the front bedroom.

'His name's Tommy Hopkins from school.'

'All right, cut yourself a coupla pieces,' she said, 'but don't be ruining the loaf by cutting it skew-whiff. There's no jam but there's a bit of margarine left in the packet, but go easy on it. We're not made of money.'

'It's OK, Kenny,' I said. 'I'm not hungry and I can get something when I get home.'

The other kids stopped their games when they saw Kenny cutting the bread. Bread and jam was a bigger attraction than bouncing a ball.

'Here,' said Kenny, cutting a couple of extra pieces and spreading them with jam. 'Share that between you.'

'I'm just going out for a bit to play on Barney's with Tommy,' Kenny called to his mam. 'I'll be back in about an hour and I'll help you to side the table and make the tea.'

'There's a three-penny bit on the sideboard, Kenny,' she shouted back. 'Get a small loaf and a quarter of corned beef from Murgatroyd's on your way back.'

'That won't be enough, Mam. I think it'll cost more than thruppence.'

'Then ask Mabel Murgatroyd to put it in the book and I'll settle up with her on Friday after the Vincent Paul have been to see us.'

Kenny and I used to play mainly in the back streets, especially in the broken-down and deserted houses on Fitzgeorge Street where we could climb and jump to our heart's content.

During that summer holiday, we played together running, jumping, and wrestling in the street. Sometimes we'd set up a little tent on Barney's waste ground using poles and a couple of bedsheets which I had sneaked out of the house when Mam's back was turned. With a couple of jam sandwiches which I also nicked from the kitchen, we dined like kings on Barney's grassy green hill. Another favourite activity was climbing. We clambered up anything and everything that offered a challenge: wooden fences, iron lamp posts, and brick walls. Though I could beat Kenny every time when it came to fighting or wrestling, I wasn't in his league when it came to climbing. He was like a monkey and could shin up the most impossible obstacles seemingly without effort. He lived dangerously and was ever ready to take chances in getting to the top of anything that offered risk and danger. He seemed to defy gravity and I once saw him vault to the top of a six-foot buttressed brick wall in a leap and a bound. He beckoned me to follow but there was no way I could have got up there without a foothold or a ladder. If ever a lad was destined to join the army as an assault force, Kenny was that lad. How I looked forward to going to school with him to St Chad's Elementary School at the end of August! But it was not to be. One day after we'd spent the afternoon running in and out of derelict houses, we parted company. Kenny didn't make it home. On the way back, he attempted one of his daring feats and came to grief. As he reached the top of a very high wall, the whole lot came down about his ears and crushed his head like an eggshell.

When I got the news the next day, it hit me like a thunderbolt and I went around for the rest of the day in a state of shock. For a short time during the day, the tragedy filtered to the back of my mind, only to return afresh to the forefront with renewed realization. Another funeral cortège to Moston Cemetery, another death of someone I had become fond of. Was there no end to it? Was I some kind of jinx who spelled disaster for anyone who came close to me? I was filled with grief not only for the loss of a friend but also because I'd seen how his mother, younger brothers and sisters relied on and looked to him as the eldest boy in the family. For days after the event I walked around in a trance, unable to believe that I would never again see poor Kenny Bogg, my newfound playmate, who would not be going on to St Chad's or indeed going on anywhere. The empty place at his desk reminded me every day.

In September 1892 we started in Sister Monica's class after the long holiday. It felt as if we'd been sentenced to two years' hard labour in her custody for crimes we couldn't remember committing. She was a very different kettle of fish from Sister Philomena and was known as something of a slave-driver. We'd seen this sister striding about the place and for us she was a forbidding figure. For a start, she was older, stricter, and nastier. I'd never seen her smile once because if she had, I'm sure her plaster of Paris face would have cracked or her teeth would have fallen out. She believed that all young children, but especially boys, had been put on earth to test her patience so earning her enough grace to take her to heaven. Furthermore, children were little ignorant savages, empty vessels or clean slates. It was her job to fill our empty heads with facts and information and to write on our blank mental tablets. Understanding did not enter into it.

'That will come later,' she said, 'when your little brains have matured and you will see the wisdom of all that we have taught you.' Her favourite verse was one she'd seen at some time in *Punch* magazine:

Sock it in, knock it in
Children's heads are empty
Stack it in, rack it in!
Still there's more aplenty!

She was around fifty years of age with sharp beady eyes which seemed to look right through you. The severe expression etched on her face was not helped by the tight wimple which enveloped her head. There were rumours among the kids that nuns had to have all their hair shaved off like Red Indians so they could be accepted into the order but there was no way of checking this out. The rest of her uniform – the starched breastplate, the heavy rosary beads, the crucifix dangling from her belt made her so intimidating, it was hard to recognize her as female. I could not believe that there were any limbs under all that camouflage as the top part seem to merge into the

131

lower half.

We'd heard all about Sister Monica from kids who'd left her class and we'd been relieved to hear that she didn't make use of the cane or the strap as forms of punishment. That is, until we found out later that she had developed more subtle, painful forms of torture. She was a compulsive leg whacker, nose pincher, ear tweaker, face slapper and, most excruciating of all and reserved for boys, sideburn puller. Perhaps the most potent weapon in her arsenal was that of ridicule and the Dunce's Cap. No wonder she'd earned the nickname 'Monica the Monster'. If she was in a bad mood or had been particularly annoyed, she resorted to belting you on the back of the hand with a ruler. I used to wonder sometimes if they made a study at the nuns' teacher training college to identify the most painful parts of children's anatomies, especially if the punishment could be delivered without leaving evidence or too much of a mark.

From day one, the new learning regime began in earnest. In religious knowledge lessons we moved on from the early baby stuff like 'Who made you?' and 'Why did God make you?' to more advanced philosophical questions like:

To whose image and likeness did God make you?

Answer: God made me to His own image and likeness.

Is this likeness to God in your body, or in your soul?

This likeness to God is chiefly in my soul.

How is your soul like to God?

My soul is like to God because it is a spirit, and is immortal.

What do you mean when you say that your soul is immortal?

When I say my soul is immortal, I mean that my soul can never die.

For the life of us, we could make neither head nor tail of what we were reciting parrot-fashion but, like most of the learning that took place in the school, we were trained to commit the sounds to memory by means of endless repetition, threats and the sundry penalties that she'd dreamed up. For us, most of the catechism answers were no more than a jumble of meaningless words and phrases.

'In the coming year while you're in this class,' the sister barked, 'you will not only learn and memorize the Apostle's Creed, you will be able to explain the meaning of the different parts to the Religious Inspector when he comes to examine you next summer. Any lazy, idle good-for-nothings who waste their time will be dealt with.'

After initial prayers, we were set to learning the next catechism quota followed by a thorough check on how much of what we'd managed to plaster on to the ceilings of our minds was still adhering there. Set prayers such as the Nicene Creed were not only longer but more complex and we were required, on pain of being whacked, to explain different aspects of the creed, some of which had taken hundreds of years for the Church to define.

What is God?

God is the supreme Spirit, who alone exists of

Himself and is infinite in all perfections.

We learned that there is only one God and there are three Persons in God: God the Father, God the Son, and God the Holy Ghost, called the Blessed Trinity. In the same way there were also three parts to our soul: memory, understanding and will.

Woe betide anyone who was not word perfect in repeating the block of answers we had been set. Some of my classmates had bitten their finger-nails down to the quick in their anxiety. Tougher kids, like Alfie and Charlie, were so stubborn that they had become resigned to the raps and slaps that followed failure to reel off the answers. They simply shrugged their shoulders and said sarcastically, 'Thank *you*, Sister,' making it sound like defiance.

In the other subjects forced down our throats, similar conditions prevailed. Our adding and take-away sums became harder, involving multiplication and division up to four figures; we continued learning multiplication tables up to the eight times. We learned to read longer passages with bigger words, to use pen and ink to copy and take dictation in fancy copperplate handwriting of morally uplifting sayings, such as 'A stitch in time saves nine' or 'Too many cooks spoil the broth' and 'Cleanliness is next to Godliness', a saying dear to the nuns' hearts, though I found out years later that the saying was attributed to John Wesley, the founder of Methodism, which wouldn't have pleased them if they'd known. The obsession with neatness meant more whacks for blots and un-tidiness because the pens given to us had scratchy nibs, boys having used them as darts, and the ink, made up by the monitors, was watery. We all did our best but it was no use. We just couldn't win.

We also learned potted versions of history and geography. Told through tales of kings and queens and some of the strange and interesting things that happened to them, for example King Alfred and the cakes; King Bruce and the spider; King Canute and his attempt to order the tide back. But facts were presented at such high speed, was it any wonder that there was much confusion in our simple immature minds? As infants, we had no sense of historical time and of how long a hundred or a thousand years were. Ten years, a hundred years, a thousand years, they were all the same. They could be simply described as 'a lot'.

Angela asked Sister where she was living when the Romans invaded Britain. Charlie claimed that a king called Canoe burned some cakes because he wasn't paying attention and received a slap round the head (Canoe, not Charlie); Doris said she didn't like King Alfred because he was a horrible man who liked playing with creepy-crawly spiders; Jimmy was sure that Queen Elizabeth rode through Coventry without any clothes on and that was why Sir Walter Raleigh had offered his cloak. Duggie said that the wife of Noah was Joan of Arc while Alfie maintained that, when Queen Victoria saw the Armada coming, she sent for Lord Nelson who put his telescope to his blind eye and said, 'There's nothing to be frightened of because I can't see nothing.'

That answer earned him the Dunce's Cap which

135

he donned proudly at a rakish angle and stood on the stool at the front grinning like a jackass.

'Although the great fire of London,' said Sister Monica desperately in one lesson, 'looked like a disaster, it was also a blessing in disguise. Why do I say that?'

'Because it cleaned up the city,' I answered promptly, thinking I was Clever Dick, 'and burned down a lot of churches.'

After Dad's death, our life at home had been completely turned on its head. The three of us, Mam, Jamesey and me, gradually fell into the new routine and time – for me at least – seemed to shoot by and, before I knew it, we were into the year 1894. The final year in Sister Monica's class! How I looked forward to going to the big school at St Chad's in the coming September.

I still went to Aunty Dorothy's house after school each day and though Zeb never hit me again (I think his brush with Mam had put the wind up him), he still gave me lots of jobs to do like sweeping the yard, cleaning windows, mopping the scullery floor, or cutting up newspapers for the lavatory. (Just call me Cindertommy, I used to think.) During the week, Mam and I got back home very late and so it was a rapid tea of soup and bread, egg on toast or chips and peas or something similar as long as it was quick and didn't require much preparation. After that there wasn't much time left before it was bedtime. Up early again the next morning and then the same routine all over again.

We were a lot better off than many who lived in

our street 'cos Mam had a job and Jamesey helped out with his wages as well. During the week, Jamesey was hard at work as a builder's labourer. He usually liked a drink after work so we didn't see too much of him. At weekends it was different. He did his fair share of looking after the house and didn't mind a bit about getting down on his knees to scrub a floor, mop out the scullery or even donkey-stone the window sills at the front in full view of all the neighbours who might have considered it odd, to say the least, to see a man performing a woman's task like this. It didn't bother him one bit and he always gave them a cheerful greeting. That was probably the most attractive feature about him, his happy-go-lucky nature, and whenever he started on one of the household chores, it was always accompanied by his singing of a popular song, usually an Irish one like 'When Irish Eyes Are Smiling'.

Although Mam was always completely worn out at weekends, she still had her various chores to attend to. On Saturday she put on her best shawl and we went shopping at the Co-op on Rochdale Road to get the groceries in.

'We need the divi more than ever,' she remarked.

I loved this visit 'cos Mr Wilson, the manager, dressed in his immaculate white coat and apron, pencil behind his ear, always let me sit on the high chair and never failed to give me a lollipop or a boiled sweet.

'There, that should keep you quiet for half an hour or so,' he'd say.

Mam handed over the list which she had written out at home and Mr Wilson hurried hither and thither assembling the various items: loaf of bread, quarter pound of Lipton's tea, bacon, half a dozen eggs, sugar, oatmeal, McDougall's self-raising flour, butter and cheese sliced off the block, and last but not least, a bottle of Scott's Emulsion. Mam continued Dad's tradition and she never missed giving me a dose every morning 'to keep my strength up'.

Saturday afternoons were spent cleaning the house from top to bottom, quite a big job as there hadn't been time during the week. I gave what help I could but as a youngster, that wasn't much. I swept the back yard, dusted down shelves and tops of furniture, but because of past experience, I didn't attempt washing the dishes as I'd found that plates seemed to have a tendency to leap out of my fingers.

After Mass at St Chad's, Sunday became washing day. Mam disappeared into the cellar and was there until late afternoon, scrubbing, rubbing, boiling, mangling, ironing. I wasn't able to help in this chore and I thought it best to keep out of the way.

Though Mam went about all these household tasks, she seemed apathetic and not really interested in doing anything, as if she'd lost heart. There were no more outings on Sundays with her but for the first year, Jamesey took me to the parks when he had the time. One Sunday, he brought in a silk kite he'd purchased in town at Lewis's department store. It was the latest model and a beautiful piece of work. At Boggart Hole Clough, it flew really well, high into the sky but it just didn't seem the same somehow as those Sundays with Dad when we had flown our rougher, home-made contraptions.

Sometimes we played football with a large rubber ball and he dribbled rings round me like most adults seemed to enjoy doing with their kids. One Sunday he kicked the ball at me and it hit me on the head.

'Why does the ball look small when it's coming towards you and then bigger as it gets nearer?' I asked him.

'Funny you should ask that.' He laughed. 'When I was a kid, I used to ask myself the same question and I could never understand why. Then one day, it struck me.'

If that was supposed to be funny, I didn't get it – at the time. It took twenty years for the penny to drop when out of the blue I suddenly remembered what he'd said.

After a while, Jamesey stopped taking me out when he found more interest in talking and playing pitch and toss with his mates on Barney's. Mam whispered that she thought he'd also got himself a girlfriend and I suppose having a little kid like me hanging on to his coat tails would have cramped his style. After that, I spent my time reading comics like *Comic Cuts* and *Chips*. Once or twice Jimmy Dixon and some of the lads from St William's came over to play hide and seek or rounders on Barney's but Mam was never too keen on letting me go too far from home in case I wandered off again. But that had been a long time ago and I was now much more grown-up. After all, I was just gone seven years of age.

Chapter Thirteen

Though there were few excursions or outings, one particular day was different from the rest. It was a Monday and the date was 21 May 1894, and it was an occasion that I would remember for the rest of my life. Queen Victoria was coming to Manchester after a thirty-seven-year absence. It was said that she'd declined to visit us because she'd objected to our statue of Oliver Cromwell, the Lord Protector of England who had presided over the beheading of King Charles I. The statue had been erected in a prominent position in front of Exchange Railway Station and Manchester Cathedral.

Today, however, she was coming to perform the official opening of the Manchester Ship Canal, thus commemorating the fact that our city, thirty miles from the sea, had become a port at the unimaginable cost of fifteen million pounds. A day's holiday was declared for all Mancunians and Salfordians to mark this engineering achievement. A huge triumphal arch of fire escape ladders was erected over Deansgate, and after the Queen had declared the canal open, a twenty-one-gun salute was fired on the Manchester Racecourse, followed by a royal procession along an eight-mile route through the town. House owners decorated their homes in honour of our royal visitor, with a keen sense of competition as to who could produce the best adornments. Public buildings were also gaily decorated with flags and a profusion of flowers and bunting. Two million people thronged the streets to cheer the Queen and to celebrate this momentous event in our city's history.

At the start of the afternoon, the weather had not been too promising and the threat of rain hovered over the town. Happily, the dark clouds did not fulfil their dark promise and even parted later for a moment or two to permit a brief appearance of the sun.

Though Mam had complained of feeling tired and not too well, she decided to join Jamesey and me in the celebrations.

'It's nothing,' she said, 'just the beginning of a cold; it'll soon clear up.'

Jamesey looked at his sister with concern. 'You've been working too hard, our Mary,' he said.

'What choice do I have, Jamesey?' she replied ruefully.

I, too, was a little worried about her as she did look pale and tired.

We'd arranged to take our places on Stretford Road, outside the School for the Deaf and Dumb, as we'd read that the Queen would be passing that way. There were no trams running and so it meant a fairly long walk to Old Trafford. Along the way we saw masses of spectators clinging precariously to buildings and balconies. We got there eventually, however, and stood with the great multitude waiting for the Queen to appear. We couldn't have found a better place for, without all the pushing and jostling, we were given a first-class opportunity to see Her Majesty when the procession was suddenly brought to a halt. This was to let one of the little girls, Annie Haslam as it was later reported, to present the Queen with a bouquet of flowers and to make a little speech. Hearing the little girl speak out so clearly, nobody would have guessed that she had been born deaf and dumb and that her ability to speak was the result of her training at the institution. The Queen acknowledged the child's presentation with a smile and a bow while the crowd responded with hearty cheers. Then a large group of Sunday School children who were assembled there raised their voices in a singing of the National Anthem. Altogether it had been a joyous day though we did hear on the grapevine, that mysterious process by which news travelled through a great crowd, that a mother and her young son had been killed on Deansgate when a massive coping stone had become dislodged and fallen on to them.

Mam was visibly upset. 'How terrible!' she exclaimed. 'A mother comes to town with her family to join in the celebrations and this terrible tragedy happens to them. Why, it could have been all of us, Jamesey! God must have been looking after us!'

After the Queen had departed, the festivities went on late into the night with a state banquet and a fireworks display at Salford Docks. At nine o'clock, we decided to call it a day because, after all, holiday or not, it was back to work and the old familiar routine next morning. Fortunately the trams had started running again and so we didn't have that long walk back to Collyhurst.

Mam now didn't look at all well; she seemed strained and world-weary as though she'd have been quite content to depart this world and join my dad.

'You'll be all right after a good night's sleep,' Jamesey said reassuringly.

After a cup of our favourite cocoa – Fry's of course – the three of us retired to bed and were soon fast asleep. It had been a long and tiring day.

Around four o'clock in the morning, I was awakened by Mam who was lying by my side tapping me gently on the shoulder.

'Tommy, love,' she whispered, 'I want you to go quickly next door and tell Jamesey to come here right away. I need his help.'

'What is it, Mam?' I asked anxiously. 'Is there anything I can do?'

'No, Tommy. Just tell your Uncle Jamesey to come here quickly.'

I ran into Jamesey who was in deep slumber and snoring loudly. I shook him roughly by the shoulders.

'Jamesey, Jamesey! Come quick! Mam wants you. I think she's very ill!'

He awoke with a start and heard the urgency in my voice. 'I'm coming,' he said. 'I'm right behind you.'

He pulled on his trousers and ran with me into the bedroom.

'Mary! Mary!' he called. 'What is it? What's wrong?'

'Oh Jamesey,' she said. 'I have this terrible, terrible thirst and a tightness in my chest; I can hardly breathe. Please go outside to the tap and bring me a glass of cold water.'

'Right, Mary! One glass of water coming right up!'

With that he charged out of the room.

While he was out, Mam said, 'Get back into bed, Tommy. Come here and give me a big hug.'

I did as I was told and hugged her for all I was worth. Then Jamesey was back with the water.

'Here you are, Mary. One glass of best Water Board pop as ordered,' he said, trying to make light of the situation. But Mam didn't answer. Still holding on to me, she had become quite still.

Jamesey touched her lightly on the cheek and said, 'Here's your water, Mary?

Still no answer. He tried several times but Mam didn't respond.

'I'll have to go and get Dr Becker,' he said desperately. 'While I'm gone, I want you to go and stay with the Kaminskys upstairs.'

It took a little time to alert the Kaminskys in the early hours of the morning to the gravity of the situation but once they realized how serious things were, they responded immediately and took me in till Jamesey got back.

Dr Becker confirmed our worst fears. Mam had died of a heart attack. She was thirty years old. 'Angina pectoris,' the doctor wrote on the death certificate but they were only words and like the words 'cerebral spinal meningitis', they didn't mean a thing to us. As far as I was concerned, she died of exhaustion, she had worked herself into the grave, and I had lost the dearest person in my life. My whole world caved in on me and came to an abrupt end, as if the earth itself had stopped turning. I was aged seven and already an orphan. At that young age, I'd suffered too much grief in too short a time. I couldn't handle it and part of me simply closed down. Jamesey was affected in the same way. He was pale and distressed; it had all happened so fast and so unexpectedly. One minute she'd been here; next minute, she was gone.

I was in such a state of trauma that I couldn't cry and even to think about Mam not being there any more was unbearable and too painful to contemplate. I walked about in a daze, unable to take in the horror and the enormity of what had happened. The procedures that had taken place when Dad had died were now repeated. Her coffin was put on display in our living room; neighbours collected for a wreath; at St Chad's Church, there was a Requiem Mass attended by many friends, neighbours, workmates, and relatives. Once again the burial was at Moston Cemetery. For me, the events seemed somehow unreal and remote as if they were happening to someone else. My mind had shut down and refused to accept the reality of the situation.

At the graveside the women cried and the men looked solemn, except for Jamesey who wept uncontrollably. As for me, it was only when I saw Mam's coffin being gently lowered into Dad's grave that I broke down and the tears began to flow. Suddenly I asked myself what I was skriking about. Throughout my life I had been taught that death was not the end but the beginning. Mam

145

had joined Dad in heaven and would be happy. Surely I should be happy too, for they were now together again. So what was I crying about? Then I realized. I was crying for myself. I was scared. What was going to happen to me now I had lost both my parents? Where could I go? Who would look after me? My grief turned to anger. What had I done to God to deserve this? It was so unfair. Some people like Jimmy Dixon had an easy ride: nice home with nice parents, father with a good job. Why was he so lucky? Why had God picked on me to be punished?

After Moston, the funeral party gathered as they had at Dad's funeral in the upper room of the Mitchell Arms in Every Street and there followed the post-interment trip down Memory Lane in which people told anecdotes about Mam, both humorous and serious, stories which began with, 'Do you remember the time that she...?' After an hour or so when the stories began to run out, someone suddenly noticed me sitting in the corner.

'What are we going to do with this poor little bugger?' Grandad Owen asked, nodding in my direction.

Good question, I thought. I felt like a piece of furniture up for auction. What am I bid for this little bugger?

Dad's mother, Gran'ma Edna, was the first to break the embarrassed silence. 'I certainly can't take him. Not at my age. I think it'd be best if we put him in a home.'

A shudder of alarm went down my spine when I heard that word 'home' which was like saying 'workhouse' to an old person. Was I to be abandoned to some cold, impersonal institution? Home was another word for an orphanage and there were plenty of scary stories of what could happen to a young kid dumped in one of those.

'Well, we're getting a bit too long in the tooth to look after a young lad,' added Grandma Bridget. 'Not only that, Owen and me have our work to consider. Remember we still have to go out to our jobs each morning and that just about exhausts us. We just wouldn't have the time.'

Uncles Patrick and Jamesey also opted out, being too busy working to offer help. Jamesey looked distraught that he wasn't able to take me on as we'd got on so well together. But what could he do? He couldn't very well give up his job to take care of me. What would we live on?

These considerations left only one person. Aunty Dorothy, a strapping, well-built woman, spoke up with authority.

'Tommy's not going into no home,' she said vehemently. 'He's our Mary's son and Brodie and me have talked it over and we've decided. We'll take him.' She looked to Brodie who nodded his agreement.

That sounded like good news until with a jolt I remembered. Old Zeb! I'd got used to going to Aunty Dorothy's after school – but living there? That was a different kettle of fish! And without Mam to come to my defence when Zeb got nasty! My mind was filled with fear and a sense of doom. I could sense dark storm clouds gathering on the horizon.

It was a week before we could organise any kind

of move. Jamesey took a week off work to keep me company and help to console me in my earth-shattering loss. He also took on the responsibility of attending to the numerous details that are involved when someone dies. He organized the business of moving by arranging for a dealer to collect Mam's furniture; members of the Mitchell family came to visit and take away her bits and pieces – 'to remember her by' they said. Dejected, I packed my own belongings, what little I had, and with a heavy heart was ready to move when Jamesey came to collect me and take me across to Aunt Dorothy's house on Angel Meadow. Dorothy and Brodie had taken time off from the market to welcome me and help me settle in, which was a big concession for them. But where were they going to put me? The idea of sharing a bed with Zeb filled me with horror. But where else could I go, since they had only two bedrooms? The basement was the answer. The front cellar was used for laundry and the back cellar was without light or any kind of win-dow. Not only was it dark, it was possibly home to thousands of spiders and maybe mice and rats. I was only seven but I wanted to die and join Mam and Dad wherever they'd gone. I only knew that I had been condemned to hell in Angel Meadow. I don't think I have ever felt so miser-able in my whole life as I did in that first week when I was finally left alone in my cellar. The furniture in the room consisted of a single bed with a straw mattress and a little chest of drawers to hold my few possessions, my clothes and one or two toys and games that my dad had bought for me oh so long ago. My only source of light would be a candle on a saucer. I determined to spend as little time as I could in this dreadful hole.

'You should be all right here,' said Dorothy, trying to cheer me up. 'You've got your own little room and at least you'll have your privacy. The light from a candle isn't very good and so we'll try to get you an oil lamp which should be much brighter. I think in time you'll be able to make yourself quite comfortable when the place is cleaned up. It was the only place we could offer, I'm afraid. The alternative would have been to put you with old Zeb and I don't think you'd have fancied that.'

Too true, I wouldn't.

During this sad week, I was given a little relief when Jimmy Dixon's mam and dad, feeling sorry for me I suppose, invited me across to their house for tea one Sunday afternoon. They lived in the end terrace on Thompson Street, not far from the Oldham Road goods yard. The house was the usual two-up and two-down with a cellar but with one difference: they had a small front garden which was something of a status symbol since it was the only one in the street. It was also well-furnished with a good solid mahogany sideboard like the one we used to have in Teignmouth Street, a pine table, and a fairly new horsehair sofa. What gave it the finishing touch, though, was the bright linoleum and new tufted rug on the stone floor.

There were two sons in the Dixon family, my

pal Jimmy and his older brother, Robert, aged fourteen, who was an apprentice at Fryers, the big engineering firm in Salford. In my honour, they had prepared a special tea of boiled ham, tomatoes and salad, a chocolate cake and, to finish off, pineapple chunks and cream. In ordinary times, I'd have considered this the feast of feasts but not on this day as I was still in that strange trance-like world trying to come to terms with the tragedy that had befallen me. Not only that, I was worried out of my mind as to what was to become of me. Living in that house on Angel Meadow with Zeb as one of my guardians filled me with a sense of dread.

'We were so sorry to hear about your mam,' Mrs Dixon said kindly. 'It has been such a terrible shock to everyone who knew her. I met her once or twice waiting outside St William's. She was such a kind, gentle lady.'

Hearing that, I came near to tears but was able to hold them back. It was something I was going to have to learn. Otherwise I'd be constantly weeping in public.

'Thank you, Mrs Dixon,' I said quietly. 'It's going to take all of us in the family a long time to get used to not having her around.'

'You do seem to have had such rotten luck,' added Mr Dixon. 'If ever there's anything we can do to help, you must let us know. Jimmy here was always crowing about you. How the two of you learned to read together and were forever vying with each other to be top of the class.'

'I think he used to beat me for top place, Dad,' added Jimmy generously.

'That's not true. I never hit you once,' I said.

My attempt at humour was really to avoid the talk round the table developing into a wake, which I'd have found hard to take.

There was a little polite laughter from them all at my remark.

'I want you to know,' Mr Dixon went on, 'that if ever you see me working on the tramways on Rochdale Road, you must let on to me because if you need to go anywhere on the tram, I can fix you up with a free ride. You've only to say the word and Bob's your uncle.'

'No, Bob's my brother,' said Jimmy, 'not my uncle.'

Jimmy was also trying to bring a little light relief into the conversation since his parents were making heavy weather talking to me. Maybe Jimmy thought I was likely to burst into tears, which would have been really embarrassing for boys of our age.

Jimmy's remark was quite funny but I could manage no more than a polite smile. I took up his dad's offer.

'If ever I do see you on the trams, Mr Dixon, I'll give you a wave,' I said. 'Are you a tram driver?'

'No, Tommy. I'm a plate-layer.'

'You mean you're a waiter?'

For reasons I didn't understand that caused more mirth all round.

'No,' chuckled Mr Dixon. 'It's my job to look after the tram rails and keep them up to scratch.'

'These tram rails sound like a bunch of monkeys,' Robert said, also doing his best to keep things light-hearted.

'Do you still go to Mass at St Chad's?' Mrs Dixon now asked.

'Yes, I do. I still go to nine o'clock 'cos it reminds me so much of the times I used to go with Mam and Dad.'

'That's understandable,' Mrs Dixon replied softly. 'We go to St Michael's now as it's so handy since we moved house. It's just across the road from here.'

'Not only that,' Robert grinned, with a twinkle in his eye, 'our Jimmy has another reason for wanting to go to St Mike's. Don't you, our kid?'

'Cut it out, our Bob,' Jimmy said, giving his brother a playful thump. 'It's not true.'

'He sees that Angela Rocca there and instead of saying his prayers, he's ogling and making sheep's eyes at his girlfriend,' Robert replied.

'I do not,' Jimmy protested, blushing all the same. 'And she's not my girlfriend. She's just a friend. Tommy here likes her just as much as I do, don't you, Tommy?'

'I haven't seen Angela since we left St William's. I forget what she looks like.'

I was fibbing of course for I'd always fancied Angela and the thought that Jimmy was seeing her and maybe chatting to her every Sunday after Mass really rattled me. But then I was getting used to things not going my way and the thought of losing Angela to Jimmy didn't compare to the pain of losing first my dad and then my mam. Life was toughening me up.

We rounded off the meal with the pineapple chunks and slices of chocolate cake for everyone.

152

The rest of the talk around the table continued on a happy note and I found the company of the Dixons a delight. I really began to warm to this family as it reminded me so much of the family I'd lost. Suddenly a mad idea flashed through my brain. Was there any chance of...? No, surely not... Would they possibly...? Would they think me cheeky if I asked? Then I thought, nothing ventured, nothing gained.

Mrs Dixon was asking me about my new home.

'You're living with your Aunty Dorothy now,' she said. 'I think that'll be much better now you're away from your old house with all those sad memories. I'm sure everything will be all right now.'

'No, Mrs Dixon,' I replied. 'I'm not happy about being there. My Aunty Dorothy and Uncle Brodie mean well but they are out for most of the day working in the market. I'll be left in the charge of Gran'pa Zeb and me and him don't get on very well. He drinks a lot and sometimes belts me for nothing. I only wish I could live in a family like yours. I don't suppose you could find room for me here.'

There, I'd said it, half-jokingly maybe, but I'd made my wish known. An embarrassed silence followed. It was Mr Dixon as head of the household who broke it.

'You're a very nice boy, Tommy. Polite, good-mannered, and you get on well with our Jimmy. But such a move is not on, son. First, because we have only two bedrooms and those are more than filled by our own two lads. But more important than that, what would your Aunty Dorothy say if you said you wanted to come and live with us? How do you think she'd feel if you told her that? It would be the biggest insult in the world that one of her own wanted to live with strangers like us, rather than with her. Why, she'd never live it down and neither would we. So, you see, Tommy, such a notion is just not on.'

'That's all right, Mr Dixon. I didn't really think it was. But Jimmy and me are such good pals, I thought that maybe it might work. It was probably a daft idea.'

Later that day, I went back to my room in the cellar crestfallen. I'd enjoyed the visit to Jimmy's home but in some ways I wished I'd never gone because seeing a happy family like the Dixons made me feel my own misery all the more. And hearing about Jimmy seeing Angela every Sunday hadn't helped either. I'd felt a slight twinge of jealousy but that was all and it soon passed. There seemed little point in caring about anything.

For the first week things went reasonably well as Brodie and Dorothy were around for much of the time but then came the day when I was left, alone in the house with Zeb. It was an afternoon and my uncle and aunt were still at the market, or more probably boozing in the Turk's Head, and I had to sit with Zeb who opened up the conversation with his usual whine.

'I didn't bloody well want you here,' he rasped as soon as we were alone. 'They should have put you in a home where you belong. If you think you'll ever be sharing my bedroom when you get fed up living in the cellar, you've got another

154

think coming.'

That was one notion that me and him were agreed on anyroad. I'd rather have slept in the privy in the back street than share a room with him. From the very first moment we were left alone in the house, he was at me as cruel as ever for he'd never forgotten or forgiven the way Mam had given him such a roasting when he whipped me round the legs for breaking a plate. I was soon to find out that he was as fond as ever of his gin and his fags and, if he had cash, as on pension pay day, he would be sending me round to the pub to buy in fresh supplies of gin or to the chemist for laudanum which was sold like aspirin.

'Why do you like laudanum, Zeb?' I asked one day.

'Because it makes you forget your troubles and takes the pain away. Now that's enough talking. Get round to Wiseman's and buy me the stuff.'

After taking the drug, he was usually in a good mood but when he was short of the readies, which was most of the time, he could turn quite vicious. On that very first day, he took up once again his old hateful routine.

'How much money have you got on you?' he demanded.

'Nowt,' I said.

'What about all the money you were given by people at your mother's funeral? What's happened to that?' he bawled down my earhole.

Next thing I knew, something hit me and it really hurt. But what was worse was the shock of the sudden slap across the face. I burst out crying.

155

'What was that for?' I whimpered.

'You're a lying little bastard!' he yelled. 'You must have a lot of cash stashed away. I saw all them mourners slipping you coppers and tanners. Anyroad, you're a big softie, whingeing like that after such a little slap. You don't know what pain and hardship are. I'll learn you to toughen up while you're here in this house.'

It was June 1894 and I had only a few weeks left at St William's and then I was to start at the big school at St Chad's in September. During the long summer holiday, I got up early, made my own breakfast (usually toast and tea) and then spent most of my time with my pals, playing football or playing street games like hide and seek or racing competitions and sometimes exploring on Barney's waste ground – anything to avoid confrontations with Zeb. This often meant staying out of the house until around four or five o'clock when Brodie and Dorothy would come home from the pub. Dorothy then cooked an evening meal, usually a couple of boiled eggs or a fry-up of bacon and eggs or sausage and mash. She always included a salad, as lettuce, tomatoes, cucumber, beetroot were so easily come by in the market.

It was around this time that I developed a slight speech defect which took the form of a stutter whenever I felt tense and uptight, usually when Zeb was at home as I never knew how he was going to behave towards me. If he had money he would send me out to do his errands but when he was short, that was when the trouble began and he could turn nasty.

This stutter didn't worry me too much at first for I seemed to stammer only when Zeb was around, and for some strange reason the problem was mainly with words beginning with an 's' or 'sh', and occasionally V. When alone I tried to overcome the problem by reciting tongue-twisters beginning with these letters. If anyone had heard me, I'm sure they'd have thought me barmy as I walked about muttering to myself things like, 'Moses supposes his toeses are roses' and 'Sister Susie's sewing shirts for soldiers' and 'She sells sea shells by the sea shore'.

The trouble was that I had no difficulty when saying these things in private. It was only in public when I thought people were looking at me that the stuttering began.

On one or two occasions, I walked over to Smithfield Market to meet Aunty Dorothy and Uncle Brodie. I usually went around 8 a.m. since their starting time of 4 a.m. was a bit too early for my liking. I was able to help them a little by carrying the occasional light box of fruit or vegetables for their customers who sometimes gave me a penny or a halfpenny for the service. Most of all I loved stroking the nose of their donkey, Crusty, and feeding him a carrot or other titbits. Once or twice they even let me handle the reins and to urge Crusty along by shouting, 'Giddy-up.' When the long morning's work was finished at around mid-day, they drove the donkey and cart back to the stables under the railway arches on Dantzig Street, after which they went to their pub on Shudehill, along with the many other market workers who liked a drink after work. On such occasions, I was left at a loose end and didn't know what to do with myself. I didn't fancy going back to share the company of Zeb and so I took to hanging around outside the pub until they were ready to go home when the pub booted them all out at 3 p.m. Occasionally I walked back to Angel Meadow in the hope of seeing some of my pals for a game of footie.

Chapter Fourteen

For months, the nuns at St William's had been talking and warning us about our projected promotion to the big school, and in September 1894 we learned what it meant and came to appreciate that our lives were to be turned upside down. For a start, boys and girls were to go to separate schools, the boys to St Chad's on Lord Street off Cheetham Hill Road, and the girls to St Michael's in George Leigh Street. I felt pangs of sorrow when I realized that I wouldn't be seeing Angela and Doris, my beloved pair, in class again although we would see them in passing when schools let out at four o'clock. I didn't mind so much about Doris as she had been pestering me to walk home with her after school. Some nights I wasn't able to shake her off but I'd rather have been seen dead than escort her home, because if any of my pals had spotted me with her, my name would've been mud. 'Go and play with the girls, you big sissy' was just about the worst insult you could receive at school. Not that Doris was a sissy; when it came to a free-for-all, she could hold her own with any of the lads.

At nine o'clock on the first day, we reported to the school yard of the boys' wing and were taken aback when we saw how much bigger our new school was. The lads aged around thirteen in the top class, Standard 4, seemed like giants to us and we were midgets by comparison. Our own age group, Standard 2, had been swelled by about twenty pupils from St Chad's Infants Department. They were a rough-looking lot, we thought, and we didn't like the look of some of them, especially one big, pink-eyed, ginger-haired kid whom the others called Ginger McDermott; he seemed to be a couple of inches taller than our own champion, Alfie Rigby. I was third in the line graded for height. My pal, Jimmy, turned out to be the shortest. The cosy little routine we'd enjoyed for two years at St William's was over. We'd entered a different, rougher world and we realized that we were going to have to make some mighty big adjustments.

In the school yard on that first morning, there was the usual chaos with kids running wildly about the place, yelling, screaming, cuffing, pushing and jostling. We new kids felt and probably looked lost as we stood there in a forlorn little group wondering what was to happen next.

On the stroke of nine o'clock, three teachers – two men, one fat, one thin, and one hefty, sour-faced woman – strode on to the scene with a tall, stern-looking man bringing up the rear. We took him to be the headmaster since he carried a cane hooked over his arm. At a nod from the tall man, the tubby male teacher blew loudly on what sounded like a police whistle and, to our amazement, the big crowd of boys running around like lunatics froze in their tracks as if struck by lightning. A second blast of the whistle and the statues came to life with the boys hurrying into lines of serried ranks, oldest at the back and youngest at the front. We newcomers didn't know what to do next until the lady teacher announced in a glass-shattering screech, 'All new boys go over to the wall and stand aside until we are ready for you.'

We did our best to obey the order but had to be nudged and pushed by the male teachers as if they were collie dogs and us sheep. Now we were out of the way, the headmaster gave a strange instruction.

'Inspection! Begin!'

The assembled boys then did a strange thing, which, to outsiders like us, looked like some bizarre religious ceremony. The hundred or so boys held out their hands, palms facing upward as if in entreaty, while the three teachers went along the lines examining not only hands and fingernails but necks, knees and footwear or, where the last item was missing, feet. Six boys obviously did not pass muster for they were pulled out of the ranks by their teachers and sent to the front. The head now reviewed each selected case.

'Cartwright, why are your neck and knees so filthy dirty?'

'No soap, sir, and me mam doesn't have no money to buy none.'

'No excuse. Next time, borrow some from your next-door neighbour. Hand out!'

The head delivered two vicious strikes of the cane. The boy yelled, 'Ow! Ow!' and sucked on his hand. 'Back to your place, Cartwright, and don't come to school unwashed again.'

'Morgan! Why are your knees so caked with dirt?'

'I've got scabs on my knees, sir, where I fell down and it hurts if I wash 'em.'

'The cane will hurt even more, Morgan. Hand out!'

The two unwashed kneecaps earned Morgan two swishes of the cane.

The other four cases were similar. One boy was punished for biting his nails, another said he hadn't had time to wash properly, another claimed the water at their house had been turned off by the Water Board, the last said he hadn't washed his neck as he didn't want to wet his clean shirt collar. The excuses counted for nothing and the cane was given regardless. We new kids observed the proceedings with trepidation, making mental notes to avoid the offences which earned the cane at this school.

The fat teacher with the police whistle now gave the command, 'On the spot, mark time!' The whole school assembly began lifting their knees high like chorus girls and stamping their feet in rhythmic time. On the order, 'Right turn!' the whole school manoeuvred smartly and then on the command of, 'Forward march!' marched off to their various classrooms with the male teachers reciting, 'Left, right! Left, right! Pick those feet up!'

It was apparent from that very first day that St Chad's Elementary School was run on strict military lines. The day had begun not with religious instruction or prayers but with inspection and military discipline.

When the older classes with their teachers had gone into the school, it was our turn for the treatment. The head addressed us. 'Standard Two! First, I want you to run about and make as much noise as you can. Imagine you're wild Indians doing a war dance. But when I blow my whistle, I want you to stand still immediately as if you've been turned to stone as you saw the rest of the school do. Ready! Go!'

We liked the idea of this game and didn't need telling twice so we leaped around the playground as if possessed by the devil. At the sound of the head's whistle, which sounded more like a football referee's than a policeman's, we turned to pillars of salt like Lot in the Bible.

'Well done!' the head called. 'Now let's try it again.'

We did the exercise several times until he was satisfied.

'Now, we'll try the next phase,' he said. 'After you have stood still, I shall blow the whistle again and I want you all to form a line in front of me as you saw the bigger boys do. Tallest boys on your right, smallest boys on the left.'

It took many attempts for us to arrange ourselves and, pushed and jostled by the lady teacher, we finally made it. Eventually the big man was happy with the result.

'Now,' he said. 'I am Mr Sullivan, your headmaster. And this lady is your teacher, Miss Florrie Corbett. Do everything she tells you; keep your noses and the rest of you clean and you won't get into trouble. She will inspect you this morning but since it's your first day here, she'll be lenient and there'll be no caning. But remember to come clean tomorrow and be early because all latecomers will be punished. The only excuse accepted is if you are dead. Then you will indeed be a latecomer.'

Florrie Corbett guffawed politely at his joke as if it was the first time she'd heard it but we had the feeling it was part of his introductory routine.

'I shall now hand you over to your class teacher,' he concluded. 'Miss Corbett, please take over.'

'Thank you, Mr Sullivan,' she simpered.

Glaring at us standing anxiously in line, she bawled in that high-pitched voice of hers, 'Standard Two! Marching on the spot! Begin! Right turn! Forward march!'

It was our first experience of training in discipline and obedience. I had the strangest feeling on that first day that I'd joined not so much a school as the army. The only things missing were khaki uniforms and rifles.

As at St William's, our educational diet was to be the four Rs plus drill, which nearly always came after religion. First our souls then our bodies. Drill was meant to give our bodies a workout but it was nothing more than synchronized physical exercises of jumping, bending, stretching and, most important, marching. We were trained to respond immediately and without question to a series of commands. 'Arms upward, bend! Elbow pressing, begin! Trunk forward, drop! Trunk pressing, begin! Running on the spot, now!' It was very similar to military training and excellent preparation for the time when we should take the Queen's shilling and join up.

Wait till I tell Mam about this, I thought. We'll have a good laugh together about all this army stuff. Then it hit me like a thump in the chest. Mam wasn't there for me to tell. It was at times like these that the tragedy of my mam and dad's deaths came home to me painfully. It was going to take a long time for me to get used to it.

Some time later was added a weekly session at Osborne Street Public Baths. Mr Dunlop, the thin one and Standard 4 master, escorted us along Rochdale Road in crocodile formation. There we were first made to strip off right down to our birthday suits and then handed over to the tender care of Mr Jack Wyngard, a sergeant major type if ever there was one. One or two lads like Gordon and Duggie were very shy about appearing in the buff and cupped both hands round their John Thomases to hide and protect them.

'Right, stand in a line by the side of the plunge!' Wyngard barked. 'Hands by your side! All of you! Don't be frightened about showing what you've got. We've seen it all before and they're all the same.' His gaze rang along the line of us standing there naked, then added with a wry grin, 'Yes, all the same. More or less, that is.'

Before we were allowed into the main plunge, we had to take our turn in one of the communal hot water baths to wash ourselves with a couple of bars of carbolic soap which the school had supplied. There followed a cold water shower and we were ready for our first swimming lesson. We were commanded to stand in the plunge to await our taskmaster's orders.

Gordon had meanwhile donned a pair of water wings.

'Where the hell did you get those balloons?' yelled Wyngard.

'Please, sir,' Gordon answered, 'me mam said I was to wear them to save me from drowning. She bought them when we went to Blackpool last summer.'

'Well, get the damned things off sharpish,' bawled our instructor, now holding a large fishing net on a long metal pole.

'Bring those things again and I'll take a personal delight in drowning you myself. We're going to learn to swim not play baby seaside games. Today, we're going to begin by practising the doggy paddle. Maybe you've all seen the way little puppies swim. Can anyone show us how it's done?'

Fortunately Alfie had been to the baths before and was chosen to demonstrate the style.

'See how easy it is,' Wyngard shouted. 'Now all of you try it and swim to the other side. Ready, go!'

Most of us managed to move clumsily in the water but one or two floundered and our martinet encouraged them along with prods with his pole. 'Swim, swim, you silly sausages!'

They had a choice. They could swim doggy fashion or they could be poked by the pole. Everyone decided that swimming was the less painful of the two alternatives. At the end of that first session, we were swimming willy-nilly breadth after breadth. Over the next year or two, Wyngard taught us to swim the crawl and the breast stroke. Maybe we weren't going to make champion swimmers of Olympic standard but we learned to be sufficiently competent in the water to survive and swim several lengths, achievements that were often recognized in official certificates of which we were extremely proud. I always suspected, however, that the real reason the authorities forced us to visit the baths was not so much for educational as for hygienic reasons. Our visits to Osborne Street gave us a thorough cleansing once a week since none of us had adequate facilities at home.

But I'm running ahead of myself. We've just arrived at St Chad's and it's the first day.

Chapter Fifteen

In the classroom we continued marking time until Miss Corbett commanded, 'Standard Two, halt!'

From there, she allocated us to our two-seater desks and Jimmy and I managed to stay together. Morning prayers followed and Jimmy tried to start me giggling again by saying, 'Our Father, who art in heaven, Harold be thy name...' This time I took no chances and kept a straight face. I was learning fast to put on a face and hide my true feelings, an essential survival skill in a school like this.

Miss Corbett began the morning by checking our names in the class register. Normally a dull routine but when she came to Gordon's name, she looked up from the page in surprise and exclaimed, 'Gordon Bennett! Is your name really Gordon Bennett?'

'Yes, miss.'

She broke out into a broad smile which was good to see on such a frosty face.

'Gordon Bennett!' she repeated.

'Present, miss,' Gordon said dutifully.

'That's a most interesting Scottish name!' she added and then turned her attention back to calling the roster.

We never understood what had caused her such amusement until many years later.

Our first lesson was religious instruction and she began by revising all the catechism answers we'd learned at St William's.

'All of you have already made your first confession and Holy Communion,' she said, 'and so I expect you to know many parts of the catechism. We shall begin by revising the Ten Commandments.' She pointed to Duggie and said, 'You there, the boy with the specs at the end of his nose. What's your name?'

'Douglas Dimson, miss, but my pals call me Duggie.'

'Duggie is not a name; it is a dreadful abbreviation of a beautiful one. I shall call you Douglas. Are you eating something?'

'No, miss.'

'Well, what's that you've got in your mouth? You look like a cow in a field, chewing the cud.'

'It's chewing gum, miss.'

'Chewing gum? I've never heard of it. Where did you get it?'

'Me mam got it, miss. It was free with some Wrigley's baking powder she got at the Co-op on Rochdale Road.'

'Well, take the disgusting rubbery stuff from your mouth at once and put it in your hankie.'

'Ain't got none, miss. I'll just put it in my pocket.' Surreptitiously, Duggie stuck it under the desk.

'Very well, Douglas, say the first commandment.'

Those of us acquainted with his intellectual ability cringed. Why did she have to pick him out on our first day?

Duggie began, 'I am the Lord thy God who brought thee out of the land of Egypt and into the house of bondage–'

'Stop! Stop at once!' our teacher screamed. She strode up to the luckless Duggie. 'Not *INTO*, you ninny, but *OUT OF!*' she yelled down his ear-hole, emphasizing each phrase with a clout across the head. 'Now, *you* say it just as I did!'

Duggie duly obeyed and repeated as instructed, 'Who brought thee out of the land of Egypt and not *INTO*, you ninny, but *OUT OF* the house of bondage.'

That error earned him another clout but Duggie eventually got it right and we proceeded to go through the rest of the commandments until we reached the ninth and the tenth, the ones about coveting our neighbours' goods and wives. We found those a bit of a laugh 'cos round our way no one had anything worth coveting and as for wives, whoever had made up that rule about coveting them obviously hadn't seen the old crones sitting on the steps along Angel Meadow.

'And if we break one of the commandments, what have we done?' she asked.

We were moving on to Miss Corbett's favourite part of the catechism. Sin! She was a world expert on the subject. No doubt learned men consulted her about it.

A forest of hands went up for we knew our stuff as the nuns back at St William's had given us a thorough grounding. 'Miss, miss,' we called excitedly, trying to win her attention.

'You will not call out like that,' she snapped.

169

'Any more of that and I'll box all your ears.'

'Box your ears' – that was a new one on us and we soon came to know that it was her favourite expression as she used it about a hundred and forty-seven times a day until we wondered if she was related to the great world boxing champion Gentleman Jim Corbett. Maybe he was her brother. Anyhow, from that day forward, we nick-named her the Bruiser and we were especially pleased when we learned later that Gentleman Jim had become heavyweight champion by knocking out a boxer with the same name as our head, John Sullivan.

'When we break a commandment, we have committed a sin,' said my pal, Jimmy, when she selected him to answer the question.

'And what is sin?'

Charlie was chosen to answer and, in parrot-fashion, trotted out the accepted response: 'Sin is an offence against God, by any thought, word, deed, or omission against the law of God.'

'When you are born,' she continued, 'is your soul without sin?'

'Yes, miss,' said Jimmy. 'You've not had time to commit any sins.'

Gordon, our class toady, was waving his hand about as if wetting his pants. 'That's wrong, miss. He's forgotten about the stain of original sin on your soul.'

Bennett's reputation had obviously preceded him, for the Bruiser said, 'Good boy, Gordon. And how do we clean that original sin off?'

'By being baptised,' the teacher's pet replied.

'Well done!' she said. 'After baptism, our souls

170

are as white as freshly fallen snow but when we commit actual sin, they become dirty, filthy slush that has been trodden on by a thousand pairs of muddy football boots. There are two kinds of sin, venial and mortal.'

'How many venials does it take to equal a mortal, miss?' asked the red-headed kid called Ginger McDermott from Chad's Infants.

'There's no equation like that,' she said. 'It's not like a table of weights and measures. Although venial sin is an offence that displeases God, it's nowhere near as serious as mortal. Why do you think serious sin is called mortal?'

'Because it kills the soul,' Alfie answered.

'Yes,' she said enthusiastically, 'it kills the soul and deserves hell.'

Then looking straight at me, she asked, 'And what will God say to someone who dies in a state of mortal sin?'

I don't know why she picked on me with this particular poser unless it was because I looked shifty-eyed and guilty, the type likely to commit grievous sins. But we all knew the answer to her question and I delivered the official line.

'God will say, "Depart from me, ye cursed, into the everlasting fire that was prepared for the devil and his angels".'

'Yes. To hell for all eternity. A great Italian artist has done a painting of what he thinks hell is like. Here it is.'

She rolled out a huge tatty reproduction of Michelangelo's 'The Last Judgement' and attached it to the blackboard. The canvas was dog-eared, no doubt from being used to terrify so many generations of pupils before us.

'See, boys, how Lucifer and his wicked angels are there with their pitchforks ready to throw you on to the hottest fire you've ever seen.'

The painting left me deeply disturbed because in my mind's eye, I could see myself as a figure like Guy Fawkes burning in the middle of that blaze with devils all round me poking with their forks to turn me over to make sure I was well done on the other side.

Courageously, Charlie raised his hand to ask a question. 'How long is eternity, miss? Is it more than a million?'

'Much more than a million,' she replied, warming to the theme. 'Imagine the sea at Blackpool.'

Not an easy thing for us to do for none of us, apart from Gordon, had ever been to that famous resort.

'If you tried to empty the sea, one eggcupful at a time, would that take a long time?'

'Oh, yes, miss!' we chorused, forgetting to raise our hands.

'Then multiply that a trillion, trillion times and you haven't even started to use up eternity.'

We were impressed. Miss Corbett got into her stride.

'Remember, boys, that the devil is everywhere. He is even sitting right next to you at this very minute.'

I took a closer look at my pal, Jimmy. He wasn't the devil, surely, I thought. Then he put his fingers in the sides of his mouth and pulled a horrible face at me. Maybe the Bruiser had a point.

'But we have a guardian angel as well as the

devil's angel always sitting on your shoulder,' she continued.

I felt sad when I heard her say that because I always thought my guardian angel had been Angela Rocca who'd gone to the girls' school and was no longer around so she couldn't very well be on my shoulder.

'When we're tempted to do bad things,' the Bruiser continued, 'it is the dark angel that is tempting us, urging us on. But you must listen to the good angel who is there by your side whispering in your ear telling you the right thing to do. If you go to hell, boys, your soul will burn in Michelangelo's fire, the one that never goes out and is hotter than anything ever seen here on earth. If you have committed a sin, what must you do?'

'Have it forgiven in confession right away,' simpered Gordon.

'Yes, Gordon, go to confession right away. I'll tell you a story. There was once a young boy who stole a bar of chocolate from a shop and his conscience told him it was a mortal sin but he ignored the voice of his guardian angel. Next day, which was a Saturday, he decided to confess it and be forgiven, but on the way there, he was knocked down and killed by a runaway horse. Where do you think he is now?'

The class couldn't stop itself from chorusing, 'Burning in hell, miss.'

This story worried me somewhat. 'What if he'd been knocked down *after* going to church, miss?' I asked.

'Then he would have gone straight to heaven,'

she replied.

'That's not fair,' I said. 'It was just a matter of luck that he was knocked down *before* and not *after.*'

'Then you should learn not to commit sin because you never know when you're going to die. You must always be ready, just in case.'

'It still sounds unfair to me,' I mumbled, still not satisfied.

'You're Tommy Hopkins, aren't you?' she said. 'Sister Monica has warned me about you.' Said you were a bit of a troublemaker. Come out here and hold out your hand.'

I got four of the strap for arguing and answering back. I learned that day that in this class, it was best to keep your mouth shut and your thoughts to yourself. In all this talk of souls burning in hell there was something else puzzling me. Where was your soul? Had anyone ever seen it? I asked everyone I knew but no one seemed to know its location. None of my pals knew. I asked Gran'pa Zeb.

'How the hell would I know?' he snorted. 'Ask your Aunty Dorothy or your Uncle Brodie.'

I did, but they hadn't a clue either.

'I only know you've *got* one,' Brodie said thoughtfully. 'Otherwise why would we have that emergency call for sailors, SOS? Save our Souls.' He made it sound like 'Save arseholes'.

Aunty Dorothy was nearer the mark when she replied, 'Your soul is a spirit and it is invisible.'

'Does it have a body?' I persisted. 'If you stuck a knife in it, would it hurt?'

'How could it, if it's a spirit?' she replied.

That was what I wanted to hear. The catechism said my soul was like God because it was an immortal spirit. In that case what was there to be worried about if your soul did burn in hell 'cos you wouldn't be able to feel a thing? I wanted to ask Miss Corbett about this but I was in enough trouble already.

Later that morning during the playtime break, the Bruiser called me back to her desk.

'I've always found that the best way of dealing with mischief-makers like you is to keep them so busy they've no time to cause trouble. From now on, you'll be Standard Two's monitor and you will be in charge of giving out things to the class, like pens and ink.'

'Yes, miss. Thank you very much, miss.'

I wasn't sure I wanted the job but what could I do? She showed me how to mix the ink from a large stone jar and how to distribute it in the inkwells of each desk.

'Don't make it too strong,' she said. 'One part water and one part ink will be quite sufficient.'

My next job was to put one pen-holder and one nib on each desk. I could see right away that there would be trouble because the pens would make ideal darts and there would soon be a run on the nibs. I was right because there was trouble after the second day when the Bruiser came to count the pens that were handed in. There were three missing! And I would probably get the blame. At four o'clock when we were due to be released from our prison, she carried out her inventory and discovered the shortage.

175

'There should be thirty pens,' she said, 'and there are only twenty-seven. Where are the others?

'Don't know, miss,' I said. I suspected Ginger McDermott but I was caught between the devil and the deep blue sea. Ginger was the devil and Corbett the sea.

'Well, you should know. You are the class monitor and it is your job to know' She turned on the class. 'Who has the three pens? Come on. Own up and nothing more will be said.'

Silence. Every face was a picture of innocence.

'Very well,' she exploded. 'Two can play at this game. I shall give everyone here two of the strap until the thief owns up.'

Miss Corbett was a strapping middle-aged teacher, that is to say, a champion strapper and could have represented Great Britain at the Olympics in this particular sport. When it came to delivering the tawse, she was deadly accurate for when she brought it down on someone's hand, it hit the mark and really hurt – every single time. She had long since learned to counter the hand-waggling of the more cunning pupils by insisting the victims place one hand underneath the other to create a firm base under the hand due to receive punishment.

Despite that, there was no chance of anyone confessing guilt and the Bruiser went round the class systematically delivering two of the tawse to each one, including her favourite, Gordon, who began blubbering.

'You have made *my* arm ache,' she yelled, 'and so in return I shall make yours do the same. All of you hold out your arms sideways till I tell you to put them down.'

Five minutes of this and arms began to wobble.

'I said arms up!' she screeched.

Another five minutes passed and the ache in the arms became unbearable.

'Very well,' Miss Corbett barked. 'Since the culprit won't own up, I shall examine each desk. Open desk lids, now!'

She went round the class peering into the interior of each desk without result until she reached that of our leader, Alfie. And there they were! The missing pens!

'I know nowt about them, miss,' Alfie protested. 'Honest to God, miss.'

Alfie was wasting his time. He'd been caught red-handed.

'Get out to the front, you nasty little thief!' she fumed. 'Hold out your hand.'

As she delivered vicious strokes to the outstretched hands she seethed. 'Here are two for hiding the pens and two for taking the name of the Lord in vain.'

We in the class could have told her who had hidden the pens as it was written on the faces of two boys, Ginger McDermott and Mick Malone, who could not disguise their gleeful expressions as Alfie took his punishment.

War has been declared, I thought.

The full complement of pens was handed across to me.

'As for you,' she snapped as I returned the pens, minus their nibs, to the box. 'You keep a thorough check on the number in future or you'll answer for it next time.'

Who would be the class monitor? I asked my-self.

Chapter Sixteen

Religious lessons then were mainly about hellfire, brimstone and rote-learning of catechism answers without any argument or discussion. Lessons in other subjects were much the same. History con-sisted mainly of learning dates – of battles and the reigns of English kings and queens. We found that the only way we could fix the characters and the dates in our thick heads was to learn them in the form of rhymes or jingles. Here are just a few of them that I can still remember.

In ten sixty-six,
Willy the Norman got up to his tricks.

John, John, bad King John,
Disgraced the throne that he sat on.
Nasty John was a right royal tartar
Until he signed the Magna Carta.
In twelve fifteen at Runnymede
'Twas there he did the fateful deed.

In fourteen ninety-two,
Columbus sailed the ocean blue.

Things were not much better in geography where

Duggie believed the equator to be an imaginary lion running around the world. The lessons were mainly about the British Empire and how great a country we were because we owned half the world.

'See all those red splashes across the globe,' Miss Corbett enthused. 'They are the countries which belong to our glorious Queen Victoria. You must always be proud to be British because the rest of the world looks up to us as their leaders.'

Charlie put his hand up to say something. We hoped he wasn't going to contradict her as that would put her in a bad temper and we'd all have to suffer the consequences.

'My dad says the white people keep the blacks as servants,' Charlie said. 'The blacks do all the hard jobs while the whites take it easy enjoying themselves and living it up in big houses. Is that true, miss?'

Charlie was trying to rattle her chain and it looked as if he was succeeding, for she said, 'Isn't your father one of those on strike on the railways?'

'Yes, miss, they're on strike for shorter hours and better pay.'

'Ah, he's one of those agitating anarchists. Well, tell your dad that he's wrong about the whites living off the fat of the land while the natives do the work. The white men supply the brains, the skill and the know-how. Just you tell him to put that in his pipe and smoke it.'

'He doesn't smoke, miss.' Charlie was really stoking her fire and we would all be the worse for it. Fortunately for us, she calmed down and

179

turned her attention to the map she had pinned up on the wall.

'As I was saying before I was rudely interrupted, the red bits are Her Majesty's possessions and they are to be found all round the world. It has been said that the sun never sets on the British Empire. What do we mean by that?'

Alfie, whose mind was somewhere else, thought he had the answer. 'It's because the empire is in the east and the sun sets in the west.'

'What stuff and nonsense some of you have in your heads!' Miss Corbett exclaimed. 'Look at the map again. Who can come out and point to Africa?'

Gordon was first with his hand up and went out and put his finger on the continent.

'Well done, Gordon. I only wish we had more like you in this class,' she added, glowering at Alfie. 'Why do we call it the Dark Continent, do you think?'

'Is it because the people there can't afford candles?' Duggie offered.

'No, not quite right.'

'Is it because the people who live there are black?' suggested Jimmy.

In geography and other subjects we were set to learning reams and reams of rigmaroles and phrases which meant little or nothing to us, like: the terrestrial core is of an igneous nature; the earth is an oblate spheroid; nature abhors a vacuum; a circle is a polygon with an infinite number of sides. Under the threat of punishment, we were trained like myna birds to regurgitate them. If there was one good thing that I could say for our education, it was that it helped to produce in us a highly trained memory, a skill that I found invaluable later in life when I took my first job.

The same teaching techniques were used in English literature where we were required to memorize yards and yards of poetry. If we had to do poetry, we preferred the stuff that appealed to our dreams of a better life, like *The Pedlar's Caravan* by William Brighty Rands.

I wish I lived in a caravan,
With a horse to drive, like the pedlar man!
Where he comes from nobody knows,
Or where he goes to, but on he goes!

Or a bit of adventure, like *The Rime of the Ancient Mariner* by Samuel Taylor Coleridge with that unforgettable line:

Water, water, everywhere, nor any drop to
   drink.

'My dad would love this poem,' Charlie said. 'Even if seawater were drinkable, he wouldn't touch the stuff, not in a million years.'

'The same goes for my Uncle Brodie and Auntie Dorothy,' I laughed.

Miss Corbett was mad keen, however, on the poems of Robbie Burns since she was from Glasgow.

'These are the most beautiful verses ever written she enthused.

First, she made us learn:

My luve's like a red, red rose
That's newly sprung in June

which Alfie immediately changed to:

My luve's got a red, red nose
That always runs in June.

'Robbie Burns didn't know how to spell, miss,'
grinned Jimmy. 'You don't spell "luve" like that.'

Florrie failed to see the funny side of it.

'Yes, yes,' she snapped impatiently. 'That's an
old joke and we all know how clever you are,
Jimmy Dixon, but Burns is writing in dialect and
that's how it's pronounced.'

Much of the poetry she made us learn was all
about love which we thought was soppy, especially
one that began:

I have heard the mavis singing
His love song to the morn ...

'My big sister's named Mavis,' Duggie told us at
playtime. 'I've heard our Mavis singing and I can
tell you, it's bloody awful!'

But Miss Corbett insisted that we commit the
poetry to memory.

'In some ways, it's like the catechism you have
to learn,' she said. 'You may not understand or
appreciate it today but there will come a time
when you will, that is if you ever come to your
senses.'

We didn't believe her one bit.

As for sex education, we didn't get any that could be recognized as such. One day, however, a lad in Standard 4 was caught by one of the male teachers looking surreptitiously at a picture postcard of Miss Irene Langhorne, the original Gibson Girl, displaying an hour-glass figure that left nothing to the imagination (or, as the caption on the card put it, 'a girl with an eighteen-inch waist, a mass of golden hair, and a low-cut gown in black velvet'). The picture was enough to sound warning bells in Mr Sullivan's head. One day, he called the school together in an emergency assembly and, having made sure that all females – including Miss Corbett and the school cleaning woman – were not within hearing distance, gave us a special talk on the dangers of sex. He warned us of the dangers of 'handling the sexual organ' which, in extreme cases, he said, had been known to fall off.

'The seed, boys,' he informed us, 'is precious and is to be preserved for fatherhood, not dissipated in carnal pleasure. I've never been guilty of the disgusting practice myself but if any of you here persist in the filthy habit, remember that it can cause not only weakness in the head and the heart but can lead to idiocy and lunacy. The asylums are filled with people who have abused themselves. Furthermore, it may earn God's severest displeasure. Consider the story of Onan in the Bible. When his older brother, Er, died, Onan was commanded by his father, Judah, to produce offspring with Er's widow as there was no male heir. Instead Onan spilled his seed upon the ground and God was so angry with him that He punished him with death.'

Many of us younger boys in Standard 2 did not fully understand what he was on about but, judging by the sheepish and embarrassed expressions on the faces of Standards 3 and 4, the bigger boys did.

'Who was that Owen man in the Bible?' Duggie asked as we came out of the assembly. 'I didn't understand what that was all about.'

'Not Owen, you ninny,' said Jimmy. 'Onan!'

'Onan? What kind of daft name is that?' Duggie exclaimed.

'It's Jewish,' I told him. 'Anyroad, it's not as daft as "Er"! Imagine being stopped by the cops and being asked your name. "Er", you would say.'

Charlie took it up. 'Then the cop would say, "What's the matter with you? Don't you know your own name? Never mind *Er*. Get on with it and give us your name".'

'And if you kept on saying "Er, Er",', added Alfie, 'you'd probably end up behind bars for giving cheek.'

Apart from some vague descriptions of reproduction by reference to examples from the vegetable kingdom, the biblical story of Onan turned out to be the full extent of our education in sex. No wonder we left school confused.

184

Chapter Seventeen

What we learned in the classroom could, roughly speaking, be called schooling. Some of it useful, some of it not. The real learning took place outside the classroom and this was called our true education, for it was something we never forgot and it shaped our lives and characters. From my so-called peer groups – both friends and enemies – I learned how to smoke, swear, fight and, most important of all, how to survive.

From the very first day, our class at school was divided into two factions: the St Chad's and St William's gangs. It was strange how our own school fellows, friends and former foes, became a closely-knit or 'in group' once we were faced by a potential outside enemy. Our little clique was made up of Alfie Rigby, Charlie Madden, Duggie Dimson, Jimmy Dixon, me and even Gordon Bennett, despite his tendency to blab on us.

It was June 1894 and we were seven going on eight. In that glorious summer – why is it that in our memories of our childhood, the weather is always sunny and glorious? – we went around together and became hunters and fishers. Our hunting consisted of leaping across Barney's waste ground like gazelles and, armed with our newly acquired butterfly nets, pursued those beautiful but tricky lepidoptera ('tricky to catch and tricky to pronounce'), as we came to call them after

Jimmy Dixon showed us the word in his *A Boy's Book of British Butterflies.* We never did anything with them after we'd caught them, like pinning them in books, for example, but simply let them go. The thrill had been in the chase.

Our fishing activity was catching tadpoles which we stored in jam jars and then waited patiently for them to develop into frogs.

'If you handle too many frogs,' Gordon warned us one day, 'you'll develop warts on the backs of your hands.'

'Rubbish!' said Charlie. 'Where do you get these barmy ideas from?'

'It's in the Bible,' Gordon protested. 'God was angry with the Egyptians and so he sent a plague of frogs and warts.'

'That may be true,' Alfie said, 'but my dad, who's a butcher and has a lot of warts on his hands, says it's due to working with meat and water.'

Duggie felt he had to add to the conversation with '*My* dad told me that you only get warts from frogs if you let them pee on the back of your hands.'

'And there's not much chance of that happening,' I said.

All this talk of frogs and warts didn't worry us one bit. Our main interest in frogs lay in another direction. When our victims were good and ready, we organized racing and jumping competitions, encouraging our own personal champions to out-perform their rivals by prodding them on the backside with a matchstick.

Alfie was our undisputed champion not only in

these competitions but also as boss of our little clique. 'Undisputed' because no one had challenged him since he'd been the tallest and had appointed himself as our cock on the very first day at school. I, being next in height, was his unofficial deputy.

In Standard 2 at school, the top dog of the St Chad's gang was undoubtedly the big lout Ginger McDermott, with Mick Malone as his sidekick, along with several other hangers-on. The most obvious bone of contention and one that hung over us like a sword during that first week was the unresolved question of who was to be cock of the whole class. It was not a question of if the top-dog position was to be fought over but when.

Being cock of something was an important and prestigious role, like a 'capo' in the Mafia, because the holder of the office could set the agenda for a gang, resolve arguments and keep underlings in line. The cock was always deferred to when it came to making decisions affecting the whole group and the status usually had to be earned in battle by fighting off potential contenders. In each class, there was a cock, and there was even a supremo for the whole school in the person of Bill Battersby, a veritable colossus, in Standard 4. But for us in that first week in Standard 2, we had the gnawing problem of who was to reign over us and be our representative in negotiations with other groups. Would it be our own Alfie Rigby or Ginger McDermott? In the first week at the big school, nothing happened. The two contenders contented themselves by throwing insults at each other as to the inferior qualities of the other gang.

'Chad's chickens – that's all you lot are,' Alfie scoffed when he saw Ginger in the playground. 'Is your mam in school with you to wipe your nose and your bottom?'

'William's whingers,' rejoined Ginger. 'Any of you wet your pants yet? Because some of you will when I get round to showing you who's boss around here.'

Gradually the bar was raised and they moved on to the next stage, pushing each other as they passed on the playground.

'Do that again, McDermott,' Alfie hissed, 'and I'll thump you.'

'Oh, yeah? It'll take a bigger man than you, Rigby. Your mam and dad must be really ugly to produce someone with a face like yours.'

Not to be outdone in the verbal battle, our leader said, 'I'd say the same thing about you, McDermott, if you had a face.'

'You tell him, Alfie,' us William's lot chorused. In the verbal battle, we were definitely on top. Could we keep it up when it came to the actual punch-up itself? I wasn't too sure as we'd never actually witnessed Alfie's fighting skills. His claim had been based on his height and his urinary skill.

As the days went by, the niggling began to hot up until it took the form of barging into each other as they ran about the playground. On the Thursday of the second week, they clashed as they both tried to get through the classroom door at the same time.

'Stand back, McDermott, and let your betters

through,' Alfie snarled.

'Stand back yourself, Rigby, you little tub of butter. One of these days, I'm going to give you such a pasting, you won't be able to walk for a week.'

'The only pasting you'll ever give is with a wallpaper brush,' retorted Alfie.

'You're asking for it, Rigby. Start saying your prayers 'cos I'm going to pulverize you.'

'You and whose army, pig-eyes? I can lick you with one hand tied behind my back.'

'You just try it, fatty, and I'll black both your eyes. I can mollycrush you with my little finger.'

'Can't.'

'Can.'

This exchange of pleasantries could have continued indefinitely but it resolved itself by resort to physical force. They squeezed the sides of their bodies against each other until they both fell through the exit. They continued the verbal interplay in the yard.

'You're nothing but talk, McDermott,' Alfie sneered. 'Just a big mouth. Why don't you put your money where your mouth is?'

'Right, that's it!' Ginger said. 'I'll give you one last chance. Say sorry and I'll let you off.'

'OK. Sorry. Sorry I didn't tell you that you and your Chad Chickens are nothing but a load of pretty boys who should have gone to the girls' school.'

'Right! You've had your chance,' Ginger snarled. 'Now you're for it. In the back entry outside the school gates on Friday after the teachers have gone. I'm going to give you the biggest hiding of your life.'

'You're on,' replied our knight in shining armour. 'But you'll be the one getting the hiding 'cos when I've finished with you, you'll want to run away and hide.'

The teachers left at four o'clock like bullets fired from a gun. After all, it was Friday and they'd had enough. But among the 'scholars' of the school, word soon spread and at half past four, a good crowd had gathered, including several from the older classes.

There were a few verbal and physical preliminaries to be dealt with before the actual fisticuffs could begin. Ginger gave Alfie a shoulder charge, saying, 'Still time for you to back down, if you want, Rigby. I'll have mercy on you.'

'Back down!' Alfie snorted. 'Back down! You must be kidding, McDermott. Is this your way of ducking out of it?'

'Don't say I didn't warn you,' Ginger rasped.

Alfie adopted a Jim Corbett boxing stance as he had seen in pictures of 'Gentleman Jim' in the newspapers. That was his first big mistake and also his last. Ginger had no intention of following Marquess of Queensberry rules or any other rules for that matter. His first move was to kick Alfie on the shins and when he bent down to rub his injured leg, Ginger elbowed him one in the guts.

'Ow! Ow!' Alfie yelled. 'That wasn't fair. You're not supposed to do that.'

'Then how about this?' bawled Ginger gleefully, giving our gladiator a fourpenny one on the chin.

Alfie went down on one knee. He was out-classed. Ginger followed up his advantage by pushing his opponent on to his back, kneeling on his upper arms and slapping him about the head. 'Now, say sorry,' Ginger barked.

'No, I won't,' our man mumbled defiantly.

'We'll soon see about that,' squawked Ginger and the punishment went on unabated.

I winced at each blow as if the thumps were landing on me.

At last our defeated champion managed a smothered, 'Sorry! Sorry!' and Ginger released him. 'Let that be a lesson to you and the rest of you William weasels. Better watch out who you're dealing with next time.'

The fight was over. It had lasted about thirty seconds. Standard 2 had been taken over by a tyrant. Not only a tyrant but a foreign tyrant, as far as us William's lads were concerned.

The consequences for our contingent were not only disappointing but humiliating and unbear-able. For the rest of that term, the Chad victors lorded it over us and pushed us around merci-lessly. In the playground, we were shoved about, knocked to the wall and taunted with catcalls of, 'Yah! William's Whingers! Your Alfie Rigby couldn't lick a toffee apple, never mind lick our Ginger.' There was little we could do because our star had been well and truly trounced and we'd been left powerless.

In the classroom, Jimmy Dixon and me got the worst of it because Ginger and his deputy, Mick Malone, sat in the desk immediately behind us and we were the constant recipients of their bullying demands reinforced by threats of what they were going to do to us.

Jimmy and I worked hard at school and in the weekly tests it was between him and me who would come top. I'm not claiming we were the brainiest in the class but we had a friendly competition going between us and, in trying to beat each other, we were spurred on to produce our best efforts. If he got eight out of ten then I had to get nine; if I got nine he had to get ten. In arithmetic, we were past the nine times table, were on to harder sums of addition and subtraction, and had even reached the dizzy heights of long multiplication. Our two neighbours at the rear of us couldn't get their sums right and were constantly being called out for the strap. The solution to their problem was to thump Jimmy and me in the back.

"What's the answer to number ten, Hopkins?' hissed Ginger.

'Do your own work,' I hissed back.

'Right, Hopkins. You and Dixon are for it!' He reinforced his threat with a dig in my spine.

His companion, Mick, was just as bad.

'You, Dixon! What've you got for number twelve? Hold up your book so's I can see it.'

'Push off, Malone. Why should I tell you? Work it out for yourself,' Jimmy snapped back.

'Just wait till playtime, Dixon. You're in for a good belting.'

Both of them got their sums wrong and were given two of the tawse which made them angrier still. They were seething and the duo cornered us at playtime.

'Next time we ask you for the answers, you'd better give 'em or you'll both get knuckle sandwiches, like this,' Ginger spat, thumping me heavily in the side. 'And it's no use going to your leader for help,' he sneered, 'for we all know what a great fighter *he* is.'

Jimmy Dixon was receiving similar treatment from Mick Malone.

The same thing was happening in English lessons when we were given spelling dictation and had to write down such words as: *separate, accommodation, committee, address, embarrass.*

Jimmy and I decided between us to resist their demands no matter how many thumps in the back it meant. For a whole fortnight, we suffered their punches but then Ginger decided on a change of tack. One morning, Jimmy and I opened our arithmetic and English exercise books to find huge blots on the pages of our most recent work. Blots like these were almost capital offences with the Bruiser and we received two of the strap for each blot. We both knew only too well where the smudges had come from. One look at the gloating expressions on the faces of Ginger and Mick was enough. It was hard to know what to do about what was little short of blackmail. Either we let them copy or they would mess up our work and get us into trouble. At the end of school that day, we decided that the easiest way out of it was to give in to their demands. After all, what did it matter to us if they copied our answers? They were the ones wasting their time at school and learning nothing. At the back of my mind, I was unhappy about it, though. Surely something could be done about it. We could report the matter to our teacher or even to Mr Sullivan himself but that would really be asking for trouble, for there was nothing worse or anyone more hated than a snitch. We'd be disowned by everyone, including our own gang, if we did that. We had to find another answer.

Up to this point in school, my tendency to stammer over certain words had remained hidden and I was eager to keep it that way. I took great care to avoid all words beginning with 'sh' by substituting other words whenever possible but it wasn't always easy. Had my minor vocal impediment become public knowledge, my reputation in Standard 2, such as it was, would have been completely destroyed. For almost eighteen months, I managed to keep it to myself though I think my pal Jimmy was aware of it. Came the day, however, when it was brought into the open.

Miss Corbett decided to introduce us to one of her favourite verses. She went into raptures describing the theme of the work.

'It is my favourite and one of the most beautiful among Tennyson's poems,' she gushed. 'It is the story of the Lady of Shalott who is a magical being who lives alone on an island not far from King Arthur's Camelot. Here is a famous painting of her by one of our best-known artists, John William Waterhouse.'

She attached the painting to the blackboard.

'See how beautiful and how lonely she is, boys. We shall take turns reading around the class and I shall choose only the very best readers. Recite in your clearest voice, boys, so as to bring out the beauty of this masterpiece.'

Quickly I scanned through the poem and I prayed that she wouldn't ask me to read as I could see so many stumbling blocks ahead. My luck was out. She announced her chosen readers and I was on the list. I raised my hand.

'Please, miss,' I said, 'I have a frog in my throat and I can't read today.'

'Nonsense, she said. 'Of course you can read. You just spoke and there's nothing wrong with your voice.'

I resigned myself to my fate. If she asks me, I thought, I'll have a heart attack.

We were some way into the poem when she pointed to me and said, 'Tommy Hopkins, continue!'

Anxiously I took a rapid look at the stanza which had fallen to me and I knew I was in trouble. I stood up, took a deep breath and forced my dried-up mouth to read.

And by the moon the reaper weary,
Piling sh-sh-sheaves in uplands airy,
Listening, whispers, ''Tis the fairy
Lady of Sh-Sh-Sh-Shalott.'

A hush fell over the class.

'Are you poking fun at this beautiful poem, Hopkins?' the Bruiser asked me ominously.

'No, miss. Honest to God. I couldn't help it.'

'Again. The last line,' she commanded.

'The Lady of Sh-Sh-Sh-Shalott,' I stammered.

'Where do you get this "Sh-Sh-Sh-Shalott"

from? If Tennyson had wanted it read like that, I am sure he would have written it.'

By now the class had begun to snigger and I prayed for the ground to open up and swallow me. No such luck.

'Now, once again. Say the verse and this time say it properly as the poet intended.'

It was no use as, by this time, I was extremely keyed up and couldn't get my tongue round 'The Lady of Shalott'.

'Right, that's it!' she stormed. 'Get out here.'

She took me by the ear and led me out to the front where she gave me a stinging slap across the face which sent my head reeling. She really believed I was making fun of the poem and was beside herself with rage.

'Hold your hand out!' she shrieked.

I stretched out my right hand and she brought the strap down with all the strength and skill acquired over twenty years' practice. Three more strokes followed and I spent the rest of the lesson kneeling at the front of the room. The punishment for my imagined crime was bad enough and I wouldn't have minded if that had been the end of it but there was more to come. My enemies in the class never let it go. For the rest of that day and the weeks that followed Ginger McDermott and Mick Malone tormented me and would not let me forget it.

'Hopkins,' Ginger sneered. 'You're useless. You couldn't even sh-sh-shovel sh-sh-shit.'

His cronies around him guffawed, enjoying my discomfiture.

'One of these days, Ginger, I'll make you eat

196

those words,' I replied, looking him straight in the eye.

'Yeah, and pigs might fly, Hopkins.'

Chapter Eighteen

On Saturdays, I continued working with Uncle Brodie and Aunty Dorothy in Smithfield Market. As a special favour, they allowed me to turn up later at half past eight.

'As you know, Tommy,' Aunty Dorothy explained, 'we start at four in the morning but that's a bit early for a growing youngster like you so you can meet us later. Besides, you'll be no use to us if you turn up half asleep, so it'll be best if we ease you into market work gradually.'

I was grateful for that as I didn't fancy getting up at the unearthly hour of three in the morning. I just thanked the Lord that market work wasn't going to be my regular job.

If I had to get up at that hour every morning, I thought, I'd be sleep-walking the rest of the day.

I met Brodie and Dorothy at the agreed time and place outside Deakin's stall. It was there that I mentioned my problem at school to my uncle.

'The only answer to bullying,' said Brodie, 'is to beat them at their own game. You have to go in there and show them who's boss. Give them a good arse-kicking. Knock the stuffing out of 'em. You have to do it yourself. It's no good asking someone else to do it for you.'

'This lad's a big bloke, Uncle. He's already beaten our best fighter. What chance would I stand? Just the same, I wouldn't mind having a few lessons from you.'

'You mean in boxing?'

'No, not boxing. That'll be no good. This lad doesn't fight by the rules. He plays rough. I hate dirty fighting but with this lad, there's no choice.'

'Then what you need is not lessons from me but a few pointers from Mad Alec in the market.'

'Who's Mad Alec? Is he barmy?'

'No, Tommy. He's called mad not because he's barmy but because he fights like a madman if he gets involved in a brawl. No one in the market can hold a candle to him when it comes to the rough stuff. He used to be a scuttler and a member of the notorious Meadow Lads that once fought regular pitched battles with the Bengal Tiger gang of Ancoats. I'll have a word with him and see if he can give you a few pointers after we've finished this morning.'

Mad Alec was a well-known figure in Smithfield Market and he had earned his title the hard way. No one ever challenged him as he knew and employed every dirty, lowdown trick in the book and I was going to receive personal instruction from the master himself. I met him after work on that first Saturday morning and I saw immediately why he was called Mad. He had a wild look in his eyes and his hands and feet twitched as if he were scrapping with an opponent and warding off imaginary blows. In, this first lesson, he said he was going to give me a few vital survival tips.

'This bloke,' I began, 'is bigger and heavier than me and he begins a scrap by kicking his opponent in the shins.'

'Forget about size because it don't matter. Remember the old saying, "The bigger they are, the harder they fall". First rule. If you're gonna have a ding-dong with someone, don't mess about talking and saying what you're going to do to each other. That's a waste of time. Get the first blow in before he has time to think and he won't know what's hit him. Square up to your opponent in the usual way but don't wait for the signal for the off. That's just asking for it. I like to open the proceedings by stamping on his toes, then kicking him in the goolies as hard as I can. Another trick is to suddenly lie down on your back. He'll be so surprised, he won't know what to make of it. While you're down there, punch upwards and thump him in the cohones. See how he likes that for starters.'

'This bloke at school begins by kicking out,' I said.

'S'easy to deal with a punter that kicks out as long as you're ready. Leap back, grab his kicking leg and up-end him. When he's on his back, jump on him good and hard with both feet. If he gets up again, give him a good Smithfield smacker.'

'A Smithfield smacker?'

'Like a Manchester kiss only worse. A Manchester kiss means nutting your opponent with your forehead as if you're heading the winning goal for your football team. That's no good. A Smithfield smacker is better. Instead of using

199

your forehead, which does *you* more damage than *him,* you use the top of your head and you charge your opponent like a mad bull at a gatepost. Use knees, elbows, feet. Gouge his eyes out with your knuckles. Make sure you are wearing big boots, though clogs are best. Jump on his toes with all your might. One of you is going to come out on top. Make sure it's you. Forget Marquess of Queensberry rules – they're too fancy and too sissy. I'm teaching you the Marquess of Smithfield rules to be used in a roughhouse or a ding-dong. Anyway, that's enough talking. Let's get down to the practical stuff. First, I want you to lie down and hook your foot behind my leg and see if you can bring me down by kicking against my kneecap.'

For the remainder of that first term at St Chad's, I received weekly, individual, down-to-earth (literally) instruction from the maestro. At the end of November, Mad Alec pronounced me ready.

'I'll put my money on you to win,' he said. 'I only wish I were there to see it. Get mad, Tommy! Get mad! Remember all I've taught you and don't forget the honour and reputation of Smithfield Market is riding on you.'

The Monday after my last lesson in dirty fighting, Jimmy and I talked it over and decided to go into the next and most dangerous phase of our counter-blackmail operation.

'I hope you realize how dangerous this plan is, Jimmy,' I said.

'I do, Tommy,' he replied, 'but there's no alternative if we're going to put an end to this bullying.'

200

In arithmetic exercises, we made sure that all calculations were the wrong answers. In English we took down dictation and wrote: 'The comitee where quite deffinate that we cud have seperate acomodashun for our meating.'

Of course we were given the strap but so were our two blackmailers and the look of anger on their faces more than compensated for the pain in our hands.

'You did that on purpose, didn't you, Hopkins?' Ginger seethed. 'Right! You're for it! I'm going to beat hell out of you on Friday after school.'

'I'm quaking in my clogs, Ginger,' I smiled. 'What time do you suggest? Will half past four suit you?'

I spoke as if I were supremely confident but inside I was a quivering jelly and I had last-minute doubts that Mad Alec's coaching and expectations would be as good as he claimed when it came to the crunch. But it was too late to back out now without losing face and wiping out completely what little status remained to us, William's Whingers.

That Friday afternoon, there was an even bigger crowd assembled to witness my execution. I must admit that when I came face to face with Ginger, he really did look formidable; he was taller and broader, with a fearsome reputation as a fighter and a bully.

'Give him one for me!' Mick Malone called to his fellow thug as Ginger squared up to me.

'Start saying your prayers, Hopkins,' Ginger hissed. 'You're going down.'

He was right in that prediction because, following Mad Alec's instruction, I fell on my back and punched him immediately in the pills. He groaned and bent double in agony. I leaped immediately to my feet and waited for the onslaught which I knew would follow. He knew better than to wait but rushed at me, kicking out with his right leg for my shins as I knew he would. Jumping back, I grabbed his foot and pulled with all my might. Ginger landed on his back with a thump and a look of amazement on his face. I leaped high into the air and came down heavily on his belly with my iron clogs, knocking all the air out of him. Panting heavily, he staggered to his feet and I gave him my best Smithfield Market smacker right on the snout.

'This is for all the thumps in the back during the last six weeks,' I said, giving him a massive punch on the jaw. He went down on one knee and I pushed him once more on to his back. Ginger's face was puffy and his nostrils were streaming blood. I sat on his stomach and forced his arms out and knelt on them with as much pressure as I could muster.

'That was for your sneers about shovelling shit,' I said.

It was time to bring matters to a head.

'Say, "Give in",' I said, pressing more heavily on his outstretched arms.

'Never!' he replied, struggling to free himself.

I gave him a few more slaps across the face, determined to put a finish to his bullying and his taunting once and for all. I continued putting all my weight on to his arm muscles until at last and much to my relief, he got out a muffled, 'Give in.'

I stood up and looked down at his prostrate figure. 'Let that be the end of it. No more copying and no more punches in the back. You and Mick do your own work from now on and Jimmy and me will do ours. And one more thing. No more sneering.'

From that day on, I was hailed as 'cock' of Standard 2, a dubious honour I could well have done without. I hoped, though, that I had done Smithfield Market proud. As for Ginger, he was smouldering with anger, having publicly accepted his defeat. But I knew that he was not the kind of lad to take things lying down. I had the feeling that he'd be back one day seeking revenge in some underhand way and probably when I least expected it.

Chapter Nineteen

Our little gang of William's lads rather liked the name that Ginger had tried to insult us with, William's Whingers, as it sounded a bit like Wingers. So we adopted it as our official title in our daily football practices after school and in our Friday afternoon matches against the Chad's Chickens on a nearby croft. We were constantly short of cash and all of us, William's Whingers and Chad's Chickens, were forever racking our brains to think up money-making schemes. For a start, we badly needed a decent football for our games of soccer. At first, we tried playing with a tin can, then a fluffy lump (I can't call it a 'ball') made up of old socks stitched together by Duggie's mam, but they were no good at all. For a start, they weren't round, so they wouldn't roll, and they wouldn't bounce, so there was no way of controlling them or practising our kicking and dribbling skills. Alfie's dad worked as a butcher in the wholesale meat market and had pull. Using his influence through his contacts, he managed to cadge a few pigs' bladders from a local slaughterhouse. These were much better but it was a dirty job cleaning them out and blowing them up. The bladders had their own drawbacks because they were more suitable for rugby than soccer and it was no easy job making them airtight so they were always popping. There were proper leather footballs, or 'caseys', for sale at Wiles's toy store in town but they cost five and six and that was for the cheapest. Since none of us had any ready cash, there was no choice but to make do with the bladders for the rest of that term.

'If only we had some lolly,' sighed Charlie, 'we could buy one of them lovely caseys. We'd have a great game of footie with it.'

'No use pipe-dreaming,' said my pal, Jimmy.

I didn't say anything but I had my regular Saturday job at the market and was still earning the odd penny or ha'penny doing errands. Secretly I decided to save up all these coppers for a football, though it seemed like a huge task to raise sixty-six pennies or one hundred and thirty two ha'pennies. I bought a money box shaped and coloured like a pillar box and hid it in the bottom drawer of my chest of drawers in the cellar. Every Saturday I 'posted' into the slot the few coppers and the occasional tanner or threepenny bit I had over after buying myself a bag of Holland toffees. It was no easy matter getting the money out once it had been posted into the money box. The only way of extracting the coins was by levering off the tin top and so ruining the box, or by patiently fishing out the coppers one at a time with a knife through the slot. I thought it was a good thing that it was so hard to get the money out because I was often tempted to take the lot out and splash out on something daft like treacle toffee. As the weeks went by, my money box became heavier and heavier and there was a truly satisfying feeling as I weighed and rattled it in my hand each Saturday. The jingle was music to my ears and I was beginning to like the idea of having a bit of cash behind me.

It struck me one day that I was getting like that bloke in the story the Bruiser was reading to us the other day – Silas Marner. But then I thought, No, I'm not becoming a miser. I'm going to use this money to buy that football in Wiles's. I can hardly wait to see the gang's faces when I roll up with a new casey one Friday afternoon.

The big day came round at the end of November. That Saturday, I withheld my usual contribution to the box as it was time to begin the joyous but fiddly task of fishing out my savings, though I was tempted to simply break off the top and pour out the lot in one go. I was really looking forward to it as it had taken me almost a whole term to build up what I judged to be enough to buy that special football.

In the evening I went down to the cellar and pulled out my box, which by now was feeling gratifyingly heavy. What a happy sensation as I rattled it for the last time. How my reputation in the gang was going to soar when I turned up with that new casey! It was going to be a long but satisfying job fishing out the coppers after all these weeks but it was one I'd been looking forward to for ages. I inserted the knife and after numerous abortive attempts, I manoeuvred out the first coin. My hair stood on end and my heart skipped a beat when I saw what had emerged. It wasn't a coin at all! It was a metal washer! Painstakingly over the next hour, I got the rest out. My cache was not cash but useless washers. What could have happened? Had some mischievous, evil gnome using fiendish alchemy transmuted my money into base metal? Then it came to me in a flash. Not an evil spirit as such but almost – Gran'pa Zeb! For weeks he'd had the whole day to practise fishing out the coppers at his leisure. But why would he do it? That was easy to answer. For gin, fags and drugs.

I wasn't going to let him get away with it. All my hopes and dreams that term had rested on buying that football and now he'd drunk and smoked my savings away. I determined to confront him right away. I found him upstairs in his usual position sitting in his battered armchair in front of the fire, clutching a glass of his favourite tipple.

'Zeb,' I omitted the title of Gran'pa, 'you pinched the coins out of my money box and replaced them with washers. You bloody old devil, you! You're a bloody thief!'

He leaped to his feet, took hold of his crook and poked me savagely in the chest, knocking me on to my back. 'You cheeky little bugger,' he yelled, standing over me. 'Don't you dare talk to me like that! Who the bloody hell do you think you are, calling me a thief? I've half a mind to thump you with this crutch. Any more of your bloody cheek and I'll take the horse whip to you. What the hell would I want with your paltry few coppers?'

'They'd help towards that bottle of gin on the table for a start,' I retorted. 'Anyway, I'm going to tell Brodie and Dorothy what you've done. Maybe they can get my cash back.'

'Tell who the bloody hell you like,' he stormed. 'See if I care.'

I have never liked the idea of telling tales about anyone, not even Zeb, despite the dirty trick he'd played. At school it was the golden rule: 'Never blab on anyone.' But this was different. In my mind's eye, for a whole term I'd carried round a picture of me going to the store, picking out that brand new casey, pumping up the bladder, lacing up the leather, and then presenting it to the two teams one Friday afternoon. How proud I'd have been to see the look of surprise and pleasure on their faces when we kicked off the match with it. Now this old man had destroyed my dream with his thieving ways and drunken habits.

Brodie and Dorothy listened to my tale of woe without interruption as if it was a story they'd heard before.

Finally Brodie spoke up. 'Leave it with me,

Tommy. I'll speak to my da. This time he's gone too far. How much was in the box?'

'About six shillings in copper and a little silver in tanners and threepenny bits.'

Later that day, Brodie reported back to me. 'He says he didn't pinch the money; he only borrowed it and he was going to put it back when he gets his next pension payment. Anyroad, your Aunty Dorothy and me have agreed to give you your six bob and we'll take it out of Zeb's pension for the next few weeks. But if you are keeping money about the house, better find a safer hiding place.'

So all was well that ended well. I got my new football and we had some great games on Friday afternoons. We found playing with a heavy leather football much harder work, though, especially on a muddy field when heading it was like bashing your forehead against a cannonball with laces. As for the old pig bladders, we kicked them into touch.

Chapter Twenty

Although we enjoyed our football, we were still desperately short of cash and we continued racking our brains for fresh ideas. Two heads are better than one and several heads are better than two, or so we thought. We decided to form a little company dedicated to finding ways of making money and as cock of the class, I was elected managing director of the enterprise. We found a dilapidated shed on Barney's waste ground and made this our headquarters to discuss ways and means of raising capital. Our first financial venture involved returning empty jam jars, mineral bottles and beer bottles when we could filch them but the grown-ups at home had this field pretty well sewn up. We thought of chopping and selling firewood but that too had been done and was an overcrowded market monopolized by men out of work. We needed something new, something different.

We looked to Charlie as our ideas man as we gathered round the table in our den.

'The other day, me and my mam were coming out of the Maypole Dairies shop with a basket of groceries,' he told us by way of introduction. 'My mam was just putting her change back in her purse when a tanner fell out of her hand and rolled down the grid in the road. She went mad 'cos, as you know, we can't afford to lose a sixpence like that. So I wondered if any of you lot can think of ways of fishing it out.'

'What we must do,' said Jimmy, the brains of our outfit, 'is get a thin rod like the kind we have on our butterfly nets and poke it down the grid.'

'But how would that work?' I asked. 'We'd need something sticky on the end of the rod to pick up the tanner.'

'We could try mashed-up soap,' added Alfie, anxious to contribute to the puzzle. 'That should be sticky enough to pick up a tanner. I'll cut some off our family's block tomorrow night.'

'Didn't know your family had soap,' grinned

Charlie Madden.

'Watch it, Charlie,' muttered Alfie, giving him a playful thump.

That Friday night, we gathered outside the Maypole shop to try and retrieve the sixpence. Alfie took the piece of Fairy soap he'd brought, spat on it and mashed it up till it was good and sticky. We stuck the blob on the end of the rod and began the ticklish operation. Taking it in turns, with sleeves rolled up, we lay on our stomachs poking down the grid as delicately as safe-breakers trying to crack a lock combination. Passers-by simply shrugged their shoulders, assuming we were a bunch of nutters escaped from the local asylum. But it was no use, our efforts were in vain because, despite our best efforts, we failed to fish out the sixpence though we did manage to lift out lots of slime and sludge. After a while, the soap became so soggy it simply dissolved and was useless for picking up anything, especially something as tiny as a sixpence. There was no alternative but to retire to our headquarters and go back to the drawing board.

'I have a small but powerful horseshoe magnet in the science set my dad gave me for Christmas,' suggested Jimmy. 'We could dangle it on a piece of string and see if that works.'

The next night, we got together at the den to conduct a scientific experiment. First, we lined up on the table as many coins as we could lay our hands on and tried to pick them up with the magnet. Like the soap, it was a blind alley. The magnet picked up farthings and a few little foreign coins like pfennigs and centimes all right but beyond those, nothing doing. No good at all for sixpences or threepenny bits.

'That's because some coins are made up of alloys that contain no iron and so cannot be magnetized,' Jimmy, our would-be scientist, explained.

But we were not in the mood for clever-clog theories.

'I have a good idea,' said Duggie.

Our little gang sighed. Duggie with an idea? No chance.

'Sometimes I have ideas,' he protested when he saw the doubtful expressions on our faces.

'Yeah, so do lunatics in the asylums,' sneered Alfie.

'Give him a chance,' Jimmy said, coming to his defence.

'Right. Let's have this brilliant brainwave of yours,' Alfie said.

'Why not use sticky toffee papers?' Duggie said, chewing for all his worth on his Wrigley's.

'That's stupid,' Alfie snorted. 'How are we going to attach toffee papers to a thin bamboo stick, I'd like to know? Where's your brains, Duggie?'

I looked at Duggie's face and at his jaws working mechanically like pistons in a steam engine. Then it struck me. Chewing gum! That was the answer.

'Listen, lads!' I exclaimed. 'Duggie's notion isn't all that bad. Maybe not toffee papers but remember when Duggie stuck his gum under his desk when the Bruiser told him to take the stuff out of

211

his mouth?'

'Yeah?' Alfie said. 'We remember. So what?'

The penny was slow to drop. Then Charlie saw the light. 'Of course! We can use chewing gum!' he said. 'It's obvious. Sticky, gooey chewing gum! That should do it.'

Duggie was made to remove the gum and we stuck it on the end of the bamboo rod. It worked! We replaced the line of coins along the table and with the minimum of effort we were able to pick up every single coin. Copper and silver! The lot! Eureka!

The next night, we returned to the grid outside the Maypole and took up our usual prone postures in the gutter where we had become an accepted feature of the place. Jimmy assumed responsibility for locating the coin and, summoning up all his concentration, took a deep breath and began gently jabbing the rod down the grid. The rest of us lay gathered around like a medical team assisting at a critical operation. After several tentative but gentle pokes, Jimmy whispered urgently, 'Don't move! Keep quite still! I think I've got it!'

Slowly, oh so slowly, he pulled up the rod and then we could all see it – the elusive silver sixpence attached to the gum. Then came the really tricky part – getting the rod through the bars of the grid. It was a tight fit and just as we thought we were home and dry, the end of the rod caught the metal bar and the sixpence fell back into the drain with a plop. We were determined not to give in. The mantle of retriever was assumed by Duggie who proved to be most adept and, after several abortive attempts, had the tanner out on the pavement and then into Charlie's hands so he could return it to his mam.

'Do you realize,' Charlie said, as he pocketed the coin, that there must be hundreds of coins and other valuable objects dropped down grids by mistake. We could make our fortune if we do the round of all the grids in the district.'

Charlie may have been right but considering the tremendous effort and time needed to retrieve that sixpence, we didn't fancy poking down every grid in Collyhurst and Ancoats in the hope of finding something valuable. Though with lots more practice and, after many failed attempts, we'd become more skilful at the job, the chief problem was the last bit of the operation, manoeuvring the bamboo rod through the narrow bars of the grid. Even here we found a solution.

After a really frustrating time outside the Co-op grocery store one day, Duggie had his second brainwave of the year.

'Why don't we remove the grid cover and then we can reach down into the water and feel for objects with our hands?'

We all stared at Duggie in amazement. Maybe he wasn't so dumb after all. The simplest solution is always the best in the end.

'Fine, but how do we do that since it's a heavy metal cover? I asked.

Charlie had the answer. 'My dad works on the railways,' he said, 'and I'm sure he'll get me a heavy-duty lever if I ask him.'

And that's what we did. We lifted the covers and

Gordon, the telltale, who had been an onlooker for most of our operations, was chosen to do the foraging as he had arms as long as an orang-utan. He plunged his right arm down the drain and was soon bringing up all manner of treasures – safety pins, occasional small coins and, on one memorable occasion, a lady's brooch. This profitable activity would have continued indefinitely but Gordon's mam found out what her son was doing and played merry hell with him and with us.

'Do you realize, you stupid little buggers,' she railed, 'that you could all catch scarlet fever or diphtheria from them drains. I won't have our Gordon putting his arm into the sewer. It's got to stop or I'll have the law on you.'

That was enough for us and we wound up that particular arm of our company – the treasure-hunting branch.

We were still short of money, of course, and a fresh approach was called for.

Once again, it was Charlie who came up with the next idea. Muck! Horse muck in particular. At first we scoffed at the notion. Trust Charlie to think of something like that, the mucky pup. The gang looked to me as the cock to deliver a judgement.

'It's a load of bullshit,' I declared.

'No,' says Charlie. 'Not *bull* shit. *Horse* shit. You know the old Lancashire saying, "Where there's muck, there's brass." Just think about it for a minute.'

We did and the more we thought, the more attractive it seemed. Not the product but the idea.

First, there was an almost limitless supply of the basic material in the stables at the Dantzig railway arches and the watchman in charge was more than willing to see the stuff carted away, especially if we tipped him a few coppers.

He told us that the average horse produced around eight or nine tons of manure a year. Since at any one time there were about ten horses or donkeys in the stables, it meant an awful lot of muck at our disposal.

'It makes excellent compost,' he explained. 'Especially when mixed with straw or hay, but you must add water to keep it damp. When it's dark, crumbly and fresh-smelling, you'll know you've got black gold.'

The big question was: who would buy it from us and how much would they be prepared to pay? Before we went into production mode, market research was needed. We decided on the name of the Manchester United Company Kollectors, or Muck for short, Collyhurst branch. As leader I divided the company into departments. Duggie, Charlie and Alfie would take charge of production and the transport, consisting of Charlie's go-cart, whilst Jimmy, Gordon and me would take responsibility for promotion and sales. We agreed on the reasonable price of a penny a bucket.

Our sales team walked the length of Rochdale Road as far as Queen's Park and discovered many churches and Methodist chapels with extensive vegetable gardens, like St Patrick's RC Church on Livesey Street, the Methodist chapel on Eggington Street, the Nebo Welsh chapel on

215

Consterdine Street and the Anglican church at St Oswald's Grove. One or two said they couldn't see why they should buy our product since there was lots of it available free of charge just lying about the roads.

'Well, just go and shovel it up yourselves,' we suggested.

They were welcome to try but we knew only too well how unpleasant a task that was. Fortunately there were many rectors only too willing to take our company's merchandise and we soon had more orders than our production team could cope with. It was hard, smelly work and in our first week our turnover amounted to sixteen buckets which gave us sixteen pence. This didn't go far after we'd tipped the watchman fourpence and split the balance between six of us. Tuppence each for lugging sixteen buckets of horse manure up Rochdale Road didn't seem much of a reward but it was better than nothing.

It was around this time – we were about ten years of age – that we discovered smoking. The notion came from Charlie, our ideas man, when he brought us a packet of Cinderella cigs which he'd swiped from his dad's overalls. He passed them around the group and we all lit up. I took a deep drag on my fag and almost suffocated on the spot. The acrid, burning smoke curled its way down my throat into my lungs and for a few minutes I could hardly breathe as I tried to suppress the hacking cough which was screaming for release. We puffed and wheezed our way through the packet and felt very big and grown-up, each of us trying not to splutter and afraid to admit to a feeling of nausea. We couldn't continue smoking these branded fags, however, since, along with Woodbines, they were too expensive at five for a penny. We had to find cheaper alternatives if we were going to adopt the habit.

We found the solution when we spotted the number of dimps or partially smoked cigarettes discarded on the streets. At first we tried to smoke the butts with the aid of a pin but this device was makeshift and unsatisfactory. It was Alfie who hit on the answer. We would slice the dimps open with a razor blade, collect the tobacco into little piles, and then roll our own fags with Rizla papers which were cheaply available at any newsagent. But hand-rolling required a manual dexterity which none of us had and the end results were liable to disintegrate when we tried to light up. To every problem there was always a remedy and this time Jimmy had the answer when he turned up with a cigarette rolling machine 'borrowed' from his dad. Now we were in business.

Our ever-efficient research department soon located places to pick up the best dimps. And strange as it may seem, the most fertile grounds were outside churches, especially after ceremonies like christenings, weddings or funerals. Before the men went into the church on these occasions, they invariably had a few last drags as if needing strength to face the coming ordeal within. After-the-event smoking was equally fruitful for they emerged with a seemingly urgent need for the comfort and relief afforded by a fag. Our pickings were rich indeed and back at our head office on Barney's, we were soon busy manufacturing an abundant supply of cigarettes. Our first forays resulted in a packet of three cigarettes for each of us and we went home feeling that we'd had a most profitable and productive day at the factory.

My euphoria, however, was short-lived. I reached home around five o'clock that particular day and Zeb was waiting for me, ready to pounce.

'I was sweeping up in the cellar today,' he said, 'and I could smell tobacco everywhere. Have you been smoking? No use lying to me.'

'What if I have?' I replied defiantly. 'What's it got to do with you?'

'You haven't the money to be wasting it on fags. Where are you getting them from? Come on, own up. Are you stealing them?'

'No, I'm not. We roll our own and so it doesn't cost us anything. We pick up cigarette butts on the street.'

'Right, you mean dimps. Let's see 'em.'

I showed him the small packet of three cigarettes I had in my pocket, my share of the day's output.

'I'll take charge of these. You're much too young to be smoking. Your Aunty Dorothy will belt you all round the houses if she knew.'

I refused to hand them over and was rewarded with a stinging, open-handed smack across the cheek that sent me reeling against the chest of drawers.

He was too big for me to take on and it was useless arguing with him so I handed over my three homemade fags in the Woodbine packet. I was fuming with anger. They say that revenge is a dish best eaten cold and I vowed there and then to get even with him. But how? A plan began to form in my mind.

Another bone of contention I had with Zeb was that whenever I was absent from the house, he'd got into the habit of going through my things to see if there was anything worth stealing. I'd had an example of that when he'd taken the coppers I'd been saving to buy a football. Now, the chest of drawers in my room had round wooden knobs and the top one had broken off, leaving a round hole. I had intended gluing it back some time but hadn't got round to it. The only way to open that drawer was to insert two fingers and give a good pull. Using chewing gum begged from Duggie, I stuck three or four drawing pins with the sharp pointed bit uppermost all round the hole inside the drawer. Any unsuspecting thief who tried to open the top drawer by yanking it would be sure to stick his two fingers into the pins. There was more to my plan than that, though. The victim would most likely suck his fingers when he felt the painful prick, so for good measure I spread a little horse manure on to the pins. Let's see how Zeb likes that, I said to myself. But wait a minute, I thought; when he's managed to pull the drawer open, he'll expect to find a few of my homemade cigarettes, won't he? Not wishing to disappoint him, I left him five home-rolled cigarettes as a reward for his labour and to compensate for his sore fingers. What he'd find would be a blend of Virginia tobacco and dried horse manure. I hoped they were to his taste. Nevertheless, I was nervous about going home after a day of foraging with my pals. What would he do after pricking his fingers and finding that the cigarettes I'd left him contained horseshit? No doubt about it, I told myself, I'm in for a good hiding. It'll be worth it, though, to get one over on him.

I got back that evening expecting all hell to be let loose around my ears and I braced myself ready to face the music.

His response took me completely by surprise. The drawing-pin ruse had worked all right 'cos the index finger of his right hand had been bandaged but I was taken aback by his reaction to the blended cigarettes.

'I found them there cigs in your drawer,' he said evenly. 'I told you that you were too young to be smoking so I've taken them off you. I've smoked them myself and the only thing I've got to say to you...'

I steeled myself and awaited the inevitable slap across the face but it didn't come.

Instead he gave me a big smile, patted me on the shoulder and said, 'I've got to say it. They are the bloody best, the strongest cigarettes I've ever tasted. What's in 'em?'

'They're a special mixture, Gran'pa, of Virginian and Turkish tobaccos. Not available in the shops.'

'Can you get any more? I'd be willing to buy 'em from you. And stop calling me Gran'pa. Call me Zeb.'

'I'll do my best to get you some, Zeb, but they'll be twopence each.'

'Doesn't matter, Tommy. I'll take ten.'

'Leave it to me, Zeb, though it might not be easy as they were made up of a rare and expensive blend.'

I could hardly wait to give the news to the rest of our company. We'd hit on a winner at last.

Chapter Twenty-One

It was July 1898 and I, along with most of my school chums, would soon be twelve years of age. It was a Monday morning and we were halfway through the month, going about our normal business at school. In time to the rhythm that Miss Corbett was beating on her desk with her ruler, we were reciting in our best sing-song voices the Imperial tables of weights and measures for the coming test.

'Twelve inches make one foot; 3 feet make one yard; 1,760 yards, one mile; 5,285 feet, one mile; 63,360 inches, one mile.'

Then we moved on to gills, pints, quarts, gallons, pecks and bushels. There was lots of other stuff about rods, perches, chains and furlongs. We didn't know why we needed all this rubbish unless we had ambitions to become surveyors, milkmen, or publicans. Ours not to reason why but simply to get on with it under the penalty of the strap if we failed to retain any of it in our over-burdened brains.

We were in full swing when we were interrupted by the head's monitor who went up to Miss Corbett's desk and whispered something in her ear. She looked up at the class and, smiling menacingly, pointed to me and Jimmy Dixon.

'Mr Sullivan would like to see you two,' she said. 'Off you go to his office.'

'Uh-oh,' Jimmy muttered. 'What have we done wrong now?'

'Don't ask me,' I replied, equally puzzled.

As far as I knew we had done nothing to merit his attention. In the school test at the end of last term, Jimmy and I had been top. Not, as I said earlier, because we were all that brainy but because we had good memories and were forever trying to beat each other in school tests.

Nervously, we knocked on Sullivan's door and waited, rubbing our hands with spit in case we were to be strapped for some forgotten, unspecified offence. That was one thing our elementary education had imparted to us: a feeling of guilt.

'Come in,' he called.

We went in and stood before his desk waiting to be accused and found guilty. Instead he gave us a big smile and said, 'You two have done exceptionally well in your class work and I am very pleased with you. I want you to take this letter home to your parents and tell them I would like them to come and see me. I may have some very good news for you and them.'

'I don't have any parents, sir,' I said.

'Yes, I know that, Tommy. Just pass the letter on to your guardians.'

Intrigued, we went back to class and sat at our desks under the sympathetic eyes of our classmates who were sure we had been caned for something or other. We didn't tell them anything because we neither knew nor understood what was going on ourselves.

Dutifully I passed the letter to Aunty Dorothy when she came home that afternoon from Smithfield Market.

'What's all this about, Tommy?' she asked suspiciously. 'It must be serious trouble if your head wants to see us. What've you been up to?'

'Nothing. Honest, Aunty Dorothy. He said it was very good news but he didn't say what it was.'

On Wednesday afternoon, a couple of days later, Uncle Brodie and Aunty Dorothy, grumbling all the way but dressed in their best, came up to the school to see Mr Sullivan. Outside his office we found Mr and Mrs Dixon with Jimmy waiting to see what the fuss was all about.

'Hello, Tommy,' Mrs Dixon said. 'Nice to see you again. I hope everything's going well for you. You must come round again to tea some time.'

'Thank you, Mrs Dixon, I'd like that. And everything's fine,' I replied.

'Any idea what this is about?' Brodie asked of Mr Dixon.

'Not a clue,' he replied.

Both sets of adults looked nervous. Mr Sullivan opened his door at last and called everyone in and told us all to sit down.

'I'm sorry if asking you to come and see me like this has caused you serious inconvenience but what I have to tell you could be of great importance for your sons. They have both done extremely well in their end-of-year tests and I now have a proposition which may be to their advantage.'

The six of us were now all agog.

'A small firm called E.H. Royce and Company has recently set up in Cooke Street in Hulme. I am a friend of a man called Vic Claremont who is a partner in the business which makes dynamos and other electrical products. It is a registered limited liability company and so very secure. According to my friend, the business has great potential.'

We sat enthralled by Mr Sullivan's explanation but what had all this got to do with us?

He continued, 'The firm wishes to offer apprenticeships to intelligent and able young pupils, and I think your two sons may fit the bill and be ideal pupils to take advantage of the opportunity. Both are bright and hard-working. What do you think?'

Jimmy and I didn't think anything as we were not accustomed to taking any part in major decisions like this.

Jimmy's dad spoke first. 'What would this, er, apprenticeship thing entail, sir?'

'It would mean that the boys would stay on here at school until the age of fourteen but would spend half their time attending the Royce factory to learn their trade. As you probably know, the leaving age used to be ten but this was raised to eleven in eighteen ninety-three and so your sons are at liberty to leave at the end of this school year if that is what you wish. There has been a move to raise the leaving age to thirteen but it'll probably amount to nothing as it's opposed by some captains of industry who believe that tiny fingers are required to keep the wheels of industry turning. And surprisingly enough, opposed also by some actors who claim that it would be impossible to perform some Shakespearean plays without them. But that's by the by. As the law stands, your boys can leave school at the end of this month. If they seize this opportunity that is being offered, however, it would mean staying on at school for an extra couple of years and then instead of earning a wage after leaving, they would be learning a highly skilled trade from experts in electrical engineering until about the age of eighteen. Then, who knows where it could lead?'

When I heard Mr Sullivan say I'd be at school until the age of fourteen and that, even after that, I should still be learning not earning, I knew for certain that it was a nonstarter. Aunty Dorothy and Uncle Brodie were expecting me to contribute to my upkeep after school.

'Henry Royce is one of the foremost engineers in Britain,' the head went on. 'There has even been speculation in some newspapers that he may go into the motorcar production business one day. Only tentative talk at the moment, I admit, but it could be the start of something big.'

'I don't think anything will ever come of these new-fangled horseless carriages,' Uncle Brodie pronounced with authority. 'They're a waste of time and money as they'll never replace the horse. But apart from not getting any wages, what else does this apprenticeship thing involve?'

'There would be an initial payment of fifteen pounds to be paid by you to seal the apprenticeship contract. Two or three years after qualification, Tommy and Jimmy here should be earning very good wages.'

The prospect of working in an engineering firm and with Jimmy seemed really exciting. But when I heard the mention of fifteen pounds due as a down-payment, that really put the kibosh on it and I knew beyond any doubt that there'd be nothing doing as far as I was concerned. The head may as well have been talking of a thousand pounds, for all the chance there was of me taking up the offer. Jimmy's dad, however, seemed interested.

'How soon would you need to have an answer?' he asked.

'Within the next week,' Mr Sullivan replied. 'I shall give you the necessary forms and if you are interested, fill in the details and let me have them back next week with the deposit. We can go from there.'

We took the forms home. Jimmy's dad completed his and returned it within a few days. Jimmy was to join the Royce company. Aunty Dorothy and Uncle Brodie brought the forms home to our house in Angel Meadow. At first, Dorothy was unsure.

'Don't you think this might be a great opportunity for Tommy, Brodie?' she suggested tentatively.

Brodie gave the forms hardly a second glance.

'Have you gone mad, Dorothy?' he exclaimed. 'Do you think we're millionaires or something? That we've got money to burn and that we can just throw away fifteen pounds on some bloody daft appendix scheme or whatever it was called. And waste a small fortune on a barmy idea like horseless carriages! Do you think I was born yesterday?'

'Very well, Brodie, if you feel that strongly about it. I just thought that it might give Tommy a big leg-up just for once in his life. After all, the kid's had some tough breaks and this could be his big chance to make something of his life. But you're the head of this house and what you say, goes.'

'And that's what I *do* say!' Brodie bellowed. 'Tommy will not be signing up for no scheme. He'll be working for us in the market and helping to pay for his keep.'

Without more ado, Brodie tore up the apprenticeship forms and threw the pieces into the fire. I watched the printed paper and my hopes go up in flames. It was a bitter pill to swallow especially now that I knew Jimmy Dixon would be taking up the offer. How I wished that my own mam and dad had been alive because I knew for certain that they'd have agreed to take up the offer no matter what the cost and no matter what the sacrifices.

Chapter Twenty-Two

As I watched that paper burn, something inside me died and I felt sick at heart.

'I think I'll go and have a lie-down,' I said.

'You do that, Tommy,' Dorothy said. 'It's been a long day.'

I went down to my dismal room in the cellar, locked the door and stretched out on the bed, arms behind my head. I was down in the dumps. I remained there for I don't know how long in the dark, thoroughly miserable and staring at the ceiling. I felt sorry for myself and the tears rolled down my cheeks when I thought about the rotten luck I'd had in my life. Then my self-pity turned to anger and bitterness. I addressed my resentment to God.

What a lousy, lousy world you've put me in, God. Everything in my life so far has gone wrong. What a bloody awful hand of cards you've dealt me. First you let my dad die, then my mam, so making me an orphan. Anyone I've liked, loved or thought anything of you've snuffed out like a candle. There was that little lad that I used to play with from Paley Street, what was his name again? Herbert Lamb, that was it. Poor kid died a horrible death drinking that carbolic acid. Then there was the case of that little girl, Josie, who I really liked; she died in that terrible accident with the fire.

What's the use of trying any more? Nothing's gone right. At school I've worked hard and been top of the class with Jimmy Dixon and a fat lot of good it's done me. He gets an apprenticeship and will end up in one of the top jobs. As for me, what am I going to get? A bloody useless, lousy, rotten, stinking job as a fetcher-and-carrier in Smithfield Market, that's what. Nothing better than a slave humping things about from place to place. No brains required for the job. I'll still be doing the same thing forty years from now. What was the bloody point of learning all that shit at St Chad's? All that history, those multiplication tables, catechism answers, spellings, verbs and adverbs? A bloody waste of time! But that's me finished with school. There's just one week of the term left but I'm not going back. Tomorrow I'll look for something else. I'll show you, God. I'll run away to sea, that's what I'll do.

I didn't sleep much that night as there were too many thoughts whirling round my brain. My thoughts were not clear but I was sure that my schooldays were behind me. I had reached a crisis in my life. In the brief time that I nodded off, I saw myself as captain of a ship commanding my crew to pull up anchor and steer a westerly course for America. The ship appeared to be a sailing vessel much like the ones I'd seen in the illustrations in *Treasure Island* and not a bit like the ones I hoped would take me on as cabin boy or something. Furthermore, I didn't have too much confidence in the crew either since it seemed to be made up of the gang from St Chad's and my bosun was Gran'pa Zeb with his wooden leg and a parrot on his shoulder that repeated over and over, 'Pieces of eight! Pieces of eight!'

Next morning, having put on my best gansey and shorts, thinking they would be the best kind of dress for someone running away to sea, I set off for school at the usual time, taking with me a piece of bread and a lump of cheese for my dinner as I intended making a day of it. How do you go about running away to sea? I wondered. Salford Docks! That was the answer. With the recently opened ship canal, there was sure to be lots of ships about to sail for foreign ports. With my head down and my hands plunged in my pockets, I began walking. And how I walked! I don't know how far but it took me along Rochdale Road, down Shudehill, past Smithfield Market, Withy Grove, across Hanging Ditch, by Deansgate and Chester Road. By this time I was famished and weary so I stopped on the grass verge and ate my cheese sandwich. Across the road, I could see a sign pointing the way to Salford Docks and in particular to Pomona Docks. Exhausted but triumphant, I made my way to the main entrance and spoke to the security officer on the gate. He listened to my request to approach a ship's captain to ask if he had any vacancies for a cabin boy.

'So you want to run away to sea, do you?' he asked with an amused smile playing on his lips. 'Do your mam and dad know you're here?'

'Haven't got any. I'm an orphan but I've got a guardian.'

'You look a bit young for joining a ship's crew,' he remarked. 'How old are you?'

'Thirteen,' I lied, sticking my chest out and trying to look taller.

'Well, you could try the shipping office over there near the dock, I suppose,' he said. 'See what they think.'

'Thank you very much, sir,' I replied, trying to make my voice sound a little deeper.

So I'd got past the security guard, the first hurdle. I was on my way. The building he had indicated was the Anglo Pacific Company with shipping to Australia, the USA, and the Far East. Just the ticket, I thought. I climbed the stairs to the office and approached the elderly clerk at the counter.

'And what can we do for you, young sir?' he asked in a kindly voice, studying me over the wire spectacles perched on the end of his nose.

'I'd like to apply for a position as cabin boy in one of your ships.'

'I see, I see,' he replied, looking a bit doubtful. 'And how old are you, may I ask?'

'Fourteen,' I answered, adding a year to my previous lie.

The old gentleman decided to humour me.

'I'm not sure there are any vacancies for cabin boys nowadays. We're looking for grown-up men with strong muscles on our ships. Before anyone would consider you, though, they'd need to see your birth certificate and a letter from your parents or guardians giving permission.'

When I heard this, I knew I was sunk and I hadn't even been to sea.

'I could try another shipping firm,' I replied defiantly.

'No use, I'm afraid. You would find the same answer at all of them. Your best bet is to come back when you're eighteen and have developed big arm muscles and a strong back.'

I came away from the docks despondent. It looked as if I was stuck with Smithfield Market as my life career.

I decided to walk back and visit Grandad Owen Mitchell to see if he could offer advice. I'd always found him friendly and helpful on the few times I'd visited him, though Grandma Bridget seemed to rule the roost there. Fortunately she was out for the day visiting a friend when I called and so I got Grandad on his own. As usual, he gave me a warm greeting.

'Top o' the mornin' to you, young Thomas. You're quite a stranger! What brings you to this part of the world?'

I felt a stab of guilt when I heard this for I'd been so busy living my own life, I hadn't seen as much of my grandparents as I should have. He and Grandma Bridget were in their mid-fifties and still working which I found surprising as I considered them to be quite ancient.

He listened patiently as I blubbered out my tale of woe: how everything in my life had gone wrong, how I'd missed out on my chance to be apprenticed to the Royce Company, how I was stuck with a dead-end job in Smithfield Market, how I felt that my life wasn't worth a light.

'Now, you listen to me, young Thomas,' he said when I finally finished my sorrowful story. 'It is time you began counting your blessings and realized what's important in your life. I know things have been tough for you, what with your mam and dad dying, but the way things have turned out, your life could have been a lot worse. You might have ended up like one of them starving beggars we see on the street and God knows Manchester has enough of them. Your home could have been a doorway in some filthy back entry or a corner of a brick kiln, along with a lot of meths drinkers. You might have been drawn into a life of crime, thieving and stealing just to survive. There'd have been only one career prospect for you then and that would have been Strangeways Prison. So, instead of reckoning up all the things that have gone wrong, start looking at the things that have gone right for a change. Look at the good things that have happened to you. Your Aunty Dorothy, my youngest daughter, remember, volunteered to take you in when nobody else stepped forward. She didn't have to do that. You could have been sent to a home, an orphanage, and then who knows what might have happened to you after that. Think about what you've got. A secure home, though I know it's no palace. You have a room, a roof and a bed. I know old Zeb can be a nasty piece of work but remember he's had a rough life too. Keep out of his way as much as you can and maybe look for ways to help him and win him over.'

'That's all very well,' I said, 'but look at the job I've landed up with. A potato-humper and no better than a mule.'

'Rubbish, Tommy! As well as a home, you've got the prospect of a job for life. I know it doesn't sound much at the moment but many workers make a good living there and I'm sure Dorothy and Brodie will see you right. Happiness isn't how much money you've got in your pocket and how important you think you are. It has more to do with having good friends and having a positive outlook on life. Always look on the bright side and that's the best advice I can give you. Be content with your lot 'cos making the best of it is the secret of true happiness. What's that old saying? "God help me to change the things that I can change, to accept the things that I can't and the wisdom to know the difference".

'Whatever you do in life, always aim to be the very best at it. If it's your fate to be a street cleaner or a dishwasher, make sure that you are the best bloody sweeper or dishwasher in the whole wide world. Aim at perfection until people around you say, "These streets are the cleanest and his dishes are the most sparkling on the planet".'

When Grandad Owen had finished speaking, my eyes were filled with tears, not of sorrow but of gladness. He was right. I'd been looking at life through the wrong end of the telescope.

'Thanks, Grandad,' I said. 'You've really got me thinking and made me see things differently. I'll start work in Smithfield Market and if I'm to be a carter like Uncle Brodie, I'll be the best bloody carter in Manchester. No, not just in Manchester but in the whole of Britain!'

Friday, 25 July 1897, was the last day of the summer term at school and the end of my elementary education. I thought it best to go back into the classroom, not that there was much choice anyway as I had to get my school leaving certificate if anyone was to employ me. Before going off to work in the early hours, Aunty Dorothy had left me sixpence on my chest of drawers with a brief note scrawled on a scrap of paper that said, 'Get yourself and your pals a few toffees to celebrate you leaving. It's a big day in your life.'

In the school yard at nine o'clock we went through the usual routine and lined up in our serried ranks when the whistle sounded. It was the day when we thought and said out loud, 'This is the last day that we'll line up, march into class, get the strap (we hoped), recite the catechism, say the multiplication tables ...' As usual there were a few latecomers but Mr Sullivan let them all off. If only he'd been so lenient the rest of the year!

On that final day, we didn't do any class work but spent our time playing games like OXO, hangman, snakes and ladders, and ludo. Miss Corbett even brought in a box of Sharp's caramels and distributed them. So she had a heart after all. There was also no need for Aunty Dorothy's tanner so I put it in my pocket. Maybe I'd take my pals out later for a drink of sarsaparilla or Tizer at the local herbal shop. In the afternoon, we had to stand up and tell everyone what we'd be doing after leaving. When it came to Jimmy, we all knew about his glittering prospects with the Henry Royce company; Gordon Bennett said he would be staying on at school as his dad was hoping to get him a job as a messenger boy in the post office. Typical, we thought, Gordon going around spreading the Good News. As we announced to the rest of the class what jobs we would be taking up, it soon became obvious that many of us would be following in the footsteps of our dads (or, in my case, guardians) and that meant one of the wholesale markets: meat, fish, or fruit and vegetable. It was natural that some of us would be employed there since we lived only a stone's throw away. Duggie and Charlie would be working on the wholesale fruit and vegetable section, Duggie helping his dad who owned the stall and Charlie as general dogsbody on Holbrook's, while Alfie would be using his strength humping joints of meat in the wholesale meat market. Ginger McDermott and Mick Malone would be working with their dads on their barrows on Market Street. So, I remember thinking, there was every chance that I'd be seeing quite a lot of one or the other of them, worse luck.

'You mean a costermonger?' the Bruiser remarked when Ginger announced what his job was to be.

'No, miss. We'll be selling fruit and veg, not custard,' he answered.

There was a final assembly for the school. I never thought I'd be sad at leaving the place but I was. Us school leavers weren't the biggest lads in the school, for some boys had opted to stay on till fourteen, which, except for Jimmy's case, I could never understand. Surely anyone with any sense would want to get out of the dump as soon as they got the chance. What was the point of learning all those useless bits of information we'd been forced to commit to memory for the past few years? To the applause and cheers of the assembly, each leaver was called out to the front where Mr Sullivan handed him the official leaving certificate.

'Good luck, Tommy,' Mr Sullivan said as he handed me my papers. 'Pity you decided not to take the Henry Royce offer. Opportunity rarely knocks twice. Let's hope you are the exception.'

I went back to my place with a lump in my throat. If only my own mam and dad had been around to witness this day. I took a quick look at my certificate and reference. It said: 'This is to certify that Thomas Hopkins attended this school from September 1893 to July 1898. During his time he made excellent progress at his studies both secular and religious and was exemplary in his general behaviour. He had almost perfect attendance and during the whole of his time at this school was absent for only one day. Signed: John L. Sullivan, Headmaster.'

The leaving ceremony was rounded off with a hymn that seemed to say it all.

He who would valiant be
'gainst all disaster,
Let him in constancy
Follow the master
There's no discouragement
Shall make him once relent
His first avowed intent
To be a pilgrim.

Though we couldn't get our tongues round most of the words, when it came to the last line, we lifted the roof off with 'to be a pilgrim'.

We shook hands and said our goodbyes at the corner of Lord Street, knowing that we would never again share a classroom or enjoy baiting Miss Corbett. But the parting was not as sad as it might have been because we made a pact that no matter what our jobs were, we'd arrange a regular game of football on St Michael's Flags every weekend. And that included pals from the St William's contingent and our rivals, St Chad's.

Most of us were not due to start our jobs for a week or two and so we were able to have a short holiday and get in a few games of football on weekdays as well as on Saturday afternoons. We enjoyed these kick-abouts, though at times it was more like a war if we disputed a bad tackle or if we didn't agree on an offside position when the ball had been put past the goalkeeper. These conflicts were inevitable, I suppose, since we never had a referee and sometimes the only way we could come to a decision was through fisticuffs. Despite that, we had some great afternoons until one day it all went wrong for me.

One afternoon after our match, I was walking along Irk Street on the way home with Duggie, our goalkeeper, and I was telling him that he would kick the ball further and with better accuracy if he used a half volley.

'Half volley? And what's that when it's at home?' he asked.

'You drop the ball and let it hit the ground,' I explained, 'and just as it's bouncing up, you wham it with all your might. Look, I'll show you.'

So saying, I dropped the ball and kicked it a beauty. It went soaring up into the sky.

'You mean like this,' Duggie said, retrieving the ball. He kicked it but he still hadn't got the knack.

'No, no,' I said. 'What you kicked just now was a full volley. For a half volley, you must let the ball hit the ground first before you kick it. Look, I'll show you again.'

I took the ball and once again punted it right up high into the air. Disaster! There was the sound of shattering glass.

'Oh no!' I exclaimed. 'I hope I haven't put somebody's window in.'

'No, you haven't broke no window,' Duggie said gleefully, 'but you have shattered the glass on that lamp post. We'd better leg it before the rozzers nab you.'

Too late. From out of nowhere appeared a constable on his beat.

'Now then, you lads,' he drawled. 'Who's responsible? Come on, come clean. Was it you?' he said, pointing to Duggie.

For some reason Duggie looked the more guilty of the pair of us.

'No, officer,' I said quickly. 'It was me. It was an accident. I was showing my pal here how to kick a half volley.'

'That's as may be but you were also demonstrating to him how to put a lamp-post glass in. So, what's your name and address?' he asked, taking out his notebook.

After giving him the information, I told Duggie to go home since he wasn't involved.

'No,' he said. 'I was just as much to blame. It was just as much my fault. I'll stay with you.'

'No, Duggie. It'll be best if you push off. It was my stupid kick that did the damage.'

I was thinking that he'd be better out of the way as his presence might make things worse. Duggie didn't need telling twice.

'OK, Tommy. See you tomorrow.'

'I'm not going to arrest you this time,' the copper continued, 'for I believe you when you say it was accidental, but you do have to be more careful in future. I'll just take you home and tell your parents to take the cost out of your spends if you get any or punish you in the way they think fit.'

'No parents, only guardians,' I told him.

'All the same to me,' he said.

We found only Zeb at home as Dorothy and Brodie were still at the market, probably in the Turk's Head. The officer explained what had happened. As the sorry tale unfolded, Zeb looked like thunder and I knew there was going to be hell to pay when we were alone. The policeman departed and I wasn't wrong in my fear.

'You're nothing but a bloody nuisance,' Zeb roared. 'Fancy being dragged home by the scruff of the neck by a rozzer! You've brought nothing but shame and dishonour on this family and I'm going to teach you a lesson you'll never forget.'

He took off his big belt and waded into me, giving me the biggest thrashing of my life, using the buckle end. After half an hour of being chased and belted around the room, I retired to my place in the cellar like a wounded animal. When Zeb said it would be a lesson I'd never forget, he was right there. He left welts and bruises all over my

240

body: legs, shoulders, and backside.

'One last thing,' he snarled, standing over me as I whimpered on my bed. 'If you're ever dragged home again like that by the law, I'll take the horse whip to you. D'you hear me? I'll not have this family's good name disgraced by the likes of you. I'll swing for you if I have to. Think on!'

And I did exactly that. I did think on. If ever he tries to do that again, I'm leaving this Godforsaken dump once and for all, first chance I get.

Part II

Chapter Twenty-Three

It was Sunday night, the first after leaving school, and I was enjoying a deep, dreamless sleep. It had been a hard, vicious game of football we'd played that afternoon on St Michael's Flags: William's Whingers against the Chad's Chickens. Result was a draw – two each – and I was happy with that 'cos it'd been a good fight, with no quarter given.

After a quick tea of toast and a couple of boiled eggs, I went down to my room in the cellar and flopped on the bed feeling content. And why not? After all, no more school. That part of my life was over and done with. I'd had a very enjoyable time since leaving St Chad's and on this particular night I must have gone out like a light. It seemed I'd just closed my eyes and was enjoying my state of unconsciousness when I felt someone shaking me by the shoulders. With difficulty I opened my eyes and gradually came to. It was Aunty Dorothy looking down on me.

'What is it? What's happened?' I demanded panic-stricken and still rubbing my eyes. 'Is the house on fire? Has someone died? Is it Zeb?'

'No, Tommy. Nothing like that.' She laughed. 'Time to get up.'

'But I've only just come to bed,' I protested. 'What time is it?'

'Three o'clock.'

'In the afternoon?'

'No, you silly. In the morning. Time to go to work.'

Slowly and reluctantly I came back to the land of the living and got up. I put on my shirt and my new overalls which they'd bought for me at Beaty Brothers on Deansgate. Going to work in short trousers hadn't seemed right and people in the market might have laughed at me. Next, I slipped on my jacket, stockings and boots and went upstairs for my usual breakfast of porridge and a quick brew. Before we set off, I remembered to put on my proudest possession – a new cloth cap, the universal symbol of the working man.

Our first port of call was the Dantzig Street stables to collect the cart and our donkey and to saddle him up. Crusty was always glad to see us and he nodded his head several times in greeting. I am sure that if he'd been human, he'd have smiled and said, 'Good morning. Nice day.'

Next, we gave him a good drink of water from a clean bucket.

'Crusty's not been too well for the last few days,' Aunty Dorothy said. 'I put it down to the water at the trough in Miller Street. We've stopped him drinking there 'cos the water's filthy with all kinds of shit that some of the other carters' horses have dropped in it. Crusty's twenty years old now which means he's getting on a bit and it doesn't do for him to be drinking foul water. Not at his age.'

'What age do donkeys live to?' I asked.

'About thirty-five to forty or even forty-five in exceptional cases,' Brodie replied. 'After twenty-five they can't cope with hard work and they're sent to the knacker's yard. A mule works to the age of twenty-two, the horse till it's sixteen or so. They're lucky in some ways. Us men have to work till we're seventy or until we drop. God is kinder to animals. Our Crusty is what we call a gelding.'

'A gelding?'

Brodie laughed. 'It means he's been castrated, had his goolies removed, so he's lost interest in the opposite sex – in mares, that is.'

'Wouldn't be a bad idea for some men I know,' Dorothy remarked, throwing Brodie an old-fashioned look.

'What made you choose the name Crusty?' I asked.

Dorothy answered. 'We thought it was the perfect name for him. First, he's fond of a nice crust if you give him one; then he's a bit like a crust – hard on the outside but soft on the inside; and sometimes he can be crusty if he doesn't get his own way. If he's ever in a bad temper, don't, whatever you do, stand behind him 'cos he can give you a hell of a kick with his hind legs. But that's unusual. Mostly he's a lovely fellah, friendly and outgoing. Aren't you, Crusty, old son?'

She said this last giving him an affectionate kiss on the forehead.

I could see how loving they were of their animal and they seemed to treat him as if he were a champion racehorse. I'd noticed on my first few visits to the market how fond the donkey owners were of their charges.

Next came his nosebag of oats, and after we'd

247

attached the harness of saddle, bridle and halter, we backed him into the shafts of the cart and secured him by his traces. Not that it took much effort for he knew the routine better than we did.

'That's good leather harness, is that,' said Brodie. 'None of your cheap coloured rubbish. That can be dangerous 'cos if the traces snap, you can have a nasty, even fatal accident.'

'Isn't that cart a bit heavy for him to pull, Brodie?' I asked.

'No, not at all. The cart has got large wheels and rubber tyres which make it a lot easier. But Crusty is a powerful donkey and could pull twice what we ask him to do.'

With Dorothy, Brodie and me sitting at the front, we clip-clopped our way to Smithfield Market. Crusty had made this trip every day for the past six or seven years and knew every inch of the way without guidance: which main roads to stop at, where to relieve himself, and how steep or easy a particular incline was. First along Miller Street, then Swan Street, finally turning into Eagle Street to join the throng of traders at the centre, the very heart of the market where we had arranged to meet our first customers. I noticed that all the market men seemed to be garbed in the same outfit: cloth cap, pullover, corduroy trousers with bottoms tied with string, and a fag inevitably drooping from the lower lip as if it were a permanent fixture of the face. In addition, carters wore a piece of sacking draped round the shoulders, perhaps as an additional symbol of their calling.

The first thing that struck me about the market was its distinctive aroma, a mixture of fruit and vegetables, fish, poultry, game, and horse dung blended into one overpowering but not unpleasant smell. Though it was only four o'clock, the market was already a whirl of activity: a hive of noisy, hustling, bustling men dashing about the place like ants upturned from their nest. Hurry, hurry, no time to stand and stare. Donkeys and carts trundled by while men with impossibly high towers of baskets balanced precariously on their heads zigzagged their way through the turmoil; impatient porters with heavily loaded barrows squeezed their way through the maze of traffic, bawling and cursing anyone that hindered their progress. Everyone was rushing about, yelling and in bad temper.

'Now then, Blundell, shift that bloody cart! You're blocking the road!'

'Not my fault if you've upset your load, mate. S'your bloody problem.'

'Clear the way! Clear the way! You're holding us up!'

'Get out my road, you dozy bugger. I'm coming through!'

'Come on! Come on! You're not at a bloody funeral!'

'Where *do* these slow bastards come from? Get a move on, Nicholson! We haven't got all day!'

Spellbound and open-mouthed, I gazed at the scene: the dozens of stalls around me each stacked with produce of every conceivable kind. Oranges and onions from Spain. Tomatoes from Guernsey. Apples from Kent and Somerset.

Peaches from Italy. Grapes from Portugal. Potatoes from Ireland. Strawberries from Evesham. Cabbages from Cheshire. Mackerel from Aberdeen, plaice from Fleetwood, haddock from Hull, and smokies from Arbroath. They'd got everything there. On the stalls, trilby-hatted salesmen in white coats, clipboards in hand, haggled with traders and took orders from the visiting greengrocers.

'Ten taters, five caulies, five cabbages, six apples, five straws, four pears!' shouted a visiting shopkeeper.

'Right, Sid! Collect five o'clock!' the salesman yelled back.

Hurry, hurry! Don't waste time! Gotta keep things moving!

Presiding over this madcap activity stood the huge figure of Big Bert O'Neil, the police sergeant, whose job it was to keep a weather eye on the market, sort out disputes, deal with troublemakers and try to keep the traffic moving. No mean task.

'Is it always as bad as this?' I asked Brodie.

'You think *this* is bad?' he replied. 'Wait till you see it a bit later on at eight o'clock when it'll be rush hour. Then nothing moves.'

'Then why call it "rush" hour?'

Brodie just grinned. 'Search me.'

On this, my first day at work, I stood in the midst of this hurly-burly, this swirling confusion, lost and bewildered. Where do I go?

What do I do?

Who'll tell me?

I didn't have to wait long.

250

'Right, Tommy!' Brodie barked. 'Go with Dorothy and collect our handcart from Deakin's stall and pick up our order for Murgatroyd's of Bolton. He'll be waiting outside the market in Cable Street. Dorothy will show you how. Come back to the centre with the stuff. I'll go to Nichol's and get the rest. At the double now!'

Dorothy and I began the hundred-yard dash to Deakin's.

'Why doesn't Murgatroyd come into the market and collect the stuff himself?' I asked breathlessly.

'He's not allowed. You've gotta have a carter's licence to work in the market. Otherwise you'll have the rozzers after you. Greengrocers and hawkers have to park outside the market and only official carters and porters are allowed into the market itself. We then take their orders out to them.'

'Why don't they get their own licences, come into the market and collect their own orders?'

'You've seen how chaotic it is in the centre, Tommy. If they let every Tom, Dick and Harry come in with their carts and barrows, there'd be a total log jam and things would come to a complete halt. It's bad enough as it is.'

We picked up the handcart and made a beeline for Deakin's.

'You load up Murgatroyd's orders here,' she said, 'and I'll go across to Stevenson's for the rest. Be quick now.'

I got to Deakin's and approached an elderly salesman whose white hair matched his coat.

'I've come for Murgatroyd's stuff,' I said.

'Right,' the old gent said. 'It's all here ready for you. Three taters, three apples, two onions, three oranges.'

I went up to a bag of potatoes and took hold of it by its ears and lifted with all my might. It didn't budge. Not an inch. Even though I almost wrenched my arms out of their sockets in the attempt.

The old gent laughed. 'You're obviously new to the game. Here, let me show you.' He wrapped both arms round the bag and hoisted it easily on to my handcart.

'When you lift something heavy like this, hold the bag firmly and close to your body. Feet shoulder-width apart and bend your knees, back straight. You try it.'

It was still too heavy and the old-timer helped me load the rest of the stuff on to the cart.

'Thanks a lot,' I said. 'I couldn't have done it without you.'

'You'll soon get used to it and you'll find it gets easier after you've been doing it as long as I have. My name's Joe Brannan, by the way.' He shook me by the hand. 'Welcome to Smithfield. Call me Joe.'

'My name's Tommy and this is my first day on the job.'

'That's obvious,' he laughed. 'You're Dorothy's boy. Tommy Langley?

'No, not Langley. Tommy Hopkins. I lost both my parents when I was younger. Dorothy and Brodie Langley are only my guardians.'

'Sorry to hear about the death of your mam and dad, Tommy. That's tough on a young kid like you. But you've done well to be taken under the wing of Brodie and Dorothy as they're well thought of here in the market. So, your first day, eh? I've been working in the market for nigh on thirty years.'

As we loaded up the handcart together, we got talking.

'I didn't know Smithfield Market had been here that long, Joe,' I said.

'There's been a market here since eighteen twenty-one and the roof was built in eighteen fifty-three. It's long been Manchester's proud boast that we have the biggest and longest covered market in the world – bigger even than London's Covent Garden. There are well over a hundred stalls here. I came to work here thirty years ago in eighteen sixty-seven and have loved every minute of it. There's never a dull moment, always something going on.'

'Wow, thirty years! That's a long time.'

'Yeah, I suppose so but it seems like yesterday that I was doing my first day like you; time has simply shot by. It's a good place to work, though it can be bloody hard at times. Today, Monday, isn't so bad. Not too busy.'

'Not too busy!' I exclaimed. 'I've never seen such rushing about! It's a madhouse.'

'Wait till you see it on Friday and Saturday, when the traders are getting ready for the weekend. Then you'll see what a real madhouse is. Every kind of fruit, vegetable, fish, meat you can think of, and some that you can't, are traded here. Somerset apples, Evesham plums, oranges and grapes from Italy and Spain, flowers from Holland, Fyffe's 'Blue Label' bananas from the West Indies. The building of the ship canal has opened up Manchester to the world and its produce.'

'Would you say you've been happy here, Joe?'

I asked him this because I still wasn't sure that I wanted to spend the rest of my life working in what I thought was complete bedlam.

'Really happy,' he replied. 'But then I like to keep busy with things going on all round me. Every day is different. You may not become a millionaire but there's good security working in the market. People will always need grub and you'll never find yourself out of a job. Not only that, you'll never go hungry in this line of work. Market traders are always generous when you do a good job for them. They don't mind if you take a few samples home, as long as you don't overdo it. You'll find that every porter and carter has a shopping bag called a "swinger" hanging on the back of his cart and in this he collects a few items as he goes around. So you can see market work has its own little rewards.'

Joe's face became serious and he looked earnestly into my eyes and said, 'I may sound like an old misery, Tommy, but one thing I think I should warn you about and that is the bevvy.'

'The bevvy, Joe? What's that?'

'It means beer, Tommy. Market workers put everything they've got into their jobs and they run themselves into the ground and work up a big sweat. Most finish at around eleven or twelve midday and then it's into the pub – the Hare and Hounds or the Turk's Head on Shudehill. No harm in that but many of them are there until closing time and they roll home pissed every day. Don't you be like that. It could be your ruination.'

'Thanks, Joe. I'll remember it. Anyroad, I've never liked the taste of beer.'

This piece of advice was one I tried to follow as a young man. After all, I'd seen how Brodie and Dorothy were and I think their daily drinking habits spoiled them as people. I determined that when I got older I might go for a drink after work with other market workers but I wouldn't overdo it by spending the rest of the afternoon in the boozer. The odd drink maybe but no more.

Joe changed the subject and continued telling me about some of the good things about the job. 'So as the day goes on, the porter adds a few things to his "swinger" like fruit and veg, maybe a fish or two, occasionally meat like poultry or a rabbit. It's one of the perks of the job.'

'I can see some of the advantages of the job, Joe, but I'm not sure I'll ever get used to getting up at three o'clock in the morning.'

'That's nothing. Us salesmen who work on the stalls are here at midnight when the wholesale deliveries are made. Big shire horses, as big as elephants some of them, bring the stuff up from the railway stations and the docks and so we've got to be here to check it in. Then sleepy-heads like you come on duty at four o'clock to see to the orders for the retailers. You've got it easy; you don't know you're born.'

'The way you tell it, Joe, makes the job sound quite interesting, even exciting.'

'That's as may be, Tommy, but there are some wicked bastards working here as well. They're up to all kinds of dirty tricks like putting faded fruit and veg at the bottom of the crates and it's only when the greengrocer gets back to his shop that he discovers the deception. Another thing is that some workers get very jealous if they think you're doing too well and they'll try to do you down, if they can.'

'How do you mean, Joe?'

'Well, if they think you're getting ahead of them or earning more than they are, they'll do their best to muck things up for you by getting in your way and slowing you down. They may even fix it so that your load is unstable and falls off. The one to look out for is a bastard by the name of Slug Bullock. Watch out for him 'cos he'll have it in for a newcomer like you.'

'Never heard of him, Joe. Who is this Slug when he's at home?'

'He was a member of the Bengal Tigers of Ancoats gang. Most of them ended up in Strangeways but Slug Bullock managed to escape prison, God knows how. He's a villain and a regular right down bad 'un. So be on your guard.'

'How will I know him, Joe?'

'He's big and ugly, has a scar on his left cheek and a large wart on his nose. You'll know him when you see him.'

As we were talking, Mad Alec passed by pushing a loaded cart.

'How are you, Tommy lad?' he shouted breathlessly. 'Brodie told me that you did well in that fight at school. So glad you didn't let the side down.'

'No, Alec. I think I did Smithfield Market proud,

256

thanks to all that training you gave me.'

'That's what I like to hear. Tommy lad. Any time I can help, you've only got to say.' Then with the speed of a Shanghai rickshaw coolie, he was gone.

'What about him, Mad Alec?' I asked Joe. 'Is he a good bloke to know?'

'One of the best,' Joe replied. 'You'll not go far wrong if you make him your friend. He'll always stand by you if ever you need him.'

'Thanks for the advice and the warnings, Joe. I'll be on my guard.'

'One thing I would add, Tommy, is that you've got to be nippy and ready to fight and elbow your way through the chaos that builds up every morning. Do you have a strong voice, Tommy? You'll need it. You've got to be able to bawl your head off at anyone gumming up the works. Let me hear you shout, "Now then, Blundell! Get a bloody move on! You're holding up the market!"

I did as he asked and shouted the command.

'That's terrible, Tommy. That's like whispering. Shout louder as if the other bloke's ten miles away and is as deaf as a post. Try again.'

I did.

'That's more like it. You'll do, young 'un. Another thing: try to get the coppers on your side. The bobby on duty will help to clear your way and it does no harm if you grease his palm with a few pieces of choice fruit or fish. Get him on your side and you'll be surprised how quickly he unblocks the road for you.'

By this time, Dorothy was back. 'Come on, Tommy, no time for idle gossip. Thanks, Joe, for

257

your help in loading the cart 'cos I'm sure Tommy couldn't have managed that little lot on his own.'

As we came away, she said, 'I'm glad you've been talking to Joe Brannan. We call him the market oracle 'cos he knows everybody and everything what's going on. If you ever have a problem about anything to do with Smithfield, Joe's the man to see.'

'Yes, he gave me lots of good advice,' I said.

'I'm glad,' she said. 'I know you were bitterly disappointed that you didn't get the apprenticeship along with your pal Jimmy but, as I'm sure Joe must have told you, working in the market isn't so bad. When you get older, you'll get the chance maybe to run your own little business and earn good money here. And one thing I'll bet you haven't thought about. While your pal Jimmy will be depending on his parents for his spends, you will be earning your own wage and will have more cash in your pocket than him. Brodie and me will see that you're all right until you can set up on your own.'

After that little speech, we charged at breakneck speed round to Stevenson's to pick up Dorothy's order and pile it up on to the cart, which by now had become so heavy that I could hardly lift the shafts. For Dorothy, it was no problem; with one heave she raised the shafts and with me pushing at the rear, we were on our madcap way back to the centre to join up with Brodie.

In the headlong rush, we passed Doonican's fruit stall and I caught a glimpse of my old friend from St William's Infant School, Doris, towering above a pyramid of oranges and apples. She'd certainly grown since I last saw her.

'Hiya, Tommy,' she bawled after me.

'Nice to see you, Doris. Can't talk now,' I shouted back. 'Speak to you later if I get the chance.'

Brodie was waiting with the main cart stacked up with the produce he'd collected. Somehow, we piled our own stuff on top and secured it with ropes. How poor old Crusty was going to pull this lot, I didn't know. But he did and didn't seem to find it a problem. With Dorothy in the driving seat and Brodie and me pushing at the back, we got the order to Cable Street where we found Murgatroyd's big cart and his shire horse waiting. We helped load him up and he was soon on his way back to Bolton, having paid Brodie's charge of ten shillings.

For the rest of our eight-hour stint, we worked almost non-stop with only one fifteen-minute break for breakfast at eight o'clock when we went to Fred's café for a mug of tea and a bacon butty. I cannot ever remember food tasting that good. On my way back to the centre, I espied what could only be Slug Bullock and he was every bit as ugly as Joe Brannan had described him. What is more, he was in earnest conversation with those two old St Chad's enemies of mine – Ginger McDermott and Mick Malone. They greeted me as I passed.

'Aye-aye, Tommy,' Ginger called out to me. 'How's it going?'

'Hard work, Ginger. All go and no mistake. What brings you and Mick to the market?'

'Have you forgot already, Tommy? Our dads have hawker's barrows just off Market Street. We're set up in Tib Street, so we should see you about the place when we come to give our orders. We're here to find a porter to pick up our fruit and veg orders from the stalls. We'll probably see you about the place every day. It'll be just like old times, eh?'

'Yeah, yeah. But why can't you pick up your own stuff, Ginger? Why throw money away paying somebody to get it for you?'

'Don't have a licence, Tommy. So we're not allowed and we have to pay a porter like Slug here to do it for us.'

'It's my job to collect their stuff for 'em and take it to 'em in Tib Street,' Slug added. 'Only licensed porters like me are allowed to do it.'

The news that I might be seeing these two old St Chad's lads almost every day didn't exactly fill my heart with joy. This pair had usually meant trouble in the past and they didn't forget old grievances easily. Still, that was all history now and it was best to forget it as I had my own work to get on with. Brodie was such a slave-driver, I wouldn't be able to give much thought to these two old rivals being around the place even if they were nursing grudges.

The rest of the morning followed a similar pattern. About eleven o'clock, the pace of activity slowed down and we were able to catch our breath. By 1 p.m., the market was almost still and it was time to call it a day. Some stallholders began winding tarpaulin covers round their merchandise as security, a sure sign that business had closed for the day. My legs were like jelly. Is this my life for the next forty years? I asked myself. Then as an afterthought, I added, still talking to myself, what if it is? It's not so bad and, as everyone keeps telling me, I'll get used to it eventually.

We rounded off the market when Brodie went for his daily ration of eight or nine pints of beer at the Turk's Head while Dorothy and me drove over to John Gee's, the hay and straw dealer on Shudehill, for supplies.

'When do we take Crusty to the blacksmith for shoeing?' I asked.

Dorothy laughed. 'We don't. Donkeys don't need shoeing but they do need a sort of manicure from time to time. We'll take him to the vets at the end of the week to be wormed and then to the farrier to have his hooves trimmed. We'll also check on his touch of the flu to see if there's anything we can do. We're lucky to have a good vet to look after him as some horse vets think it's beneath their dignity to attend to a donkey. After that, it's back to the stables 'cos Crusty here needs a feed and a rest. He's worked hard today. Then, my lad, it's home to bed for you. I dare say you're ready for a good sleep. It's been a long day, especially as it's your first time.'

'It most certainly has, Aunty,' I said, stifling a yawn.

As we clip-clopped our weary way down Miller Street before turning into Dantzig Street, we were passed by three or four other donkey and carts, obviously in a race to get back to the stables.

'One day,' she said, 'when you've learned the ropes, you can take Crusty back to the stables by

261

yourself, but I think you'll find old Crusty here is not up to joining in any of those races the stable lads like to get up to. He likes a more sedate pace, especially if he's worked hard as he has today.'

'I'd love to take the reins, Aunty, and I think our Crusty is a bit past it to think of racing him back. When do you think I'll be ready?'

'Not for some time yet, Tommy,' she laughed. 'You've got a lot to learn before we can hand over the reins, my lad.'

'When do you think that'll be? Next month?' I was impatient for responsibility.

'Not a chance, Tommy. I'd say more like eighteen months, when you'll be gone thirteen or so. Driving a donkey on a public road is a skilled art and you need to learn how to control him from the driving position. Crusty has to learn to respond to your particular instructions which may be a bit different from mine or Brodie's. Only when we and Crusty have full confidence in your skill can we let you do the driving.'

I think Aunty Dorothy was keen to hand over the reins to me so she could join Brodie in the pub at the end of each day's work. But wisely she decided that that particular day would have to wait until I was good and ready.

When we reached the stables, we gave Crusty a good brushing down to make him clean and neat once more before settling him down for his feed of cereal mash, pony nuts, and a few of his favourite fruit and vegetables like carrots and eating apples. Finally, after checking that he had clean straw and a bucketful of clean water, we left him to his well-earned rest.

262

'It's important to keep him well groomed,' Aunty told me as we walked away from the stables. 'Not only does it keep him clean, it discourages lice and gives you the chance to spot any small cuts or bald patches. So we brush out loose hair and mud and keep his eyes and hooves clean.'

Aunty told me that she usually joined Brodie in the pub after seeing to Crusty but since it was my first week in the market, she would accompany me home to see me settled in.

At the house, we found Zeb waiting to greet us. He was reeking of gin and tobacco as usual.

'Got any fags?' was his first question to me. 'Got any of them special fags I bought from you the other week? Best fags I've ever smoked.'

'Sorry, Zeb,' I said. 'The tobacconists who manufactured them have ceased trading. But I do have a few things from the market to put in the larder.'

I handed over the bag of freebies – fruit, vegetables and fish – which we had collected in our 'swinger' over the course of the morning. These perks, I thought, are the best features of working in Smithfield Market.

In the kitchen, I made myself a mug of tea, went down to the cellar and collapsed on to the bed. I was asleep in about twenty seconds, the tea left untouched on my bedside table.

That first day at work was typical of the days that followed and I soon fell into the market routine. Time went by so quickly that weeks seemed like days, months like weeks, and before I knew where I was, a year had passed. Although I started work

263

as a general dogsbody and did many of the more menial jobs, like sweeping out the stable, bringing in the straw and hay, polishing the harness and washing the cart, I learned lots of other things during those first twelve months. Brodie and Dorothy taught me how to drive the donkey and cart safely and skilfully by, for example, not holding the reins too tightly or overworking Crusty.

'Remember Crusty's a donkey and not a steam engine that can pull any load at any speed no matter how heavy. Be considerate. If you're going up a steep hill, get off the cart and walk. Crusty'll have enough to do pulling a heavy load without having to carry you as well. And if you're going down a steep hill, put on the brake to stop the cart running away and, very important, when you get to the bottom of the hill, don't forget to release the brake again or the poor donkey will be straining against jammed wheels.'

Apart from all this donkey craft, I absorbed a lot about the market business too – the names and locations of most of the stallholders, how to load up and secure the goods on the cart, how to watch out for the underhand tricks some salesmen could get up to, like giving short weight, and, most important, which evil bastards were the most likely to try it on.

Chapter Twenty-Four

1 January 1900 was a day of great celebration throughout the British Isles, though some believed that the new century was not really due to begin until January 1901. Just the same, for most people the air was full of promise and everywhere there was a feeling of great expectation and excitement at the breathtaking inventions that science was creating almost on a daily basis: motor cars, photography, moving pictures, X-rays and wireless, to name but a few. Victoria was still on the throne and Britain was at the peak of its greatness though we were still involved in a war in South Africa. From the pubs along Shudehill could be heard the strains of 'Goodbye Dolly Gray' and the marching song written by Manchester's Leslie Stuart, 'The Soldiers of the Queen', with its jingoistic claim:

...when we say we've ALWAYS won
And when they ask us how it's done,
We'll proudly point to every one
Of England's soldiers of the Queen!

For me also the year 1900 was full of promise. But not of great scientific or technological achievement. My hopes were more modest but nevertheless just as exciting for me. This was the year when Aunty Dorothy made good her word.

Eighteen months had passed and she now judged me competent enough to take over the task of driving Crusty and the cart back to the stables after work. For me, it was a big day 'cos it meant I was no longer a child but a young man who could be given the responsibility of driving a donkey and cart on a public road. I had arrived! I was on my way!

First thing in the morning, the three of us – Brodie, Dorothy and me – arose in the early hours and collected Crusty together as usual, but at around eleven-thirty, as the market became less busy, Brodie and Dorothy went to join their friends and workmates in the Turk's Head where no doubt they sank several pints of Mitchell and Butler's ales and bottles of Guinness stout to replace, as they claimed, the 'gallons' of sweat they had lost during a morning's hard grafting in the frenzied atmosphere of the market. When they'd finished their marathon drinking session in the pub, it was usually the donkey that took the pair home and not the other way round.

The pub, along with the Hare and Hounds, was an important meeting place for various market workers, a place where they could place an illicit bet with a bookie, relax and enjoy gossiping about market affairs and the latest goings-on of who was sleeping with whom and whose wife had walked out on her husband. I never begrudged Dorothy this chance to go off and relax with Brodie for an hour or two because she worked so hard during the week. Even on Sundays there was no respite, for she had to see to the weekly wash in the cellar just as my own mam had done in happier times.

Taking Crusty back to the stables was an easy task as the donkey knew the road and the routine inside out and we went back to Dantzig Street at a steady trot. He was a very even-tempered donkey and remained calm and unperturbed no matter what the distraction – such as a mad dog barking at his hindquarters or rag-a-muffins throwing stones at him. There were one or two things that I had to keep in mind on the journey back, though, like remembering not to pull the reins too sharply and to apply the cart brake on the downhill slope along Miller Street. Crusty seemed sometimes to have a sixth sense when it came to spotting hidden danger. On one occasion, when we turned into Dantzig Street, we were faced with a gushing flood of water due to a burst water main. That didn't seem like a problem to me and I thought we could simply drive through it. I urged the donkey forward with a 'Giddy up, Crusty' but he came to a dead stop and refused to budge. I gave him a little touch of the whip but he still wouldn't move. He stood motionless and no matter what I tried, he remained rooted to the spot. Just then, a workman came running up to us, waving at us frantically.

'Go back! Go back!' he shouted. 'The road has collapsed under that water.'

It was a good job Crusty had stopped as he did or I am sure he, the cart and me would have gone right into the deep hole and turned topsy-turvy. We went back on our tracks and returned to the stable via Corporation Street.

When we reached the stables, I had the pleasant job of removing his breast harness and settling him down in his stall. I patted him on the forehead and stroked his mane, keeping up a flow of talk as I did so.

'Well, you really saved our bacon today, Crusty, old son. Let's remove your halter and bridle and that nasty bit from your mouth. I don't know how you manage to do all that work with that cutting your mouth, I really don't. You've worked hard today, my lad, and you deserve a good feed of this special bran mash I've had made up for you. My, that was a big load you had to pull to that shop in Oldham Road today! I don't know where you get the strength, I really don't. You're a good donkey, always patient and gentle. You're getting on a bit, though. You'll soon be twenty-one. Why, that's like an old, old man in human terms. I can't see myself pulling loads like that when I get old. I hope I never have to, Crusty.'

Throughout this little speech of mine, the donkey regarded me with his big sad eyes as if he understood every word. There was something very lovable about this donkey. He had great strength and was capable of kicking out, but his behaviour was never less than exemplary. If I had to choose words to describe him, they would be: 'gentle', 'loyal', 'obedient'. I had the feeling that he'd be always like that, patient and resigned to his fate no matter how he was treated. As the months passed by, a strong bond of trust and affection grew up between us. There were other donkeys in other parts of the stable and I could hear the occasional braying from other stalls and I often felt that another donkey as companion would have been welcome. I raised this matter with Brodie and

Dorothy but they said one donkey was about all they could afford at that time. Maybe if business picked up a little, they mumbled, they might think about it.

The other stable lads often told me stories of the cruel ways that donkeys were sometimes treated and my blood ran cold when I heard them. Like the little donkey that had his nostrils slit in the belief that it would help him work harder or the lame donkeys that were made to go on working by ignorant, cruel owners who believed the remedy was to brand their animals with red-hot irons. Such beasts were forced to go on despite their agony.

It was towards the end of November in 1900 that I noticed that Crusty's appetite was not as keen as usual and he wasn't looking so well. We'd come back from the market as we always did towards 1p.m. and I was going through the normal routine of settling him down. We had all worked hard that day but not unusually so, though around ten o'clock when I was having breakfast at the café, some urchins wandering through the market on the cadge had been feeding him sour cooking apples and I'd had to chase them off. Now back at the stables I could tell from his strange behaviour that he was experiencing some discomfort for he kept nodding and lowering his head as if trying to tell me something. Several times he lay down and rolled from side to side, got to his feet again and, twisting his head, looked at his stomach. Once or twice he tried to bite at his belly as if attempting to ward off pain. Then, he became calm again and I heaved a sigh of relief – the trouble seemed to have subsided.

'Poor old Crusty,' I said, patting him on the forehead and stroking his mane. 'Maybe a good night's rest will put you right.'

I helped him lie down and wrapped a couple of thick blankets round him, hoping against hope that he would be recovered by next morning. Later that evening, when Dorothy and Brodie were back from the pub, I reported Crusty's condition.

'Ah, nothing to be concerned about, Tommy lad,' Brodie said reassuringly. 'When you go to collect him tomorrow, you'll find him right as rain. You'll see.' I was so worried that I didn't sleep at all well that night. I said a few words to God, hoping He might help to pull Crusty through.

'Come on, God. Please make him well again. Every time I get close to someone, they've gone and died on me. Surely not this time! It's only an innocent, hard-working donkey that's done no harm to anyone. And didn't Christ once ride on a donkey? How did that poem by Chesterton that we learned at school go again?

When fishes flew and forests walked
And figs grew upon thorn,
Some moment when the moon was blood
Then surely I was born;

With monstrous head and sickening cry
And ears like errant wings,
The devil's walking parody
On all four-footed things

Fools! For I also had my hour;
One far fierce hour and sweet:
There was a shout about my ears,
And palms before my feet.

'So, if the donkey was once chosen to carry Christ, surely you can let our Crusty survive this sudden sickness? Just this once, let someone I love get better.'

I said this prayer and maybe I didn't carry enough conviction because, deep down, I had a sixth sense that Crusty might not make it. Maybe I was asking a lot of God, for I had never seen Crusty looking so poorly and, after all, he was getting on a bit.

Next morning, Dorothy, Brodie and I walked over to the stables. Me, fearing the worst. My instincts proved right 'cos Crusty's condition was definitely worse. He was restlessly thrashing about in his stall and he was clearly in distress.

'I think we should send for the vet right away,' Dorothy said. 'Crusty obviously can't go to the market today.'

'I'm sure his sickness is only temporary,' Brodie, forever the optimist, replied. 'He'll be fine after a day's rest.'

Dorothy was adamant. 'No, Brodie. Crusty is very sick. To me it looks like a severe case of colic. He needs expert attention.'

After much persuasion along these lines, Brodie reluctantly agreed to fetch Mr Elliott, the local vet. While we waited for him to arrive, an agonized Crusty continued to roll over and over

271

in the straw. We found it harrowing to watch him as there was nothing we could do to relieve his agony.

When the vet arrived, he gave Crusty a strong sedative to alleviate the pain and then carried out a thorough examination while we stood by feeling helpless. Then Mr Elliott gave his diagnosis and for me the news was like a hammer blow in the chest.

'There's no doubt,' the vet said, 'that your donkey is suffering from an advanced form of colic. My recommendation is that you have him put down as soon as possible for he is suffering badly. In my experience, donkeys rarely recover from cases of colic as bad as this. It would be a mercy to have him put out of his misery.'

'But we had no idea,' Brodie protested. 'There was no sign to warn us.'

'I'm not really surprised,' Mr Elliott said. 'Donkeys can be less expressive than horses and symptoms can easily be overlooked until the problem has overwhelmed them. Colic may not be identified until the donkey is in the terminal stages of the disease.'

Brodie paid the vet his fee and the rest of the day passed as if we were in a nightmare. A man from the Collyhurst knacker's yard came and led Crusty away and we were left in a state of shock as if we'd lost a close member of the family, which, in a way, we had. There was no funeral, no ceremony but Aunty Dorothy wept copiously because Crusty had been an endearing creature who had given them hard work and loyalty over many years. It all happened so quickly, there was hardly time to take it in. Brodie and Dorothy had had Crusty as a colt and broken him in and trained him from the very beginning. The sight of Crusty with his long ears and soulful eyes being taken away in the van was one that none of us would ever forget. As for me, I had become so used to losing good friends and those close to me that I'd become case-hardened. I heaved a deep sigh and something inside me seemed to switch off as if I'd become resigned and reconciled to a life that was both cruel and unfair. I had come to the conclusion that it was perhaps best not to form deep, loving relationships with anyone or anything since it always led ultimately to pain and sorrow.

'Ah well,' said Brodie solemnly. 'That's that. We'll just have to soldier on with things as best we can. Life has to go on.'

We didn't go to the market that day and our thoughts turned to finding a replacement donkey for, without one, we were out of business.

A couple of days after Crusty had been taken away to the boneyard, Brodie and I paid a visit one afternoon to John McCarthy, a reputable horse dealer and auctioneer, situated at the corner of Thomas Street and High Street.

Brodie had already visited the auctioneer's stables earlier that morning in order to look over the donkeys that were coming up for sale.

'There were some poor specimens that didn't look too healthy,' he told me. 'But there were two geldings that caught my fancy. Both nine years old and of standard size, that is about ten to eleven hands' (40 to 45 inches) '–one black, the other grey. We'll see how much they go for.'

The auction began at two o'clock and a good crowd of prospective buyers had gathered there arguing, laughing and shouting.

'Most of these blokes are here for the horses and the ponies,' Brodie said. 'Donkeys are last on the list.'

I looked around the auction stables and most of the customers seemed to me to have horse-like faces except for one or two who looked like donkeys. There was a great deal of excitement as the auction proceeded and the rubicund, bushy-browed auctioneer banging his mallet had difficulty making himself heard above the babble of voices.

We had to wait awhile before the two donkeys that Brodie was interested in came up for sale. Both were superb specimens and I'd have been happy if Brodie had bought either, though I think he was inclined to go for the black one. At first. For some strange reason, Brodie changed his mind when it was offered for auction and it was sold to an old greengrocer for seven guineas.

We weren't sure whether *we* had selected the grey donkey or whether it was the other way round and the donkey had selected us, for throughout the bidding, the grey gelding had looked at us steadily as if saying, 'The black donkey is not for you. *I* am the one you want and *you* are the owners I've been looking for all my life.' I could see from the glint in Brodie's eyes that he'd not be able to resist the charm of the donkey's white nose, dark muzzle and light rings round the eyes.

'Next donkey to be offered,' the ruddy-faced auctioneer announced, 'is a ten-year-old grey gelding. You've all had the chance to examine him and you must be aware that he is a superb specimen in beautiful condition. He is called Prince after Edward, the Prince of Wales, and what a good name that is for he's a donkey suitable for royalty. Can we open the bidding at five guineas?'

A young farmer dressed in deerstalker hat, Norfolk jacket and gaiters and with a face not unlike the animal he was hoping to buy got into competition with a market carter. The offers soon rose in half-guinea leaps until the price reached eight guineas.

I wondered if this was beyond Brodie's pocket but he stayed in the background and gave the impression of being uninterested in the proceedings. He talked quietly to me and paid no attention to the bidding.

The auctioneer had reached the stage of accepting the last bid and had raised his mallet to seal it.

'At eight guineas. Are you all done? Then at eight guineas, going, going–'

'Ten guineas!' Brodie's voice rang out across the room.

A jump of two guineas was too much and the competitors shrugged their shoulders and dropped out. The hammer was brought down and Brodie was the new owner of this magnificent beast. Though he'd paid a little more than he'd intended, he was a happy man when he collected the various documents about the donkey's origin, health and history.

'He's a fairly strong donkey,' Brodie said happily when the deal had been duly signed, sealed and delivered, 'and he should give us many years of service.'

I was happy too and could hardly wait to get Prince back to our stable. What an exciting day! It would take some time to absorb it all. But the day was not finished because Brodie had another surprise up his sleeve and when he sprang it on me, it fair knocked me for six.

'You've worked very hard for us, Tommy,' he said, 'and what's more you've shown yourself to be an excellent donkey handler. I know it's not been very easy at home and my father can be a cantankerous old bastard, but remember he's not exactly had much of a life, being wounded and all that in the American war. But his nasty ways are only words; at least he's not become violent or tried to hit you or anything. You must tell me if he ever does.'

I said nothing. It had been obvious to me for some time that neither Dorothy nor he knew about Zeb's tendency to use the belt or the whip. And I wasn't going to be the one to tell them.

'Yes,' Brodie continued, 'our carting business in the market has been doing very well, thanks to the efforts the three of us have been putting into it. Now, I've talked it over with your aunty and we've decided to promote you. In the coming year, you'll be fifteen and you've proved to me that it's time for you to take on some real responsibility in our business. At present we give you free board and lodging and a wage of three and six a week but we're going to raise this to five shillings. We're setting up a second arm to the business and putting you in sole charge. I've already arranged it with John McCarthy and I've bought a complete outfit comprising donkey and cart and I want you to take over and run this second wing of our little enterprise. Come with me and I'll show you what I have in mind.'

We went to the back of the McCarthy stable and there stood the most beautiful black donkey I had ever set eyes on. His long ears and handsome face won my heart right away.

'He is an eight-year-old gelding,' Brodie told me, 'friendly, amenable, thoroughly trained and ready to go to work. I bought him from Brendan Clancy, an old friend who's about to retire and whose word I trust implicitly. The donkey's name is Clancy after his owner and he comes complete with cart and all the trappings.'

I was overwhelmed when I heard this. Me with my own donkey and cart! I could hardly believe it, for it was my dearest dream come true. How things had changed! When I'd first realized that I had lost my chance with the Royce Company, I'd been as mad as hell but gradually, thanks to Grandad Owen, Joe Brannan and Aunty Dorothy, I'd come to see sense and to see that my best hopes lay here in the market.

'Uncle Brodie,' I said warmly, 'I don't know how to thank you. I'll work hard for you and you'll never regret what you've done today. But one thing puzzled me when you were buying Prince. How come you hardly seemed interested in him during the auction? Why was that?'

'It doesn't do to show your hand at an auction, Tommy,' he said with a broad grin. 'If the other blokes had thought for a minute that I was interested, they'd have upped the price with a few mock bids.'

'You're a crafty old devil, Brodie, and no mistake.'

Judging by the satisfied smile on his face, Brodie liked being called crafty.

'Anyroad, Tommy,' he said, 'you'd better take Clancy on his first drive back to the stables. Tell me how he shapes up.'

It's a funny old world, I thought. One day I'm down in the dumps when our donkey dies. The next, I'm over the moon as my fortunes are reversed.

I drove Clancy carefully at first and I found him a joy to handle. A perfect gentleman. The slightest twitch of the reins and the order, 'Giddy up, Clancy', and we were off. It soon became obvious that he had been well trained by the way he took the corners in response to the merest flick of the reins. Brodie had already got back to the stables when Clancy and I arrived.

'Well, how did you find him, Tommy?' Brodie asked.

I replied with a simple thumbs-up. 'The previous owner, your friend Mr Clancy, obviously knew about donkeys and how to break them in. The donkey responded beautifully and never made a single mistake on the way here. I just know the two of us are going to be happy together.'

'You make it sound as if you're getting married to him.' Brodie laughed.

Gran'pa Zeb seemed a bit put out by this development with the new donkey. I think he'd become jealous of the attention I was getting.

'They're too soft on you,' he grumbled. 'Why should you get all this fuss made of you? You're not even their son but a bloody orphan that's been dumped on them. Anyroad, what's the name of this bloody donkey they've put you in charge of?'

'He's called Clancy after the name of the previous owner.'

'That's a bloody stupid name if ever I heard one. I'd never call a donkey Clancy – not in a month of Sundays. I was in charge of a troupe of donkeys when I was in the American army and we never gave a donkey such a daft title. Clancy, I ask you. We used the names of brave leaders, like Caesar, Napoleon, or Washington. Couldn't you choose a better name than Clancy?'

'We didn't choose it, Zeb. It had already been given when Brodie bought it and we're stuck with it.'

'Then you should change it.'

'The donkey's eight years old, Zeb. Isn't it a bit late?'

'Nonsense. The donkey will accept whatever name you give it if you go about it the right way. Now I learned about horses, ponies, and donkeys from the Indians. There's a special way of teaching a donkey its new name. Something what I learned from the Apaches. A good name for a donkey is Geronimo.'

'Why Geronimo, Zeb?'

'Because Geronimo was the leader of the

Apache tribe and famous for his courage and in a way he was as stubborn as a mule. You couldn't have a better name than that. I'll show you how to make the donkey learn his new name.'

I realized that there would be no peace until I agreed to Zeb's demand though I doubted that our donkey would ever forget his old name after such a long time.

'Yeah, you may as well humour the old bugger,' Brodie said when I told him. 'He's got nowt else to do with his time.'

'Very well, Zeb,' I told the old man. 'If you'd like to try, I'll bring the new donkey and the cart round after work tomorrow. And we'll drive over to the meadow on Barney's and you can demonstrate this special training method of yours.'

The next day after work, I collected Zeb and we drove over to Barney's waste ground. I was curious to see this Apache method of teaching a donkey a new name.

First we took the donkey from the shafts and on Zeb's instructions I held him by the halter. Then the old man took out a long bamboo cane which he had hidden under his coat and began striking the donkey on the rump. After each blow, Zeb lifted one of its ears and whispered the word 'Geronimo' down our poor animal's lughole. He did this several times as if beating a carpet, each time repeating the chosen name into its ear in order to drive home the lesson that its name was no longer Clancy but Geronimo. The donkey looked at me with what I thought was a pained but puzzled expression as if wondering what this was all about. After a few repetitions, I couldn't stand watching this stupid procedure any longer, so I said, 'Right, Zeb, I think he's got the idea now. Let me see if you've convinced him.'

I stepped away from our donkey and walked about ten yards across the meadow, holding out a juicy carrot.

'Geronimo,' I called out sweetly, at the same time offering the carrot.

Our donkey trotted across to me happily.

'That's it, Zeb,' I said. 'Well done! He knows his new name now. What an amazing method you've learned from the Apaches!'

I returned the donkey to the shafts and drove Zeb home, then took Clancy back to his stable where I made a big fuss of him with a couple more carrots and by patting his forehead, stroking his mane and talking to him in soothing tones.

'Never mind what that stupid, nasty man did to you, Clancy. It won't happen again. And you such a good donkey who's going to work so hard for me and will never harm anybody in your life.'

Clancy looked at me accusingly as if wondering why I'd let that cruel old man belt him so undeservedly.

I determined there and then that henceforth Zeb should never be allowed near my donkey again. What was more, I never used the name Geronimo in Clancy's presence again. If my donkey had learned anything that day it was to fear the Apache leader's name and to associate it with pain on its rump.

The next day was to be the donkey's first day in

the market and I worked hard cleaning and polishing the cart and the harness until they shone and the leather was a gleaming black. Clancy had been thoroughly brushed and his coat had a superb sheen. I gave him the once-over before we set off and I was well satisfied with his appearance and our overall appearance. I was as proud as a peacock as I drove along the familiar route to Smithfield. I had the feeling that people in the street were pointing us out. 'Look at that young boy with that magnificent donkey and cart. What a beautiful picture they make!'

In the market itself we created something of a stir as other carters, stable boys and stallholders congratulated me on my promotion to running my own little outfit. Mad Alec broke off from his portering to inspect my new set-up.

'Lovely specimen,' he said. 'Make sure you take care of him. Be on your guard for those who'll try to do you harm. Let me know if you ever need any help.'

I thanked him but I didn't understand what he meant by that last warning. Then I thought, That's Alec – always suspicious of the people around him and ready to have a fight.

My old St William's buddies also took time off to gather round to admire the donkey and the cart.

'You really have moved up in the world,' remarked Charlie when I stopped outside Holbrook's stall. Duggie left the family fruit and veg stall to come over and pay his respects and approval. Word went abroad and reached the outer reaches of the meat and fish market where Alfie humped boxes of herrings and barons of beef and, of course, he too had to leave off his work to add his awe and fascination.

'I suppose you'll be too high and mighty to speak to the likes of us labourers,' he said.

'I have no objection to addressing you,' I replied haughtily, 'as long as you remember to touch your forelock when I pass by.'

'Gercha,' he said, giving me the lightest sock on the jaw

Word went out as far as Doonican's fruit stall and Doris had to leave off selling her merchandise to come and express her amazement.

'Now you're a man of the world,' she said, fluttering her eyelashes. 'You'll soon be taking me out to celebrate your new position.'

'Sure, Doris. In about three years' time maybe. At the moment I'm frightened of girls.'

'Yeah,' she retorted, giving me one of her friendly thumps. 'Pull the other one, it's got bells on.'

There was a certain amount of truth in my statement. Doris did make me a little nervous as she was the pushy type and had a tendency to be not so much a 'touchy-feely type' as a 'punchy-thumpy type'.

Most of the lads I went round with were in awe of girls 'cos we didn't really understand 'em and there was a code among us that to go out with a girl was a sort of betrayal and would let the side down.

So all in all, the new donkey and cart caused a bit of fuss. But it also brought a word of warning from my old mentor and adviser, Joe Brannan.

'By all means, Tommy,' he said, 'enjoy the open mouths and the popping eyes at your newfound status in the market, but remember that certain people will be as jealous as hell of your success and will try to do you down, given half the chance.'

I basked in the glory of that first day but the work was still organized and managed by Brodie, who found the commissions. My job was simply to deliver the orders and now that he had an extra carter to help out, he was able to go further afield. I found myself delivering a wide variety of produce – fish, meat, fruit, vegetables – to more distant places in districts all round Manchester and Salford. Brodie handled all the money and kept the books of account. I think we must have been doing quite well, for after three months, he raised my pay to eight shillings a week, for which I was grateful though I still found things quite tight as I paid for my own breakfast, tea breaks, and lunch at Fred's café. But of course I got lots of free food in the form of fish, fruit and veg, which Dorothy showed me how to cook at home.

Time passed and I became good at my job. Soon I knew not only where every stall was located but also the retail shops that we served. All this time I'd built up a warm, loving and trusting relationship with Clancy. In the afternoons when I had finished work I often had my lunch with the donkey boys in their makeshift kitchen above the stables. Our meals were of the simple variety usually involving eggs prepared in one way or another – boiled eggs, poached eggs on toast, bacon and egg, cheese omelette – and occasionally we introduced some variety into our diet by buying fish and chips from the local chippie. Sometimes if I felt really tired after a hard morning's graft, I simply lay down in the straw and slept next to Clancy with my head on his belly. Often I found myself talking and confiding in him as I patted and stroked his mane.

'One day, Clancy,' I would say, 'you will retire from all this hard work and you will spend your retirement in a lovely meadow with lush grass to eat. You won't have to do all this rushing around and you'll be able to take things easy. If I get married and have kids, I'll bring them out on a Sunday afternoon to visit you and bring you apples and juicy carrots. And my wife will also take you for walks through the countryside. My wife will be kind and soft-hearted like me. You'll see.'

In the summertime when there were lots of flies buzzing around his stall, I spent my time swatting them and keeping them off him.

'Push off, flies,' I yelled. 'Go and pester some other donkey. You're not wanted here.'

I stopped one day and realized what I was doing.

'Do you see what I'm doing, Clancy?' I said. 'I must be going mad. What am I doing, talking to flies, as if they understood what I was saying?'

Not only did I spend time with Clancy after work. If the weather was nice, I visited him on Sunday after Mass at St Chad's and took him to a meadow on Barney's fields where I let him feed on the grass and run around freely without the cart.

Chapter Twenty-Five

The period 1901 to 1902 was strange in many ways. For a start, on 22 January Queen Victoria died, surrounded, Buckingham Palace reported, 'by her children and grandchildren'. The whole country went into mourning. In the market the carters and porters wore black armbands, stalls were draped in black, and donkeys, including our two, were decorated in black silk ribbons. Some horses had their hooves padded to muffle the sound of their clippety-clops. There was great demand for door wreaths and the florists were kept busy for the week leading up to Victoria's funeral on 3 February 1901. I wouldn't have minded all this but it wasn't long after that that we had to switch mood in order to celebrate the coronation of King Edward who'd had to wait so long for his mother to die so that he could take over. Even that wasn't straightforward, for first the coronation was on, then it was off. In June 1902, it was away with the miserable mourning hues and on with the brightest coloured ribbons and rosettes we could find to dress up our carts and donkeys. Then the news came through. It was all off! The new king had to have an emergency operation for appendicitis. Coronation visitors from as far away as India and the African colonies had to pack up and go home by the long sea journey. In the market we took down the gay decorations and blew the dust off the black ribbons and armbands in case we needed them again. Two months later, in August, it was a goer again and we had to get the bright silk ribbons out of storage and put them on once more.

'I wish they'd make up their bloody minds,' Brodie said. 'Does this Eddie fellah want to be king or not?'

'It's not his fault he had appendicitis,' Dorothy protested.

'Maybe not,' Brodie said, 'but he could have timed it better.'

In my own life, everything had been going smoothly for most of the year but then things mysteriously started to go wrong and I was at a loss to understand what was happening. At first, that is, because it wasn't too long before I got to know what was going on. I was taking a fairly big load of produce to Ernie Entwistle, a greengrocer on Hendham Vale off Queen's Road, Smedley. We had just turned left from Rochdale Road into Topley Street leading to the place where Ernie's shop was located. The street was a steep downhill gradient and so I took special care in applying a light touch to the brakes and negotiating the corner. I twitched the rein for the left turn and we made the manoeuvre normally but, as we did so, I could feel something sliding off the cart. Frantically I pulled on the brake but too late. A moment later there followed an almighty crash as the left-handed section of the load came adrift and landed up in the roadway. Boxes of fruit and vegetables were strewn everywhere, with apples, oranges, lemons and onions rolling mockingly down the gutter. Pedestrians on the pavement watched the disaster unfold and then many of them began picking up the fruit. Ah, good, I thought. They're going to help get the stuff back in the boxes. No such luck. The onlookers stuffed as much as they could into their pockets and shopping baskets and were gone down Rochdale Road before you could say Jack Robinson. Oddly enough, given the circumstances, I was reminded of lines from 'The Wind in a Frolic' by William Howitt, yet another verse we'd been forced to memorize under the regime of Miss Corbett at St Chad's.

> There never was heard a much lustier shout
> As the apples and oranges tumbled about;
> And urchins, that stand with their thievish eyes
> Forever on watch, ran off each with a prize.

With the aid of an old man who had been watching the proceedings, I managed to scramble some of the merchandise back into the crates and the baskets. The fruit was bruised and of no value but I reloaded what I could back on to the cart and secured it tightly. I had lost nearly a third of the order.

Brodie hit the roof when I reported back to him.

'Do you realize that your carelessness has cost us around fifteen shillings?' he stormed. 'How many times have I told you to make sure that you don't build up the load too high, that you secure it thoroughly with the ropes I've given you, and that you don't take corners too fast? Anyroad, that's your wages gone for this week. It'll teach you to take greater care in future.'

It was pointless telling him that I had *not* piled up the load too high, that I *had* secured the load with ropes, and I *had* rounded the corner with all due caution. I was at a loss to explain the mishap. A few weeks went by and everything seemed to be getting back to normal. That is until I was delivering a load of fruit to the shop on Victoria Station. Once again this meant going down a steep hill at Balloon Street. This time I was extra cautious as I descended with my load of boxes and baskets. To my horror, as I made the turn, the load became detached and I found myself having to rescue what I could of the fallen merchandise. Though not as bad as the first, this was my second catastrophe in completing an errand. I delivered most of the order intact and made my way back to Smithfield. I reported once again to Brodie and Dorothy.

'Before you go off at the deep end again, Brodie,' I said, 'let me assure you that I took every precaution to avoid another accident. Something's going on and I think we should try to find out who's got it in for me.'

Dorothy agreed with me. 'There's only one man who knows what's happening in the market and you know who that is.'

'The Oracle. Joe Brannan,' Brodie and I echoed.

We were right. Joe seemed to have access to the mysterious market grapevine and the latest gossip and who were friends, who enemies, and who lovers.

'I don't have proof, of course,' he told us when

we went over to Deakin's stall to consult him, 'but I have it on good authority (that is Mad Alec) that two young hawker lads from Tib Street have a grudge against Tommy for some reason. As for Slug Bullock, he's jealous of anyone who seems to be doing well. These three lowlifes were seen messing about with the ropes on Tommy's load when he left his cart for a moment or two to answer a call of nature the other day. I should look in that direction if I were you.'

Brodie was ready to go in like a bull. 'Let me get at that bastard Slug Bullock,' he fumed. 'I'll knock him and them two lads into the middle of next week.'

'No,' Dorothy advised, placing a hand on his arm. 'We'll have a word with Big Bert, our market sergeant. These troublemakers should be warned properly and legally to keep off once and for all.'

And that's what we did. Big Bert caught the three of them together, laid the charge before them and warned them off. Of course they protested their innocence and denied everything.

'Why are you picking on us?' Slug Bullock whined. 'We didn't do nothing.'

Big Bert poked him roughly in the chest with a huge forefinger. 'Don't you dare speak to me like that, you worthless piece of trash.'

The Manchester police had a reputation of using strong-arm methods when dealing with criminal types and here was evidence.

'We haven't touched anything,' Ginger McDermott said.

'That's as may be,' said Bert, staring at him aggressively, 'but it has been reported to me that you three were seen fiddling with the ropes on Tommy's cart. What I'm saying is, if ever any trouble like this comes to my attention again, I'll know where to look.'

Then addressing Ginger and Mick, he said, 'As for you two, you should be careful whose company you keep. This man will take you down with him. And Slug, if you're not careful you're going to land up behind bars like the rest of them Bengal Tigers you used to go around with. They were a right bunch of thugs and no mistake.'

After this severe warning there was no more trouble and Brodie very kindly recompensed me for my loss of pay.

'All's well that ends well,' I told Clancy in the stable that night. He looked at me solemnly as if he understood what I was talking about and sympathized with my position.

Chapter Twenty-Six

There was more to my life than working in the market, of course. Every Saturday afternoon, after settling Clancy down in his stall for the day, I used to play football on St Michael's Flags with the old gang plus a few newcomers. Including me, there were usually six of the old gang, consisting of Charlie who was still working at Holbrook's fruit and vegetable stall as a trainee salesman, Big Alfie who'd grown to an enormous size and was still portering in the meat and fish markets, Duggie who was working on his dad's fruit stall, and Jimmy who had taken up the apprenticeship with Henry Royce but still wouldn't miss his weekly game of footer with us for the world. We were joined also by Gordon Bennett who'd been in our class at St Chad's and had stayed on till the age of fourteen. Gordon had been a bit of a 'Holy Joe' and a tell-tale at school but he'd grown up a bit since then and was more acceptable. He was working as a messenger boy in the post office and was hoping to become a postman one day.

After our game we had taken to retiring to a wooden hut in the old church cemetery. A funny place to have a shed, you may say, but it was ideal for meeting up and resting our weary bones after a hard-fought match. We'd found it quite by accident when wandering through the cemetery looking at some of the inscriptions on the gravestones. The hut was a ramshackle affair and just about big enough for the six of us to squeeze into. It had probably been used by the grave-diggers between jobs, I suppose, but we saw that, with a bit of work, it could serve as our little gang's headquarters. A place where we could tell stories and generally chew the cud.

One Saturday we were gathered together in the hut getting ready to go down to the Flags for our game when we saw a middle-aged bloke with a droopy moustache heading towards us.

'Uh-oh,' I murmured. 'Looks like trouble coming to tell us we're trespassing and shouldn't be here.'

The man knocked on the door and said, 'Good

afternoon. May I come in?'

When we heard this courteous inquiry, we knew we'd be all right.

'By all means,' said Charlie, ever the polite one.

'My name is Tommy Johnson,' the stranger said. 'I'm superintendent of Charter Street Ragged School, just over the road there. I've seen you lads playing football on Saturdays and I've noticed that you never seem to have enough for full teams.'

'That's right,' said Jimmy. 'A few more generally join us on the pitch and then we manage to have five or six a side.'

'Would you be able to take a few of our boys from the school to make up the teams?' the stranger asked.

'That seems like a good idea,' I said warmly. 'We often feel the need for a few more players.'

'Right then,' said Mr Johnson. 'I'll send one or two across next Saturday and I dare say we can run to a new football as our way of saying thanks. The lads'll be glad of a game. Coming from the Ragged School, they don't get much of a chance of playing on a team.'

'What exactly is a Ragged School?' Duggie asked. 'Are all the kids dressed in rags, or what?'

Mr Johnson laughed. 'Not exactly, but the Ragged School gives free education and help for very poor, abandoned children in this area. We've been here over thirty years and there's another branch over the road in Sharp Street. You've probably seen it. Anyway, our lads would love a game of footy with you next Saturday. I must say it's good to see the Flags being used for games of football again. It's not so long ago that they were used for the most vicious fights between scuttling gangs in the area, who came armed with knives, hatchets, bicycle chains, and buckled belts. Some of these thugs are now in prison, others in the army.'

'Yeah, we've heard about them,' said Alfie. 'Didn't they come from different parts of Manchester and Salford?'

'They did,' said Tommy Johnson. 'There were nearly fifty of these gangs, with names like Meadow Lads, Bengal Tigers, Beswick Scuttlers, and the Greengate Gang. They fought regular pitched battles and sometimes nearly killed each other. So you can see how relieved the people of Manchester are to see the Flags being used for peaceful pursuits like football. Do you know much about the place where you are playing, I wonder?'

'Not a great deal,' said Charlie.

'Well, as you know, the Flags are over the burial ground where forty thousand paupers were buried between seventeen eighty-eight and eighteen sixteen, when it was finally closed. The ground was unpaved for nearly forty years until the flagstones were laid over them. That's how it got the name of St Michael's Flags or simply the Flags.'

'I often wondered about that,' Duggie said, 'for I couldn't see any flags like the Union Jack flying from no flagpole.'

'Before they put the flags over the bodies,' Mr Johnson continued, 'the place was nothing more than an open cesspit, a dumping ground that spread the most terrible diseases like cholera, and there were rats and other vermin running freely about the place. It's not so long ago that the bones of the dead would come to the top and it was not unknown for a human skull to be kicked around as a football.'

'Thank the Lord it's not as bad as that nowadays,' I said. 'But it's quite a thought that when we play football we're playing over the bodies of forty thousand corpses.'

'Is the place haunted?' asked Gordon, aghast.

'I doubt it,' replied Tommy Johnson, 'but who knows? Some local people say they've seen apparitions of angels who've been sent to guard the thousands of infants buried here.'

Our little gang listened to Mr Johnson's descriptions with awe.

'What did they all die of?' Jimmy asked.

'From dysentery, cholera, smallpox, diphtheria and goodness knows what else. But the Flags cover the bodies of the very poor, the paupers, who couldn't afford any kind of stone to record their graves. The cemetery around St Michael and All Angels Church – where this shed is located – is quite different, for it houses the bodies of the better-off who had the wherewithal to buy gravestones, some of them quite elaborate. If you get any spare time, you might find the inscriptions on the headstones interesting to look at.'

The following Saturday, Mr Johnson came over to the football pitch with five new players to join our game. They were a friendly lot if a bit anxious-looking, which was understandable, I suppose, since many of them had had rough lives – broken homes and so on. Mr Johnson also brought with him a new football and some exciting news.

'I've been doing some checking around,' he informed us, 'and you may be interested to learn that there is a league of teams like your own being formed. It will include clubs like the Ardwick Lads' Club and the Salford Lads' Club plus a few streets such as Livesey Street, Monsall Street and others that have formed teams like your own. Here's the address of the man who's organizing it and I'm sure if you write to him, he'll be able to give you details of fixtures and rules for joining.'

'That sounds great,' said Jimmy, 'but won't it require us to stump up some cash? If it does, that means we're out 'cos none of us has any money.'

Tommy Johnson smiled. 'I think you'll find that Manchester City Council is eager to promote the league and may provide you with a grant for kit to get you started. I'll try and pull a few strings for you and, if it comes off for you, we have a teacher at the school who says he'd be willing to act as referee for some of your games.'

And that's how our little football team got started. We had a meeting that afternoon in our hut and I was elected as secretary and given the job of writing to the league organizer.

'Ta very much,' I said. 'If there's any work to be done, give it to Joe Muggins here.'

'You're the only one around here who can write,' said Charlie.

Setting up the team officially with Manchester City Council was not as straightforward as I'd hoped. I needed two rate-paying sponsors to support our application. The first was easy as Tommy Johnson was more than willing to support us. Finding the second was the snag. It was Jimmy who came up with the solution. On cold winter days we had taken to retiring after a game to Franco Rocca's ice-cream parlour on Great Ancoats Street not only for drinks of hot Vimto but also because he had a coke fire in the shop. Franco was Angela's uncle and since Jimmy was knocking about with Angela, it was an easy matter for Jimmy to persuade him. Franco not only sponsored us but supplied football boots to those players who couldn't afford them.

After press-ganging me into the job of secretary, we elected Alfie as team captain as it was agreed he was the best footballer. Finally, after a great deal of argument and discussion, we chose a name for our team 'cos William's Whingers didn't seem right somehow and, apart from that, we now had players who were from Charter Street. We kicked a lot of suggestions into touch, like William Wanderers and the Ludgate Hill Lads. It was Gordon, our Holy Joe, who came up with the name we liked best.

'Look he said, 'our hut is in the cemetery of St Michael's and he's known as the Archangel. Why not call ourselves the Archangels?'

As soon as we heard it, we knew that was the name for us and it was adopted without argument. As instructed, I wrote to the league organizer and soon had a list of fixtures which kept us occupied on most Saturday afternoons during the football season. Furthermore, the City

Council, anxious to avoid a repetition of the scuttler wars that had given our town such a bad name, awarded us a small grant towards the cost of football outfits, mainly shirts and shorts.

On free Saturday afternoons we managed to see our favourite Manchester teams in action. Some of the lads, especially those from Gorton and Ardwick, favoured the newly titled Manchester City and went to watch their matches at the Hyde Road ground. Of course they reckoned their team was not only the greatest on the planet but that the captain, Billy Meredith, was the most stupendous man who'd ever graced the earth. Alfie and Duggie were the fiercest City supporters.

The other lads, mainly from the Clayton and Newton Heath districts, claimed that nothing could compare with their Manchester United and that their captain, Charlie Roberts, was greater than Generals Gordon and Kitchener rolled into one. At times when we, the Archangels, were trying to establish ourselves as a team, the rival supporters nearly came to blows and I had to remind them we were playing on the same team. I could never understand the enmity between the two sets of supporters because I was proud of both teams as they represented our city of Manchester which, of course, after London and Paris, was the most civilized place in the world.

So that was how we spent our Saturday afternoons but even when there was no football, we found plenty of things to do and I cannot ever remember a time when we were bored. One sunny afternoon we took up Tommy Johnson's suggestion about looking at the grave inscriptions in the upper cemetery where the well-to-do were buried. The churchyard had been closed to further burials in 1854 but there remained many fascinating gravestones. We decided to set up a competition among our little gang to see who could find the most unusual inscription as judged by majority vote, first prize to be a packet of Player's Weights cigarettes, paid for by the losers, of course. Notebooks in hand we scattered around the graveyard on the lookout for interesting epitaphs, arranging to meet after an hour to report back.

I must confess I found it an extremely cheerless business going round the gravestones reading the various things that people had written about their loved ones who had been snatched from them. It brought back so many unhappy memories of the sad things that had happened in my own life: the untimely deaths of both my parents, the tragedies of Herbert Lamb who'd died drinking carbolic acid, and Josie O'Gara whose dress had caught fire, Kenny Bogg crushed under a wall, and more recently the agonizing death of our donkey, Crusty, that I'd become so fond of. I couldn't help wondering what would be written as my own epitaph when the Grim Reaper called. I wouldn't want poetry carved on *my* headstone. It would have to be brief and to the point. Maybe something humorous like: 'Here lies Tommy Hopkins, aged 105. Shot by a jealous husband.'

Or maybe a little more serious such as: 'Did his best at each task, so what more can you ask?'

Or on an even more serious note, considering

all the rotten things that had happened in my life: 'Now no fear of the morrow, for he's safe from all sorrow.'

I forced myself to snap out of this black mood and cheer up. After all, this was supposed to be a light-hearted way of passing an hour or two, not a time for giving in to miserable thoughts like this.

A little later in the afternoon, we got back together in the shed to compare notes and found that we'd gathered an impressive collection of inscriptions.

'Did you notice,' said Jimmy, 'the big difference between inscriptions for men and those for women? The man is always listed first in the family even if he died last and his name is always in bigger letters.'

'As for me,' said Gordon, 'I was shocked by how many young kids are buried here, some only a few months old. There must be thousands of 'em. One grave I saw had twelve babies from the one family; they'd died one after the other in quick succession.'

'And did you see,' added Alfie, 'how many people died in great pain? I lost count of how many times I read, "Lo the pain of life is past" and "Peace at last after agonies bravely borne".'

'Very interesting and all that,' Alfie said impatiently, 'but what's your unusual inscription for this here competition we're suppose to be holding?'

'All right, keep your shirt on, Alfie,' Gordon retorted. 'On the gravestone I've picked, it said:

Happy infants, early blest!
Rest, in peaceful slumbers, rest.'

'I can beat that,' I said, consulting my notebook.
'How about this?

Come near, my friends, and cast an eye;
Then go your way, prepare to die.
Learn here your doom, and know you must
One day like me be turned to dust.'

'Huh, cheerful, I must say!' Alfie replied.
'I've got one of those "prepare to meet thy
doom" ones as well,' Jimmy said, 'reminding us
that we're all going to snuff it someday. Here it is:

On these lines do cast an eye
As you are now, so once was I
As I am now, so must you be
Prepare for death and follow me.'

Alfie laughed. 'It's all very well, saying "follow
me" but he didn't say where he'd gone, did he?
Now I think I've found the most unusual one.
Mine reads:

Grim death took him without any warning
He was well last night but dead this morning.'

'Not bad,' Charlie said, in that self-satisfied tone
of voice we all detested, 'but I think the ones
we've had so far are too miserable and depressing.
Mine's not only more cheerful but funny. Listen
to this.' He read from his notes:

301

'Lived his days in stress and worry
Rushed through life in a hurry
He had no time to smell the roses,
Now he feeds them as he decomposes.'

It was no competition. Charlie was awarded the prize and was given the fags which he thrust in his pocket without offering us one of them. The selfish bastard, we thought.

One form of entertainment that was becoming popular around this time was the cinema. Our little gang had attended one or two performances of films made by a couple of Frenchmen called the Lumière brothers. While at first we gasped in amazement at the idea of moving pictures, they never lasted more than a minute or two and we never thought much of the subjects on offer. One was called *Watering the Gardener*, a comedy in which a passer-by accidentally steps on to a hosepipe and when the gardener looks down the nozzle to see what's gone wrong, he gets a jet of water in his face; another was about a train arriving at a station, and a third showed a baby having its breakfast. The films did get better after a time, for example one called *Mary Jane's Mishap* telling the story about a girl who dies in an explosion and returns as a ghost to haunt those who are being warned against repeating her stupidity.

Another, titled *The Great Train Robbery*, was quite good but still very short.

We preferred by far going to the music halls to

302

see blood and thunder melodramas like *The Face at the Window*, *The Ticket of Leave Man*, and our favourite, *Sweeney Todd, the Demon Barber of Fleet Street*. The theatres were always packed out at the weekends with rowdy spectators who had come to take an active part. The more murders the better, but our main enjoyment was joining in with our comments. The dramas usually featured characters who were more or less the same in each play. There was always: a handsome hero with a name like Hector, a moustache-twirling villain called Jasper, a beautiful damsel in distress named Angelina, an old lady or man, and a comic character of either sex. The plots were simple, involving an innocent hero who's tricked by the cunning villain until fate intervenes and good triumphs over evil. The villain dies a hideous death and our hero gets the girl.

Some serious newspaper writers were worried that witnessing horrible murders and blood-curling deeds on the stage was dangerous and might result in us young people imitating the violence in the back streets of Manchester. How wrong they were! We never took these plays seriously and regarded them as one big joke, like a pantomime. In the middle of a melodramatic scene, a voice was likely to call out: 'Look out! He's behind you!'

Our greatest pleasure was pitching in and shouting out comments which were supposed to be funny. Sometimes they were; sometimes not. For us, the story wasn't very important; the play was a kind of safety valve, allowing us to let off steam and giving us the chance to show our feelings about the characters. And *how* we showed what we thought of them as soon as they appeared on stage!

When an evil face appeared at the window in *The Face at the Window*, someone bawled, 'It looks like our window-cleaner.'

'It probably *is* your window-cleaner working overtime,' a voice replied.

In *Sweeney Todd, the Evil Barber of Fleet Street*, Sweeney invited the customer into his shop with, 'How about a nice shave, sir? I can guarantee the closest shave you'll ever know. Sit down in the chair here, sir...'

'...I'll soon polish you off, sir,' a hundred voices finished with him.

One Friday night our gang of six handed over our tuppences for seats in the gods at the St James's Theatre on Oxford Street and settled down to take part in the evening's entertainment. There were usually two plays on offer: one a short performance by way of introduction to set the mood and warm up the audience, as well as giving latecomers time to settle into their seats. This was followed by the main feature. This night the show opened with a play entitled *Pay the Rent or Else*.

The lights dimmed and there was the sound of a violent storm with thunder and flashes of lightning off-stage. The curtain opened slowly to reveal the bedroom of a very poor family. In the bed was an old lady who was obviously very ill, as revealed by her rasping cough.

'You want to get something for that cough, darlin',' someone cried out. 'Try Scott's Emulsion!' The someone was our Alfie.

Charlie had to say his piece of course. 'It wasn't the cough that carried her off,' he shouted.

'It was the coffin they carried her off in!' cried the audience in unison.

Next on stage was the lovely heroine, Angelina, with her long flowing locks and wearing a beautiful silk dress. Her appearance was greeted with loud whistles and a few bawdy comments, such as, 'Show us your legs, luv.'

There's a loud knock at the door.

'It's the rent man, Mother,' says Angelina. 'We must pay the rent.'

'We can't pay,' says the mother. 'We have no money.'

'Then put it on tick,' calls a spectator.

'What shall we do?' cries the daughter.

'Better open the bloody door, luv,' calls a voice, 'before the rent man knocks it down.'

The door is opened at last and a gust of wind and snow blows in. There is a blizzard outside and we know that this is where the mother and daughter must go if they do not stump up with the rent.

Enter Jasper Hawkins, the landlord. This was the signal for the audience to raise the roof with loud catcalls, booing, and hissing, together with a hail of over-ripe tomatoes and rotten cabbages. Our little group was of course well supplied with these missiles.

'And now,' hissed the villain, 'I go to find and ravish the maiden.'

'Oh, no, you won't,' cried Duggie.

Stepping out of character, the villain replied,

305

'Oh, yes, I will.'

'Oh, no, you won't!' roared the audience.

And so the play proceeded with full audience participation to the bitter end when the hero leaps on to the stage and saves the damsel from the wicked clutches of Jasper. Once again good triumphed over evil, as it did every week. I found it hard to see how such a play could corrupt young people and turn them into ruffians.

Chapter Twenty-Seven

On the Sunday after the visit to the music hall, I attended nine o'clock Mass at St Chad's as usual, not so much because I was a Holy Joe but more because I always associated the church with those happy days when I used to go with my mam and dad. After Mass, I visited the stables to give Clancy a thorough grooming and to give him my weekly talk.

'You've worked so hard this week, old son,' I'd say as I brushed his coat. 'Time to give you a little break from pulling those heavy loads of fruit and veg about the place. One day, you'll be able to retire and take things easy and spend your days in a lovely field with lots of other donkeys, you'll see.'

Then I led him to the meadow on Barney's where there was sweet, lush grass and where he could run free without the encumbrance of having to pull a cart. How he enjoyed his freedom, jumping and leaping about like a young two-year-old colt!

After I'd settled him back in his stable with enough feed and water, I made my way to the Flags where there were usually five or six schools of pitch and toss in progress on most Sunday afternoons. Brodie had raised my pay to eight shillings a week and I was very grateful to him for that, but the wage simply wasn't enough to manage on. I was no spendthrift but the cost of buying a daily morning snack of tea and toast, the occasional dinner plus the fact that I smoked five Player's Weights a day meant I was constantly short of the readies. Add to that the need to buy every now and then replacement clothes like a shirt or a pair of boots and I found it impossible to make ends meet. Last night's visit to the music hall had knocked my finances for six and I had only three shillings to last the rest of the week. And now the football team had been set up, I needed extra cash to buy football gear since I didn't qualify for financial help from the Corporation because I had a job.

I thought I might make a few bob in one or two games of pitch and toss. On these Sunday visits to the Flags, I usually went to Artful Archie's ring because I trusted him and knew I'd get a fair deal. And very important, he had a reliable lookout ready to shout a warning if the rozzers suddenly appeared. I'd never been able to understand why the game was against the law unless it was that some men gambled their wages away, leaving their families destitute.

I joined Archie's little school which had half a

dozen men gathered round.

'Are you on, Tommy?' Archie asked.

'I am, Archie,' I replied. 'What's the limit?'

'No limit, Tommy. Bet whatever you like.'

I reckoned that there was a fifty-fifty chance of winning something and I really was desperate to supplement my wage. When the two pennies were flipped, there were three possible outcomes: 2 heads (the flipper wins), 2 tails (the flipper loses) or 1 head and 1 tail (nobody wins) and the coins are flipped again.

'I'll start by just watching, Archie,' I said.

Two other punters put threepence each on the throw.

Archie placed the two coins tails up on the index and middle finger and flicked them, sending them spinning high into the air.

The first throw resulted in two heads. Archie won.

I watched for two more turns and each time they came down heads. Archie won again. He can't go on winning time after time, I thought. Law of averages, but I won't risk too much. Just a few coppers will do.

'I'll start with twopence, Archie,' I said.

'Last of the big spenders,' Archie replied sarcastically. 'Right, any more for any more?'

A few others joined in. The coins came down head and tails. No winner. Archie threw them again. This time they came down tails. Without any effort, I'd doubled my bet already.

I watched a few more turns and for three consecutive throws, they came down heads. It's bound to be the tails' turn next, I told myself. Why not go for broke? Nothing ventured, nothing gained.

I had three shillings and tuppence left.

'I'll have three shillings on the next throw,' I said, hardly able to believe what I'd just said.

Archie tossed the coins. They came down heads. I'd lost the whole of my worldly wealth in one throw. Archie pocketed the money and I was just wondering whether I should chance my last tuppence when a shout came from the 'dogger-out'.

'Rozzers! Run for it!'

I turned on my heel and dashed for all I was worth towards Irk Street. Right into the arms of a giant policeman.

'Where do you think you're going, my lad?' he said, grabbing me by the collar.

'Home!' I gasped breathlessly.

'And where is home, may I ask?'

I gave him my address and he escorted me by the scruff of the neck along Angel Meadow until we reached our house. He banged on the door which was opened after a long interval by Gran'pa Zeb.

'What the bloody hell's been happening?' Zeb shouted. 'What's this little bastard been up to now?'

'Are you his father?' the copper asked.

'Do I look like his father?' Zeb snapped. 'No, I'm his gran'pa, worse luck. His guardians are out at the moment.'

'Well, this grandson of yours has been nabbed playing pitch and toss on the Flags and it's a very serious offence. I'm going to let him off this time. But if he's caught again, it could be a fine of up to five pounds or a month in jail or both. Make sure you keep an eye on him from now on. As for you, young man,' he said, giving my collar an extra tug, 'don't let me catch you again playing pitch and toss or you're for it.'

With that, he pushed me down the lobby of the house.

'Leave him to me, officer,' Zeb said ominously. 'I'll see to him good and proper.'

After the policeman had departed, Zeb turned on me fiercely.

'You stupid little bastard,' he roared. 'I told you that if ever you were brought home by the police again, I'd teach you a lesson you'd never forget.'

He took the horse whip down from the nail on the wall and took a vicious swipe at me, catching me on the shoulders, sending a searing pain across my back.

'We're a respectable family in this house and you've brought disgrace on us again. I told Brodie not to bring you here in the first place as you'd be nothing but trouble. And I was right. A good belting is what you need and I'm going to see that you get it.'

He raised the whip once more but before he could bring it down on me again, I seized it from his grip and pushed him into his rocking chair.

'That is the last time you'll ever hit me,' I yelled at him. 'I'm not a young kid any more and I've had enough of this. I'll not stop a moment longer in this lousy, rotten, stinking hole of a house.'

I went down to my room in the cellar and gathered up my things such as they were: a couple of shirts, a towel, my overalls, my cap, my football kit, and a few odds and ends. The twenty fags I'd been saving for the rest of the week had gone and it wasn't too hard to work out what had happened to them. Zeb's light-fingered touch at work. Again. I packed what was left of my stuff into a bag and slung it over my shoulder.

'Tell Brodie and Dorothy when they come in from the pub that I've gone to stay at the stables and will be living there from now on. I'll be at the market as usual in the morning.'

I stalked off and, if truth be told, I didn't know what I was going to do or what was to become of me. I was sixteen years of age, had no money, but I felt I'd had enough of living in that cellar and suffering from Zeb's cruelty and his pilfering of my belongings.

I walked over to the stables and let myself in. The other donkey lads immediately came to my assistance. They lived above the donkey stalls and were very comfortable and self-sufficient with a large kitchen equipped with a small cooker, a couple of gas rings and a big cold-water slop stone. They even had facilities for washing and ironing their clothes. They listened to my tale of woe and then made me a meal of two boiled eggs, toast and a pot of tea.

I lay down that night in the stable with my head on Clancy's rump. So it had come to this! I wondered what my mam and dad would've said if they could have seen me with my unusual four-legged bedfellow. I'm sure this is not what they meant when they said that some day I would find a suitable life companion. I lay awake in these strange quarters for a couple of hours and took stock of my situation. I didn't want to go back to live in that cellar on Angel Meadow. I'd had my fill of Zeb and his violent ways. He was permanently high on laudanum or gin or a combination of the two. Brodie and Dorothy had been generous in taking me in when my mam had died and, in many ways, I was sorry to be walking out on them. They both worked hard in the market but, on the other hand, they too were half-drunk much of the time. They spent most of their spare time in the Turk's Head on Shudehill. No wonder they were always short of money. My wage of eight shillings a week just wasn't enough to manage on. But I couldn't see any prospect of a raise in pay as long as they spent every day trying to drink the brewery dry. No, it was time to think about a complete break and a new start. I'd be really sorry to leave Clancy, of course, as I had developed strong affection for him and thought of him as a good friend. But that's life, I said to myself.

Next morning in the market I met Brodie and Dorothy and confirmed what Zeb would have told them, that I'd be leaving and looking for a new job and that maybe they should start searching for my replacement.

'I'm not happy to hear that, Tommy,' Brodie said, 'but I can't see any way that I can increase your wage as the business isn't doing so well, specially now that we have two donkeys to feed.'

I thought to myself: You mean it isn't making enough money to cover the cost of sixty pints of beer and thirty Guinnesses a week. Instead, I simply said, 'I understand, Brodie, and I shall never be able to thank you and Dorothy enough for all you have done for me, taking me in and all that. If it weren't for you two, I might have ended up on the streets and then it'd have been all up with me.'

Aunty Dorothy seemed more upset than Brodie that I would be leaving.

'When our Mary died and we took you on, Tommy, I never for a moment imagined that Zeb would behave towards you as he has. I can well understand how you feel and I am so sorry that things didn't work out between the two of you. I only wish I could have done more for you. If only we'd been richer, we'd never have torn up that apprenticeship form with the Royce Company. But remember, Tommy, that you're always welcome to come back and we'll keep a bed warm for you in the cellar in case you ever do.'

I never did go back to live in Angel Meadow but spent the whole of my time away sleeping in the stables cuddled up to the donkey and making full use of the kitchen and washing facilities over the stables. I'd have been perfectly content to tick over like this forever but I was stopped short in my tracks one morning when Dorothy met me in the market and said, 'Tommy, it's time you took a bath. You are beginning to smell like a donkey. God knows what your mam would've said if she'd been alive. Next thing you know, you'll be looking like one of them gypsies that never washes from one year to the next!'

'Thanks a lot for that, Aunty Dorothy. Good of you to tell me,' I said sarcastically.

She was right of course and the message hit

home. I realized that it was time I started giving some attention to personal hygiene, especially as me and the lads were becoming interested in girls, though it had got no further than talking about them in our gang hut.

'Tommy here won't be interested in girls,' Charlie scoffed. 'He lives with his donkey friend, Clancy. So he's already in a stable relationship.'

The gang guffawed at Charlie's wit.

'Not funny,' I answered, unable to hide my own chuckle.

Corrective action was called for and I began going every Friday night to Osborne Street baths where I shared a hot slipper bath with several other men. I followed this by swimming a few lengths in the plunge and I emerged from the baths feeling like a new man.

Meanwhile I was still scouting around in the market looking for a job. As was usual when I had a problem, I ended up talking to my good friend and mentor, Joe Brannan.

'Leave it with me, Tommy,' he said, 'and I'll ask around. You've proved to be a hard worker and you've got to know the market well. I'm sure most stallholders would be glad of someone like you. As soon as a suitable job turns up, I'll give you the nod and I'll be happy to recommend you.'

It was three months before anything did turn up and it was on Deakin's stall. I was overjoyed for it meant I'd be working with Joe Brannan and a team of people I'd got to know on my daily rounds. Meanwhile, Brodie found another young lad called Dan, fresh from school, to take my place at work, my room in the cellar, and at the paltry wage of five shillings he'd once paid me. I spent a few days showing him the ropes and getting Clancy and him used to each other. He was an intelligent lad and soon picked up the routine. It would be a painful parting when the time finally came to say goodbye to Clancy. But maybe it wouldn't be as bad as it seemed because I'd be seeing Clancy every day in the market when Dan collected produce from our stall. I would still be able to pat his head and give him a carrot. I mean Clancy, of course, not Dan.

In many ways, working on Deakin's stall meant a step up the social ladder, I suppose. For a start, I'd be wearing a white coat instead of the old togs that carters were accustomed to going around in, and the wage was higher at twelve shillings a week. The work involved being present on the stall to check deliveries of produce coming in from all over the world, my job being to make sure that delivery notes tallied with the amounts that came off the carts. Later that day, I checked the stuff against invoices as retailers arranged for collection of their orders through carters, such as Brodie, and porters like Mad Alec and Slug Bullock. Though the hours were much longer, the job meant more responsibility since it was open to dishonest practices. Slug approached me one day with Ginger McDermott and Mick Malone in tow.

'What about slinging an extra crate of apples on to my cart, Tommy?' he said, giving me a broad wink. 'I'll split the profit on it with you. If you do a bit each day, it'll add to your wages as I know you don't earn all that much as a checker.'

'Nothing doing, Slug,' I answered right away. 'It's more than my job's worth and I've only just started.'

'Aw, c'mon, Tommy,' he urged. 'Everybody's doing it.'

'No way, Slug. I'm not everybody. What about Bert O'Neil, the copper? He's got his eyes skinned for pilfering like that and he'll have you as soon as look at you.'

I found that this petty pilfering went on all round the market and even Brodie suggested it to me.

'No one'll ever know, Tommy,' he whispered one morning. 'It's standard practice and one of the perks of the job. How do you think we make a profit?'

But I was firm in my refusal. I didn't claim to be a saint but stealing went against the grain, especially since Deakin had given me this chance to better myself.

I still had the problem of finding a place to live as obviously I couldn't go on living in a stable, especially if I was going to be accused of smelling like a donkey. But where could I go? It was Charlie who came to my rescue.

'Look, Tommy,' he said one day as I went past Deakin's stall. 'One of the lads on our stall, Willie Ingrams, said his mother sometimes takes in lodgers and could offer you a bed at their house if you like. They live in Style Street, only a short walk from the market.'

I liked the sound of that. I could tell people I was living in 'Style'.

'I'm interested. Tell me more, Charlie,' I said.

'It's like this, Tommy,' said Willie when I met

him. 'My dad had a blazing row with my mam a few months ago. He walked out on us and we've heard that he's now living with another woman somewhere up Miles Platting way. There's just me and my mam and my three little brothers. You could share my big double bed and my mam would look after you. A paying lodger would be a great help since my family has only my wage to live on.'

As an only child, I'd never had to share a bed with anyone before but it seemed to be common practice in big working-class families, and life with a normal family sounded like something I'd been looking for.

'What would I have to pay, Willie? I asked.

'Say three bob a week for board and lodgings. How does that grab you, Tommy?

'That'll be great, Willie. I accept.'

The arrangement should work out well, I thought, because Willie and I shared the problem of most market workers, that of getting enough sleep, given our unusual working hours. We worked a twelve-hour day from midnight to mid-day. So we both needed to get our shut-eye in the afternoons.

The next day I turned up at his house around 1 p.m. Willie had been at home for an hour or so and had already had his dinner.

I should have been aware what to expect even before I entered the house for it stood out like a sore thumb, being the only one on the street that did not have donkey-stoned pavement flags in front of the house. Just the same I was taken aback when I actually went inside. I always thought families like ours had been hard done by when living in Angel Meadow but the Ingrams were so deprived, they brought back memories in so many ways of poor Kenny Bogg's family in Hannah Street. Uncle Brodie and Aunty Dorothy were rich by comparison. At the Ingrams' front windows hung dirty torn curtains, while the back windows were covered with cardboard. The only floor coverings were a few hessian sacks strewn about the bare wooden boards. Orange boxes were their furniture and their table was a large upturned crate which I recognized had once belonged to Edward Farrand & Co., a well-known market dealer.

Despite this extreme poverty Willie was still able to pull a joke out of the hat when he said to his little brother, 'Look, our Sammy, you've spilled your tea on the clean tablecloth and I haven't read it yet.'

The *Manchester Evening News* was their table cover and on the flat surface were several jam jars which obviously served as their crockery. It took strong facial control to hide my feelings of revulsion. I sat at the table on one of the boxes while the three little boys, their noses running in snot, stared at me as if I were something from a zoo.

'We've already had our dinner,' said Mrs Ingrams. 'We had fried bacon and cheese. Will I fry you some, Tommy?'

'Sounds like a good idea, Mrs Ingrams,' I said heartily.

Then I saw the dog licking the frying pan on the stove and I suddenly had a change of mind.

'I don't want to put you to any trouble, Mrs Ingrams,' I said quickly. 'A cheese sandwich will do fine.'

'Are you sure, Tommy? It's no trouble.'

'Sure, Mrs Ingrams. I had a snack at Fred's Café in the market just before I left.'

I ate my sandwich at the table watched by the three young lads who eyed every mouthful. I had the impression that they hadn't had anything that dinnertime.

As agreed, Willie and I shared the big double bed in an upstairs bedroom while Mrs Ingrams had the other room with the youngest lad who was no more than a year old. The other two slept top and tail on a mattress on the floor in the cellar.

Even this would have worked out fine but unfortunately the house, the wallpaper, and the mattresses were infested with bugs, a common problem in that part of the world as little Herbert Lamb had so tragically found out all those years ago. The result was that it wasn't easy to get even a few hours' sleep because of insect bites. Once again Willie revealed a sense of humour even under such trying conditions.

'Pull the bed away from the wall,' his mother shouted up to him when he complained about the bugs.

'I have,' he replied, 'but they keep pushing it back again.'

We found the best way to get away from the pests was to forget the mattress and sleep on the hard wooden floor. We got used to it and managed a few hours' rest but it was far from ideal. In addition to the bug problem, the three youngsters were normal lively little boys and couldn't be expected to go about on tiptoe. Often they rushed about the place, yelling and screaming with excitement in one of their games, with the result that I was nearly always tired and drowsy. Not a good condition to be in if I were to do my job properly and remain alert at two o'clock in the morning when checking newly arrived consignments at the stall.

After three weeks or so, I decided to leave the Ingrams and started looking for new accommodation. Finding fresh digs, though, wasn't as easy as I thought and I remained an unwilling lodger for longer than I'd hoped. Occasionally I even spent a night at the stables with the donkey boys, talking and laughing about some of the weird market characters, like Mad Alec or Slug Bullock. I had to admit, too, that I'd been missing the satisfaction of working with Clancy and of dealing directly with greengrocers who'd always been so appreciative when I delivered their orders to their shops. They'd usually rewarded me with an item of fish or fruit for my 'swinger' on the cart. Sometimes I went to visit Clancy on Sundays to take him for a run on Barney's meadows as it always gave me a kick (not literally, of course) to see him galloping happily around the field.

Chapter Twenty-Eight

I continued to go swimming at the Osborne Street baths as those remarks about me smelling like a donkey still rankled and, as I said earlier, our little gang of six were becoming interested in girls, not that we knew much about them or had any experience of them. On wet Sunday afternoons, we met in our little hut to chew the fat and to talk about things that interested young men the world over: jobs, football, girls, sex.

On one occasion, we quizzed Jimmy about his big job at Henry Royce and Company and I have to confess to a feeling of envy. After all, I'd been given the offer of a place there too and, had it not been for Brodie, would have been working alongside him. How differently my life would have turned out, but it was no use crying over what might have been.

'So what is it you do over there in Hulme, apart from sitting around drinking tea?' I asked.

'Big plans are afoot,' Jimmy said. 'I thought when I joined the company that I'd be doing mainly electrical engineering but we now spend more time on developing a car engine.'

'Do you really think this horseless carriage rubbish will ever amount to anything?' Charlie asked.

'I'm sure it will,' Jimmy replied warmly. 'One day horses will be seen only in the history books or as curiosities in the zoo. Everyone will travel in motorized transport of one kind or another. It used to be that cars could only travel at four miles an hour and had to be preceded by a man with a red flag. Now cars are allowed to travel at twenty m.p.h. although it has to be admitted on the quiet that many travel much faster than that. It's said that one racing driver got up to ninety m.p.h.'

'Come off it, Jimmy,' Charlie said. 'That speed would take a man's head off.'

'From what I've heard,' I said, 'cars will never be fully accepted. They raise clouds of dust everywhere that gets in people's eyes and noses. Not only that, they shake and rattle and make one hell of a noise. Sometimes drivers have to push them up steep hills and one journalist advises always having a bicycle strapped to the back just in case. They're just a music hall joke and even the cartoonists in *Punch* are poking fun at them.'

'But motor cars will get better and better, you'll see,' argued Jimmy, getting hot under the collar. 'Why, even King Edward drives a twelve horse-power Daimler, though I believe he gets furious if anyone tries to overtake him. And then there's the annual London to Brighton run and everyone now accepts that. There are already horseless buses running in London. As for the dust, that's because we don't have proper roads yet but they'll come. More and more people are buying cars and there are lots of new makes coming on the market, like those from the Benz factory in Germany, the De Dion Bouton from France, the Model T Ford from America, and in this country we have the Lanchester, Austin and Morris. We may join forces with a man called Charles Rolls to produce our own Manchester car. Now that would be something.'

Charlie remarked, 'Cars might be all right for ladies who are brave enough to go out in one and don't have the strength in their legs to ride a bicycle.'

'My big worry,' Alfie said, 'is that although cars will never take the place of the horse, they might ruin the bike trade just as I'm thinking of buying one.'

'In my opinion,' Duggie said, 'cars are nasty; noisy, smelly things. Just annoying playthings for cigar-smoking toffs. They'll never replace the horse, not in a million years.'

'And as for the idea of women driving about in these things,' Gordon said, anxious to say his piece, 'it doesn't bear thinking about. It's immoral and it's...'

'Disgusting!' we all chorused.

Our shed meetings weren't always as serious as this and we often spent our time swapping gags – occasionally of the dirty variety but not always. Those they told were usually pretty corny.

For example, Alfie said, 'My girlfriend said, "Why don't you come over to our house tonight. There'll be nobody in." I thought, I'm on a winner here. So I went over and she was right. There *was* nobody in!'

'Here's one with a market flavour that I heard on our stall,' said Charlie. 'A man goes to the doctor's with a banana in his right ear, a carrot in his left ear, and a cucumber up his nose. "What do you think's wrong with me, Doctor?" he asks. "Easy," says the doctor. "You're not eating properly".'

I did warn you that the jokes were pretty awful.

'Anybody fancy cruising down Oldham Street tonight?' Charlie asked one evening. 'You never know, we might pick up something.'

'Yeah, a nasty disease,' Alfie said, quick as a flash.

On Sunday nights, droves of young lads and lasses promenaded up and down Oldham Street and Market Street flirting and making suggestive comments to each other. The girls, mainly mill workers, always stuck together, for protection I suppose, as they strutted along the pavement singing bawdy versions of songs like 'Sweet Rosie O'Grady' and 'She's a Lass from Lancashire'. Arm in arm and dressed in their garishly-coloured coats, they flaunted themselves on parade before the gangs of lads on the other side of the road going in the opposite direction.

'Any of you girls fancy meeting up with a likely lad for a bit?' Charlie called out to a passing group.

'A bit of what?' the more forward of the girls shrieked.

'Depends on what you fancy, lass,' Charlie answered. 'Satisfaction guaranteed. All shapes and sizes on offer, darlin'. You know what they say: "A little bit of what you fancy does you good".'

The girls squealed in mock horror and disgust.

'You don't half fancy yourself, don't you?' another girl called across. 'What have you got that I would fancy?'

'Why not come over and sample the goods?' Charlie replied.

'Go home to your mam and have your nappies changed,' added her female companion.

Always keen to have the last word, Charlie shouted back, 'Why not come over here and do it for me, love?'

And so the exchange of suggestive banter continued. As usual, that was as far as it got, though occasionally one of the more daring lads would cross over to the girls, tear off a bonnet or a shawl and run off with it.

'Those girls are not my type,' I remarked one afternoon in the shed.

'Type? Type!' Charlie exclaimed. 'Lads like us can't afford no types. We have to take what we can get. Anyroad, what *is* your type?'

'I dunno,' I said, 'but certainly not one of those girls on Oldham Street. They're too common for my liking.'

'Too common? What's that mean?' Charlie persisted.

'Too noisy and brash for a start. Their screechy voices go right through me and they've no manners. They're coarse and not a bit ladylike. And their faces are plastered in thick make-up and some of them even paint their nails bright red. Why, I've even seen some of 'em eating fish and chips out of newspaper in the street. Now the sort of girl I'd go for would be quieter and more refined. She'd be good-looking and have a friendly, kind face.'

'Me, I go for the glamorous, curvaceous type with an hour-glass figure like Marie Lloyd or one of the Gibson Girls,' Alfie replied.

'Have you ever thought what women with the hour-glass figures have to suffer getting into those tight corsets?' remarked Jimmy. 'The corsets are like body crushers straight out of a medieval torture chamber.'

'They must think it's worth it,' Charlie said, 'otherwise they wouldn't do it. Their idea is to attract the men's attention 'cos they're aware that the first thing men look at is their figure. I know that the face isn't the first thing *I* look at.'

'I suppose you look at the bosom,' commented Gordon. 'I don't know why we men are so interested in a woman's chest. Maybe it's to check that she's got one but they all have two breasts, one on each side. So what's the big attraction? Beats me.'

'Maybe men look at the breasts first 'cos they were weaned too early,' said Charlie. 'Anyroad, who cares about the face? Isn't there a saying somewhere? Something about not looking at the mantelpiece?'

No one recognized the reference or knew what he was talking about.

I felt it was time to air my views on the subject. 'My mother always said beauty comes from within and is not just the outside shell. My mam and dad weren't bad looking, they were no oil paintings or anything like that but they not only adored each other, they were also great friends. Always kind and both with a great sense of humour. If either of them felt depressed, they would cheer each other up. Those are the things that really matter, not just being glamorous or good-looking.'

'Give me a Gibson Girl any day of the week,' Charlie replied.

'Supposing you marry one of these charmers,' I said, warming to the subject. 'What if she turns out to be a nasty piece of work, bad-tempered, selfish and thinks only of herself. Maybe she'll always be looking in the mirror, going on about what she looks like and what she's going to wear, what then? Remember, if you marry one of these dazzlers, you may have to live with her for forty years or more. She may not look so good after all that time.'

Duggie joined the argument. 'The kind of girl I'd like to have is one who is strong-willed, knows what she wants, and goes out to get it. Doesn't dither and doesn't mess about.'

'I read somewhere,' Jimmy said, 'that when a man chooses a girlfriend, he is really looking for his mother or at least someone like her to replace her.'

'That's rubbish,' Alfie said. 'I mean to say, my mother doesn't look a bit like Marie Lloyd. I only wish she did.'

'I don't know why there's such fuss about Marie Lloyd,' Charlie said. 'I once went to see her at the Grand and there was nothing to see. She kicked up her legs but she had so many silk petticoats underneath, I couldn't see nothing. Not even her drawers or even if she had any legs at all.'

'But you said she kicked up her legs!' exclaimed Gordon. 'That's disgusting. Why, we even cover up the legs on the furniture to avoid giving scandal, so the very idea of women displaying their limbs is going a bit too far. I don't know what the

327

world is coming to, I really don't.'

'Who'd want Marie Lloyd as his mam?' I said, taking up Alfie's argument. 'And anyroad, would you fancy a Marie Lloyd lookalike sitting at your breakfast table when she's old and grey?'

'You are an old misery, Tommy,' said Charlie. 'If you're looking for someone quiet and refined, then you're looking in the wrong places. Maybe you should be looking in a convent or an upper-class drawing room to find that kind of girl.'

'Here,' said Jimmy. 'Talking of upper class, you'll never guess what I saw last weekend.'

'Don't tell us you were at a ball at the Victoria Hotel?' Gordon said.

'No, nothing like that. I went with my dad to watch a ladies' football match.'

'Pull the other one,' said Duggie. 'Ladies playing football! Impossible! No such thing. Why, it'd be against the law.'

'But ladies aren't supposed to show their legs or their ankles,' Alfie chuckled. 'Don't tell us they played in them long dresses with corsets and all that. They wouldn't be able to run.'

'Say what you like,' said Jimmy, 'last week, my dad and me went to watch them at Giggs Lane in Bury. The captain was a lady called Nettle Honeyball. About five thousand, mainly men, turned up as spectators.'

The gang exploded in laughter.

'Now we know you're having us on,' I guffawed. 'Nobody but nobody in this world has a name like that. Nettle Honeyball!'

'Laugh all you want,' Jimmy said in even tones, but there were two teams: the Reds against the

Blues, and the Reds won eight to three. Best player on the pitch was a woman called Daisy Allen, playing for the Reds. She should be playing for England on the men's team, if you ask me.'

'Go on then, we'll buy it,' Charlie chortled. 'What were they wearing? Crinoline dresses?'

'No, nothing like that. They wore loose embroidered blouses and knickerbockers with shin pads.'

'That dress would be enough to get all the men excited, a real turn-on,' Alfie commented. 'But I'm against women playing football on principle. They should stick to their own games – netball and lacrosse.'

'I agree with that,' said Charlie, 'but if ever women take up rugby, then count me in. Imagine tackling one of them girls in knickerbockers and bringing her down. Now that would be something.'

'What next!' Gordon exclaimed. 'I wouldn't be surprised if they weren't soon riding bicycles!'

'You're out of date, Gordon.' Jimmy laughed. 'It's already happening. Women have been seen lots of times cycling in Hyde Park wearing their rationals.'

'Rationals?' Gordon asked aghast. 'What are they, in God's name?'

'A sort of two-piece costume with culottes or whatever they're called, allowing their legs to move on the pedals.'

'You mean you can actually see their legs! That's disgusting,' Gordon said. 'Such loose women should be locked up.'

'Quite right. Absolutely disgusting,' agreed

Charlie. 'How far is it then to this Hyde Park place?'

We knew little about girls but when it came to sex, we knew even less and some of the gang held some very strange ideas on the subject. I suppose it was understandable in many ways, for our only instruction had been by Mr Sullivan when he'd warned us about touching ourselves. I think we were more worried by the topic than we were entertained by spicy conversation about it. Take the subject of how babies were conceived. In this regard, I think Gordon and Duggie had the weirdest notions.

'I think babies are made simply by a boy and a girl sleeping together,' Gordon said one day.

'Where did you get that idea?' Alfie asked.

'I read it in a Sunday newspaper. In a court case, it said, "The accused slept with the female defendant and a child was conceived".'

That had Duggie worried. 'In our house I used to sleep with my sister, top and tail, as we had only the one bed. Does that mean my sister might have my baby?'

'I'm bloody sure there's nowt to be worried about.' Alfie laughed. 'Why, I've often slept with my brothers and I'm sure they're not going to conceive because of that. I'm sure there's more to it than that. I've been told that a baby is made when the urine of a man is mixed with that of a woman and the woman then drinks the mixture.'

'That's the biggest load of rubbish I've heard in a long time!' Charlie exclaimed. 'Where did you get that from, for God's sake?'

'A fellah on the fish market told me,' replied Alfie.

'I wouldn't believe all that the older market men tell you,' Charlie said. 'They're just having you on. Now we have a man on Holbrook's stall called Jake Duckworth, he's thirty years old and he's read books like the *Kama Sutra* on the subject, so he should know what he's talking about. He says a baby is made when a man puts his *yang* into a woman's *yin*.'

'What's a yang?' Duggie asked.

'I think it's an Indian word meaning a penis,' said Jimmy 'Brains' Dixon in answer.

'I always thought a penis was someone who played the piano,' Duggie said innocently.

'Anyroad,' Charlie continued, 'the man and the woman then get an orgasm.'

'An orgasm!' echoed Gordon. 'What use is a musical instrument if they don't know how to read music or how to play it?'

'Look,' said Charlie, 'I'm only telling you what he told me. After the man has passed on his life force, a baby grows in the woman's stomach.'

'I think I like the theory about drinking the mixed urine better,' said Gordon. 'But if a baby grows inside the woman, how do they get it out, I'd like to know.'

Charlie was stumped. 'I dunno the answer to that. Jake didn't tell me but I'll ask him tomorrow when I see him.'

'If we know so little about what it's all about and what we're supposed to do,' Duggie said, 'then what'll we do on our wedding night?'

'I suppose we'll have to do what I imagine most

men and women do,' Jimmy replied.

'And that is?' I asked, wondering how Jimmy came to say this as he knew no more than the rest of us.

'Just close our eyes and hope for the best,' he said.

'Anyroad,' said Charlie, 'this Jake gets a men's magazine that really gives the lowdown on the subject. For example, he told me what really gets a girl all excited and turned on so she's going mad for it ... but you won't believe it.'

'Go on, Charlie. We're all ears,' we chorused.

'Very well. But no laughing, mind you. It's sucking her big toe.'

The gang broke down in helpless laughter.

'But how,' I chortled through my tears, 'are we supposed to get at the girl's big toe? I mean, do we say something like, "I really love you, my darling, so would you mind removing your shoes and stockings so's I can kiss your big toes?"'

'Do girls have a preference for a particular toe?' Jimmy giggled. 'Left or right?'

'And it's to be hoped that she's washed her feet,' said Duggie. 'Otherwise I wouldn't fancy it one bit.'

'And cut her toenails,' added Gordon.

'All right, don't believe it then,' said Charlie, a little peeved, 'but this magazine is for adults. Jake Duckworth also collects art postcards sold by the magazine. Take a squint at these.'

Charlie showed us some postcards with pictures of scantily dressed women. We gasped in shock.

'You could go to prison for having pictures like

that,' said Duggie.

'Jake says there's nothing wrong with them 'cos they're artistic,' Charlie said.

'Artistic!' echoed Gordon. 'They're immoral and disgusting and you could burn in hell for looking at them.'

'You're right, Gordon, they *are* disgusting,' Alfie exclaimed. 'Here, Charlie, let's have a closer look.'

Charlie didn't seem in the least worried about the prospect of going to hell.

'When you say hell, Gordon, do you mean like that picture of Hades that Miss Corbett once showed us with all those devils with horns and men in ragged clothes with the pitchforks and all that?' Charlie made a gesture of horns on his head by wiggling both forefingers. 'If so, it doesn't worry me one bit because that's where all these glamorous women will be.'

You may think from our conversation that it was only the boys who were ignorant in the matter of sex but so were the girls of the time and they were the ones, after all, who were going to actually give birth to the next generation.

I spoke to a woman in the market about it a few years later and she told me, 'I knew nothing, not even when I was eighteen. Never knew what sex was. Never heard the word as it was never spoken of. I didn't know where babies came from. When I went on my honeymoon, my mother said, "Take a towel." That was all and it just goes to show how much I knew about the subject. I used to ask myself where babies could possibly come from. I looked down at my body and studied my belly button and I thought it must be there for a reason. Maybe it expands and opens up. I asked my mother about it and she said, "Leave it to nature. You'll find out soon enough when the time comes. Babies come out the same way as they went in." That really was a puzzle and it filled me with fear for a long time to come.'

Chapter Twenty-Nine

It took much longer than I'd thought to find a place of my own and I'd been staying with Willie Ingrams' family for over three months. It really was time to move on. I'd seen how poor the Ingrams were and I worried for a while that they would miss my weekly rent of three shillings. My conscience was eased a little, however, when some weeks later, after I'd moved out, Willie told me his mam and dad had become reconciled and were back together.

Soon I would be seventeen and I belonged to no one and nowhere; I was rootless, with no place to go, until Charlie told me that he'd heard good reports of a place called McGurk's Lodging House or Hostel on Victoria Street near the cathedral, close to Chetham's College of Music, and opposite the River Irwell.

It was wedged between a pub and a tattoo parlour. 'Clean Rooms at Reasonable Prices' it said on the board outside. I went into the office to make arrangements and sign the register. From the interior of the building, there came a vile, sour stench – a mixture of slops, soup and rancid cabbage. 'Hostel' was a polite word for the place; dosshouse or what the Americans called a 'flophouse' was a better description. The owner, a fat man with a cigarette dangling from his thick lips, sat behind a counter separated from his customers by a protective steel grille. On the wall behind him were a number of notices prohibiting various kinds of activities.

NO SPITTING. NO GAMBLING.
NO DRUGS.
NO DOGS. NO WOMEN.
HOSTEL OPEN 6 A.M. TO MIDNIGHT.
RESIDENTS MUST CLEAR THEIR
ACCOUNTS BEFORE LEAVING.
LET US KNOW ABOUT
BED BUGS AND FLEAS!
WE WANT TO ATTACK AND
GET RID OF THEM

'I'd 1-l-like to b-b-book accommodation and would like to sign the register,' I stammered. There was something about this man that made me tense and uptight.

Without looking up from the newspaper he was reading, he said, 'Pay half a crown and you'll get a bed and a locker with a key. You buy your own grub and cook it yourself in the communal kitchen.'

I explained that I worked unusual hours and sleeping in a packed barrack-like dormitory (with maybe more fleas and bed bugs) with a lot of other men would be no good 'cos I had to go to

335

bed in the afternoons and be in the market ready to start work at midnight.

'In that case you can rent a cubicle for an extra two shillings. You still cook your own food, though.'

I paid over my four and six and received a rent book and a key in exchange. I discovered later that the key in fact opened every other locker in the place. Not that it mattered, for my personal belongings consisted only of three shirts, three pairs of socks, and three lots of underwear, following my mam's advice: one on, one in the wash and one in the drawer.

Looking at the crummy, lowdown place around me, I felt as if I'd really reached the bottom, and all at the cost of over forty per cent of my weekly wage. I had to fight off the depression I felt creeping over me. At least I'm independent, I told myself, and this lifestyle cannot last for ever. There must be something better. However, at that time I had no alternative but to accept my lot even though a rent of four and six out of a wage of twelve shillings didn't leave me much to live on. I thanked God that I worked in the market where there was always plenty of fruit and vegetables available, even if only of the faded variety. The cubicle was a bit of a luxury, I thought, but at least I'd have a little privacy. The room was smaller than a prison cell with hardly room to swing a cat, and offered nothing more than a bed, a locker, and an oil lamp. The thin partitions between cubicles extended only partway to the ceiling, so each room was topped with chicken wire to discourage the light-fingered from climbing over and rummaging through your belongings. I found, too, that good earplugs were essential for a few hours of decent sleep.

I discovered that the hostel had accommodation for forty-eight men. Thirty-six were housed in the main dormitory in a large upper room and the other twelve in the cubicles on the ground floor. We cubicle dwellers were something of an elite as we had our own washroom/privy and a kitchen consisting of a cold-water slop stone, a wood stove and a couple of gas rings with meters. As for the facilities that the poor dormitory men shared on the floor above, it didn't bear thinking about. One morning I walked the length of the upstairs dormitory and the pong almost knocked me over. At the back of the hostel was a large covered courtyard, reminiscent of Strangeways Prison, I thought, where we were supposed to socialize and get a bit of exercise.

It may be an odd thing to say but in many ways we residents of McGurk's were the better off in a city-wide population of drifters and down-and-outs. At least we had a roof over our heads and, in order to pay the rent, must have had some kind of income though it was perhaps best not to inquire too deeply into the sources. Outside in the Manchester streets, sheltering in doorways, brick kilns, railway arches, abandoned cuttings, back alleys and courts, were the truly destitute. Among them were the luckless, the alcoholics, the drug addicts, the brain-damaged, those made insane by war or prison, or victims of unimaginable horrors. For the most part these people on the lowest rung were invisible to the general public unless they attracted attention as public nuisances by lying prone on the pavement outside hotels and public buildings. I often counted my blessings and whispered to myself, 'There but for the grace of God and Brodie and Dorothy go I.'

On my first day at McGurk's, things did not turn out so well. I came back from work just after midday, opened my locker to take out my loaf of bread and cheese to make some tea with the other men. Imagine my horror on finding that both the bread and cheese were covered in black beetles and had to be thrown away. I went into the kitchen to brew some tea anyway and got talking to a fellow resident. He was a thin, you might almost say emaciated, man who looked world-weary. He wore a strange fixed smile on his face and it was hard to tell whether it was closer to tears than to laughter.

'You must keep all your food in an airtight tin,' he told me. 'Anyroad, my name is Lennie Burke but people call me Laughing Lennie on account of my cheerful-looking face but I'm the most miserable bastard in this godforsaken place. I've hated it from the first day I came here and I hate it more every day.'

'My name's Tommy Hopkins,' I told him, 'and this is my first day here.' Then taking up on what he'd said, I asked, 'Why do you always look so happy and cheerful if you feel that miserable?'

'It's my job. I'm a barrel-organ grinder and it wouldn't do for me to look miserable, would it? So I keep up this pretence when I push this bloody machine round the streets entertaining the kids and their parents to earn a few coppers.'

'Is there much money in it?'

'Not much. I pay five shillings a week for the hire of the organ and, after that, what I earn is clear profit. Here, if the beetles got your bread and you've got no grub, have a piece of my toast. I can soon make some more. I've got plenty. How about a couple of boiled eggs as well? You can pay me back when you get fresh supplies.'

I thanked him for his kindness and offered to pay him back with a few things I'd brought from the market, like apples, bananas, oranges, and Victoria plums. I determined to get myself better organized with a few airtight tins but there was no need because when word spread that I had access to fresh fruit and vegetables, I became the most popular man on Cubicle Row and I found myself presented with more tins than I needed.

'So how come you landed up at McGurk's, Lennie, if you hate it so much?' I asked as I tucked into the toast and eggs.

'I'm forty years of age and you wouldn't believe it to look at me now but once I had it all. It's an old, old story. I worked on the cotton exchange for a firm of brokers and I had glittering prospects moving up the corporate ladder as an executive. Had a wife and two lovely daughters, and a big house in Victoria Park. But somehow, deep down, I felt I was a failure. Doesn't make sense, I know, but I began hitting the bottle hard. Was so depressed I tried to finish myself off by drinking rotgut whisky but I couldn't even do that properly. Couldn't even succeed at being a failure. Anyway, I lost the lot: job, house, family. So I came in here to get out of the cold, as it were, and to hide myself away. I've stayed ever since.'

'So, how long have you been here, Lennie?'

'Let's see. I came here in eighteen ninety-three and what's it this year?'

'Nineteen oh four.'

'Then I've been here for about ten years. That's one thing about this place: people lose track of time. Residents here are waiting to die and they've lost hope. They come for a short stay and forget that they planned to move out. Ten years go by and, like me, they find they're still here. Some residents go for months without ever leaving their cubicles. I often run errands for some of them to bring them food, drink and cigarettes. This place is a cross between a prison, a mental hospital, an old age home, and a bug hut. As for me, I've been and still am a slave to the demon drink and I can easily get through a couple of bottles of cheap whisky a day, two on Sundays when I'm not working. Just can't pack it in.'

We were joined by a dark-haired, olive-skinned man obviously of Latin extraction. Lennie introduced him as Enrico Frascati.

'We call him the Canary,' Lennie said.

'I'm notta like these others,' said Enrico in a melodic Italian accent. 'I am an opera singer and have a-sung the operas of all the great composers: Verdi, Schubert, Puccini, Mozart. Have performed in all the great opera houses: La Scala in Milano, the Met in New York, the Royal Opera House in Londra.'

I was intrigued. 'So what happened, Enrico?'

'Before every performance I was always very nervous, so I began to take laudanum for my nerves. That was my undoing. Now the drug is my prima donna and I cannot live without her. Like all women do, she has led to my ruin. My last booking was in Verdi's *Rigoletto* at the Manchester Opera House. For several nights I forgot my lines, my cues, and even the melodies. One night I didn't turn up and they gave me the sack. That was five years ago and now no one will book me. I am finito. But I can still sing as well as ever. Listen!'

Enrico broke out into *'La Donna è Mobile'* and to me his voice sounded wonderful. I applauded.

'Grazie tante,' he said. 'Now I have ended up in this terrible place among these *mendicanti* and *lazzaroni*, these derelicts, liars and cheats. I can still earn a living by singing in the streets, though only a tiny fraction of what I used to get. Today the peasants of this city do not want to hear opera; now it is only popular religious songs like "The Rosary" or "Because God Made Thee Mine".'

Over the next few weeks, I discovered that the kitchen was the meeting place for the cubicle residents and while cooking and frying there I heard a succession of heartbreaking stories. McGurk's seemed to be full of eccentric characters who had long given up trying to be normal and decent. Some residents were very old and incapable; others were mentally ill or suffering from terrible wounds received in the Boer War. These, I discovered, depended for survival on various religious charities like Christian Aid or St Vincent de Paul. In one of the end cubicles was a man still fighting the Afrikaners.

'The Boers are bastards!' he yelled. 'Shoot the lot! God Bless you, Lord Kitchener! God Bless you, Baden-Powell!'

He then broke out into one of the many Boer War songs he knew, like Rudyard Kipling's and Arthur Sullivan's 'The Absent-Minded Beggar'.

When you've shouted 'Rule Britannia':
When you've sung 'God Save the Queen'
When you've finished killing Kruger
  with your mouth:
Will you kindly drop a shilling in
  my little tambourine
For a gentleman in khaki ordered South?
He's an absent-minded beggar
  and his weaknesses are great.

He continued with a complete rendering of the thirty-nine lines until his next-door resident bawled: 'Shut your big mouth, General Kitchener! The Boer War ended in nineteen hundred and two! It's all over and we won!'

At the other end of the row of cubicles was a poor demented man, nicknamed unsurprisingly the Messiah since he was convinced he was Jesus and had the divine command to preach at us residents from morn till night. He would rant on until some irate neighbour, sometimes me, would finally blow his top with: 'Put a sock in it, Jesus. Some of us have to go to work tomorrow.'

'What doth it profit a man if he gains the whole world and suffers the loss of his own soul?' the Messiah replied in his sing-song voice.

'All the same, we'd like to get some sleep!' the

angry resident would yell back.

The Messiah always had an answer ready. 'Can you not watch with me for just one hour? I tell you solemnly that before the cock crows, you will deny me thrice.'

Lennie explained to me that the Messiah used to be a tub-thumper in Platt Fields Park and could be seen there surrounded by a crowd of hecklers every Sunday afternoon until one day he'd finally flipped and landed up here.

Every trade as well as every fraudster was represented at McGurk's. Professional men rubbed shoulders with con artists; lawyers with thieves and pickpockets. There were buskers, cobblers, navvies, merchant seamen, students, and ragpickers. I'm tempted to say they were down on their luck but many of them were there through their own fault, being addicts of one kind or another. The damage they suffered had come from their own hands. As well as the usual drunks, there were other kinds of addict like the doctor who'd fallen from grace when he became hooked on morphine which he'd sampled at his own hospital; or the gambler who had lost control and the family fortune at the dog track.

There was also an assortment of con men staying in the dosshouse, from card sharps who made their living going from pub to pub, to shoplifters who worked the big stores in teams of two or three. There was even one man who claimed to be royalty. He had visiting cards printed announcing himself as the 'Duke of Connmannara' and 'Lord of the Manor' but no one spotted the double meaning of the title. He had all the props necessary for the role – dark suit, white shirt, bow tie and, to finish it off, a monocle secured to his lapel buttonhole by a gold chain. His method was to steal an overcoat, the best he could find, from a pub, then go into a top restaurant and order the most expensive meal from the *à la carte* menu, having deposited his overcoat as a mark of good faith in the cloakroom. After finishing several courses, accompanied by a few bottles of the rarest wines, he'd send his visiting card to the head chef complimenting him on the excellence of his cooking. After a liqueur or two, there followed a visit to the gents from which he never returned and the restaurant never saw him again. Of course he was running out of posh restaurants to swindle and pretty soon would have to venture a little downmarket or go further afield and out of the city.

Incidentally, I've never been able to understand this routine of sending compliments to the chef. Did he think the waiter took the message back to the kitchen where he would say something like, 'Hey, there's a duke out there who says he likes your soup.' 'Likes my dish-washing water!' the chef would exclaim. 'He must be as mad as a hatter.'

'And he obviously doesn't know what's in the soup,' the under-chef would add.

But the accolade of 'con man of the year' must go to the most enterprising and creative resident in the place. He was known as Postcard Pete, for he had invented a surefire way of extracting money from the punters, as he called them. He had obtained a number of picture postcards which he sold in the red-light district around Piccadilly. The postcards were sold in sealed envelopes with suggestive pornographic titles like 'Saucy French Postcards'.

'This little number has been a real winner and must have netted me a small fortune over the years,' he told me one day.

'But what's actually in the package?' I asked, though I already had a shrewd idea of the answer I was going to get.

We were frying our staple diet of bacon, egg and sausage in the communal kitchen at the time. He looked up from the pan and grinned cheekily.

'Why, what it says on the label. Saucy French postcards! That is to say, pictures of famous French chefs, such as Escoffier, Carême, and Brillat-Savarin who have created world-celebrated sauces, like bordelaise, hollandaise and mayonnaise.'

'But don't you get any complaints?' I chuckled. I really did admire his cheek and enterprise.

'None so far. The punters discover too late what's in the envelope and then they're too embarrassed to complain. Anyway, they get what they've paid for. I have other cards for sale which are selling almost as well. There's "Spicy Pictures" containing lists and photos of well-known spices like cinnamon, cloves, fennel and black pepper. Another is labelled "Racy Postcards from Paris" and contains photos of Alfred Tysoe and Charles Bennett, winners of the eight hundred and fifteen hundred metres at the 1900 Olympiad games which were held in Paris.'

'But surely your customers would be expecting photos of racy *women*,' I protested.

'Well, that's what they get 'cos there's also a picture of Charlotte Cooper, the first female Olympic champion,' Pete replied. 'She won two gold medals for Britain at tennis. What more do they want?'

Residents of McGurk's entertained themselves in various ways. I was going to say in 'their spare time' but most of their time was spare. They filled in their leisure hours by playing dominoes, card games like pontoon, cribbage, poker, or board games such as draughts, ludo, snakes and ladders. The more intellectual among them played chess, while others preferred to do nothing but lie on their beds staring at the ceiling. The favourite activity, however, came on Friday afternoon when practically the whole of the company gathered in the covered courtyard at the back of the hostel for rat-baiting.

In the eighteenth century, the most popular sport had been bear-baiting but the sport had gradually died out as the supply of bears dried up. In the Manchester underworld, it was still possible to find lots of illegal fights of one kind or another if you knew where to look: there were always dogfights, cockfights, even bare fisticuff prize fights between men. But these were for the better-off who could afford the costly entrance fees of anything from one shilling to five. For the poor, there were alternatives like rat-versus-dog competitions held in low dives like McGurk's where admission cost only threepence. There were always plenty of rats available from the nearby River Irwell and I'd noticed the number of fat toms prowling around the hostel, obviously seasoned rat-catchers.

The 'pit' at the back of our dosshouse was a large unscreened box with wooden walls eight or nine feet long and four feet high. The dogs, always fox terriers, were brought in by professional trainers who raised them with the express purpose of fighting rats to the death. A prize of ten pounds would be offered for a winning dog that took on and killed up to ten rats at a time. Spectators could place wagers on how many rats the dogs would kill in a given time. The sport was a cruel and vicious one that turned my stomach and I attended only one session but I noticed that among the spectators was Mr McGurk himself, accompanied by several policemen who enjoyed the sport and the gambling. A good rat dog could kill ten rats without too much trouble but the record was held by McGurk's own dog, Lupus, which he told us proudly was Latin for 'wolf'; his pet had sunk its fangs into twenty-five in a matter of ten minutes. I heard later that it became popular to use men wearing big clogs or hobnailed boots against the poor old rats which didn't stand a chance.

So much for all the prohibitory notices that adorned McGurk's office.

I'd been staying at McGurk's for over nine months and had settled into a comfortable routine. So why change? I asked myself. After all, I was well fed, had made one or two good friends, and was enjoying a happy life. I still played football on Saturday afternoons, only now our league had entered the higher division of the Lancashire and Cheshire Amateur Youth Association where standards were more demanding and the game better organized. We'd found ourselves playing in distant places like Stockport, Macclesfield and Chester. The old gang still met up in our hut and we still laughed and joked as usual. Things were ticking over and I couldn't see any need to alter my way of life. I was always short of ready cash but somehow that didn't seem to matter. Then one day I got chatting to a new cubicle resident who had come down from the dormitory section and my whole attitude changed. Had it not been for my little *tête-à-tête* with him, I might still be at McGurk's today.

His name was Tim Farrell, and when I'd heard his story, I knew it was time to snap out of the cloud cuckoo land I'd dozed off in. As usual I got talking with him in the communal kitchen over the standard meal of bacon and cheese which we were cooking together, having agreed to share the cost of the gas meter.

'So what brought you here to McGurk's?' I asked, the usual opener with a newcomer.

'I've come down, thank the Lord, from the dormitory wing upstairs after living up there for what seems like forever,' he said. 'It's been like hell on earth, I can tell you. In many ways, I think I might have been better off in Strangeways. At least there you don't have to share a dormitory with thirty-odd decrepit old men. I'm forty-seven years of age and I came here in eighteen seventy-three at the age of seventeen so I've been here for I don't know how long.'

He paused for a moment while he carried out the calculation on his fingers.

'My God!' he exclaimed. 'I've been here for thirty years! I tell you, once you fall into the rut here, you forget to look at the calendar to check how long you've been stewing in the McGurk juice. After a while, it doesn't seem to matter.'

'So what's your story?' I asked, thinking to myself, thirty years in this dump and still sane! Amazing!

'I left school at twelve years of age,' Tim said, taking up his story 'and went to work for the Lancashire and Yorkshire Railways as a carter's boy. An easy job, just delivering parcels, but when I was seventeen, I had an accident. A heavy cartwheel ran over my foot and I was crippled. That's how I got the nickname Tiny Tim after the character in Charles Dickens' book. I got a little compensation but that soon ran out and I had to look around for something else. Not easy 'cos no one wanted to employ me once they found I limped and they looked for any excuse not to take me on. Once I tried to get a job as a porter on Exchange Station but I couldn't lift the big crate they asked me to move as a test. Later, I saw that it took three men to lift it on to the cart. It was their sneaky way of rejecting me. Then I nearly got a job as a waiter at the hundred-room Victoria Hotel on Deansgate. I tried to hide my handicap but it was no use. Once they saw that I limped, they didn't want to know.'

My heart went out to him for he'd had rotten luck.

'There was no opening in the catering trade

and I had to settle for a job as hotel lavatory attendant cleaning out the bogs on each floor. I did that job for nearly ten years.'

'So what are you doing now, Tim?'

'I was moved to general duties as a scullion, washing down the tables, polishing the cutlery and doing all the dirty work at the newly opened Midland Hotel. The job was as bad as the first one. I used to get really depressed when I thought about where I'd landed up. So I turned to laudanum to cheer myself up.'

There was that word 'laudanum' again, I thought.

'Why does nearly everyone in this place seem to go on laudanum?' I asked.

'They call it God's own medicine and it's the poor man's opium. Not only that, it's so easy to buy it at any chemist's shop. I read in the paper that lots of famous people like politicians and poets use it, including the famous Samuel Taylor Coleridge. If it's good enough for them, it's good enough for me. It gives you a lift when you're feeling down in the dumps.'

When I heard that bit about Samuel Taylor Coleridge, I was taken aback 'cos he'd written one of my favourite poems from St Chad's, 'The Rime of the Ancient Mariner'.

'Anyway,' Tim continued, 'then I was promoted to dishwasher, where I am today. I have to work in sweltering temperatures down in the bowels of the building and I think that's how I'll end my days – a dishwasher. But the pay was slightly better and that's when I improved my standard of living by moving into the cubicles.'

'So what are your plans for the future, Tim?'

'Plans? I don't have no plans! Nobody in this dump has plans! I'll never be anything but a dishwasher and I suppose I'll spend my life in a flea-bag hole like this. What else is there?'

Of all the life stories I'd heard in McGurk's, this was the one that upset me most and the one that had the deepest effect. Tim had come here at the age of seventeen – about my age. He was now forty-seven and still here thirty years later. Is this what was to become of me? Is this what my mam and dad had given their lives for? To raise a deadbeat? I made up my mind there and then that I would do everything in my power to get out of the place and do something useful with my life.

Chapter Thirty

It was 1904 and I was approaching my seven-teenth birthday when I would be entitled to apply for a licence to operate as a Smithfield Market porter in my own right. I had been working at Deakin's stall for well over a year and, while I'd been happy there, the pay of twelve shillings a week just wasn't enough to lead a full life. By a full life I meant sufficient money to feed and clothe myself decently, to pay rent on clean lodgings, to cover the cost of fares to play at football matches in far-flung Cheshire outposts, to go to places of entertainment like the music hall or the theatre, to pay for personal expenses, cigarettes for example, and finally to take a girl out if I were to meet one.

The job of porter was much better paid as you were working for yourself and not stuck on a fixed weekly wage. As well as being seventeen in order to apply for a porter's badge, you had also to be in good health (a medical was required to prove, I suppose, that you wouldn't be breathing germs on the fruit and vegetables), and of good character as testified by two upstanding rate-paying Manchester citizens. I thought of using Brodie but then realized that he wasn't a rate-payer and furthermore was rarely upstanding as he spent so much time and money in the Turk's Head. Joe Brannan, who had paid rates for many years, agreed to give me a good reference, though he said he would be sorry to lose me from the stall.

'I understand your position,' he said. 'Working for someone else means you'll never get rich. Doing portering jobs is clear profit and so I don't blame you wanting to work for yourself.'

I was one referee short, however, until Joe suggested Sergeant Bert O'Neil of the Manchester Constabulary.

'You couldn't find a Mancunian more reputable than that,' he said. 'I'll have a word with him and assure him what a good, honest worker you are.'

I was overjoyed when Bert agreed to write a few words in my support. Only two snags remained. I needed to borrow some money: a pound to pay for the licence fee and a further five pounds as deposit on the hire of a hand barrow from the

Shudehill Cart Company Limited. The rental would then cost only one pound a week and earnings should cover that quite easily. No point in asking Aunty Dorothy or Uncle Brodie as they were always broke, having donated most of their earnings to the local breweries. Once again, Joe Brannan came to the rescue.

'I don't know how I'll ever repay you,' I said. 'I'll see if I can't pull a few strings with Saint Peter and get you a place in heaven for all your kindness.'

Joe laughed. 'Don't put it like that, Tommy. You should be able to start paying me back as soon as the greengrocers begin hiring you. That shouldn't take long if I'm any judge. As for a place in heaven, I'll start polishing my halo in readiness.'

I put in my application and three weeks later I received my brass armlet bearing the Manchester Corporation coat of arms and the engraved inscription:

MARKET PORTER
NO. 591
SMITHFIELD MARKET

At last I was somebody! I was a market porter and, as such, an independent operator who could set my own rules, my own hours and my own fees. The first morning, I was in the main market square at 4 a.m. with my handcart, waiting eagerly for my first customer. I had to wait a long time 'cos no one knew me. Around nine o'clock a greengrocer named Ernie Ogden from up Miles Platting way approached me.

'My usual porter isn't here. Could you take up a load to my shop in Gaylor Street? It's just off Oldham Road. Usual charge is five bob.'

Could I! The way I was feeling, I'd have done it for nothing.

'No problem,' I said. 'Just give me your order.'

Ernie read it out from his list. 'Five spuds, six tomatoes, five straws, five caulies, eight cabbages, six peas from Holbrook's.'

I jotted them down in my notebook. The list seemed to go on and on and involved several other stalls, but I got them all down. I must try to save time by memorizing these orders, I told myself. After all, if I'd learned anything at all at St Chad's, it was how to commit stuff to memory. I whipped round the stall as fast as my legs would carry me and an hour later I had them all safely stowed on my cart and tied down securely. I was in business. It took me an hour and a half to get to his shop and back again but I'd earned my first commission. I was five shillings up!

'That was very good service,' said Ernie after I'd unloaded the last item. 'Look, the porter I've been using, a bloke called Bullock, has been most unreliable. Sometimes he's there; sometimes he's not. How would you like to do the order at the same time every day at the agreed figure of a dollar?'

My first customer and now my first regular. And at five shillings! Why, that was half my weekly wage at Deakin's! I attracted a smaller job with one more customer that day for half a crown. I'd made seven and six. Not bad for the first day.

At midday, I stopped work with a feeling of joy

and contentment in my heart. My first day had been a success and I now had my own little business and could stand on my own two feet without depending on others for survival. I even had my own 'swinger' hanging at the back of the cart. With permission of the customers I'd served of course, I collected a few items of faded fruit and vegetables plus a couple of plaice which Alfie had 'found' for me. I parked and chained up the cart on a small croft opposite the Hare and Hounds pub and went back to McGurk's happily to rest my weary bones.

Next day, Tuesday, I was in the market square bright and early ready to pick up business. But it wasn't business I picked up. It was trouble in the shape of Slug Bullock who came at me like his angry namesake, snorting angrily.

'You bastard, Hopkins,' he bawled, raising his fist as if to punch me.

'Why, what have I done?' I asked though I had an idea what was riling him.

'You've only gone and poached one of my best customers, Ernie Ogden, from right under my nose. I've half a mind to give you a good hiding. But I have my own ways of dealing with bastards like you.'

With that, he stalked off to deal with one of his customers.

Feeling a little shaken, I got on with my work. It didn't do to vex ugly characters like Slug and I wondered what he meant by that 'I have my own ways' threat. I was new to the job and didn't want to mess it up before I'd really got started. I forgot about the incident for the rest of that day as I was busy with orders from two new customers as well as completing the daily commission for Ernie Ogden which was well paid. I counted up my takings for the second day and, to my joy, found I'd made a total of ten shillings. A fortune! I repaid five of it to Joe as part payment. If I keep this up I'll soon be clear of debt, I thought.

'Stay on the alert,' Joe warned me as I handed over the instalment. 'As you build up your little business, you will cause jealousies among other porters and they'll try to do you down, if they can. Just keep your weather eye skinned.'

On my third day, business was definitely better for I had four commissions by nine o'clock. Only small jobs admittedly but I was building up a customer base and was becoming known and trusted. I was pulling the Ogden order up Rochdale Road when I noticed that some of the crates behind me were wobbling unsteadily. I stopped, rested the cart legs on the road and went back to examine the load and found that the ropes I'd used to secure the cargo had become loose. I could have sworn that I'd tied them tightly but the knots had been tampered with. It had happened once before when we'd been breaking Clancy in, getting him used to the cart. Then as now, suspicion had fallen on Slug Bullock and on that occasion it had been left to Brodie to give Bullock hell. But this time I couldn't rely on Brodie to pull my chestnuts out of the fire. It would be up to me to do something. Since I had no definite proof, I decided to leave it until such a time as I had. I continued taking Ernie's goods and received the usual five shillings but now I was on the alert for possible further trouble.

Next day on my way up Rochdale Road, the next phase of the suspected sabotage moved up a notch. I was just passing Zinc Street when it happened. The left wheel of the cart came off and the load landed up on the road with fruit rolling in the gutter, just like the accident in Topley Street with the horse and cart. I'd been careful never to leave my loaded cart untended but this was a new development. Slug must have nobbled my cart when it was parked on the croft opposite the pub. It was difficult to know what I could do about that, short of watching the cart throughout the night. If I found another parking place, I'm sure Slug would have discovered that too and continued doing his dirty work.

I was not prepared, however, for the next piece of sabotage which definitely upped the stakes. For a week, nothing had happened. Then on the Monday morning I turned up as usual to collect my cart and was shocked by the hideous sight which met my eyes. Spread-eagled and nailed to the wooden base of the cart was a dead cat. Written in chalk on the front were the words: QUIT THE MARKET. YOU HAVE BEEN WARNED. Before beginning work that morning, I called over Sergeant Bert O'Neil to witness the latest outrage. He wrote a few details in his notebook and said, 'We must keep a weather eye open to find the evil-minded sod who did this. Whoever it is has a twisted mind and he'll be for it when I find him. And find him I will. And to think that the lunatic might have been doing this while I was having a drink in the Hare and Hounds. Whoever it is was really pushing his luck.'

I had the feeling that there was no need to voice my suspicions 'cos Bert was no fool and he had a good idea of who was behind it. An important part of his job was keeping an ear to the ground and being aware of goings-on among market folk, which was why he had made the Hare and Hounds and the Turk's Head his local pubs.

I gave the cart a thorough hosing-down and asked the market cleaners to deal with the feline corpse. Then I set about my morning's work but the incident had shaken me to the core and I wondered what sort of sick mind could have committed such an atrocity of killing a cat and nailing it to my cart in order to warn me off.

I decided that we had to find the criminal somehow and my pals working in the market – Charlie, Alfie, Duggie, plus our two non-market chums, Jimmy and Gordon – agreed to set up a roster to watch the cart each night until eleven p.m. when the boozers shut. It wasn't such a great hardship 'cos we were able to meet in the pub and have a drink or two before taking our turn to go out and watch the cart from the shadows of a door hole on the other side of Shudehill.

Three nights passed. Nothing happened. Then on the Wednesday, Duggie rushed into the pub hardly able to control his excitement.

'There's three of 'em!' he yelled. 'Three of 'em!'

'Right, right, Duggie,' I said quietly but urgently. 'But keep it down. We don't want the whole pub to know. Any idea who it is?'

'Looks like Slug Bullock and the two hawkers from Chad's, Ginger McDermott and Mick

Malone. They seemed to be sawing something.'

I went round the other members of the gang. 'Don't jump up excitedly to attract attention but it looks as if our birds have arrived. We must tell Bert.'

Bert was having a pint in the saloon bar with another market worker.

'Right, Bert,' I said. 'I think we've found our culprits. They're doing their dirty work at this very moment just across the road. If we go quietly now, we should catch them red-handed.'

And that's what we did. Bert and I crept across the road in the shadows and found the three of them busy sawing through the shafts of my cart.

'Now then, young men,' Bert said, coming up to them from behind and catching them un-awares. 'What's going on here?'

It was pretty obvious what was going on here. The three of them were caught in an act of mali-cious vandalism. Bert arrested them on the spot and they were taken to the City police station to spend the night behind bars. They appeared a few days later at Minshull Street magistrates court where they were charged with causing criminal damage to the property of the Shudehill Cart Company. Ginger and Mick were each fined thirty shillings – a huge sum for them – and let off with a caution. I suspected, though, that that would not be the end of it for I'd learned a long time ago, way back at St Chad's, that neither of the pair was a good loser and would be back to do more mischief.

As for Slug, he had a long criminal record and was sentenced to six months in Strangeways and deprived permanently of his porter's licence. It was all quite dramatic and too bad for the criminals but it made my own life a little more peaceful.

Chapter Thirty-One

My earnings as a porter were much higher than those as a salesman/checker on Deakin's stall. I found that my income from Monday to Wednesday, though fairly modest at about five to six shillings a day, was a great improvement on what I was used to. On the last three working days of the week, however, Thursday to Saturday, my earnings were much higher at around twelve to fifteen shillings a day. I *felt* rich and I *was* rich for I was able to start paying Joe back his loan at a pound a week. After five weeks, I was free of debt and felt like a millionaire 'cos I had a few bob in my pocket. Now I had more money, I began looking for better lodgings. I found what I was looking for at the corner of Thompson Street and Oldham Road, a block of flats called Victoria Square. I celebrated leaving McGurk's by throwing a farewell party of fish and chips for the cubicle dwellers.

'God bless you, Tommy,' one or two called as they tucked in.

'You earned your nickname of the Fruit King,' others bawled from their alcoves. 'We'll miss you, Tommy, as well as your fruit and veg.'

My new digs consisted of a furnished room with its own little kitchen of slop stone and two gas rings. There was also a large window that looked out on to the Oldham goods yard so that in my few leisure hours I was able to watch the traffic flowing down the main road and the busy activity of the yard. My life was so much better and I was content.

There was only one thing missing. A girl! But who? I didn't know any as I'd never been able to even think of taking one out because of the expense. Now it was different. I was flush. For years in the market I'd been approached, I don't know how many times, by my old school friend, Doris Doonican.

Nearly every day she'd called out to me from behind the pyramid of fruit on her father's stall, 'When are you going to take me out, Tommy?'

There'd been no chance of anything developing since I was constantly broke. I could hardly feed myself let alone think of taking Doris out for a slap-up meal. Taking her out isn't such a bad idea at that, I thought. She's quite presentable, looks healthy enough though a bit on the big side, and her father owns a flourishing fruit stall which she might inherit a share in one day, along with her four brothers, so she might be a good catch.

The trouble was that I was always shy in the presence of girls and I still had that stutter which lay dormant but was liable to appear when I was nervous. But now, with a bob or two rattling around in my pocket at the end of the week, I decided to pluck up courage on the Friday afternoon and ask her.

'Do you fancy going out with me tonight?' I said as I passed the Doonican fruit stall. Doris couldn't believe her ears.

'Are you having me on, Tommy? I've been asking you for years. What's brought this on? What's happened?'

'I've got a bit of dosh, that's all.'

'I'd love to go,' she said. 'You know I've always fancied you ever since we were kids at St William's.'

'Sh-sh-shall we go to the Band on the Wall? We could have a couple of drinks and maybe a b-b-bit of dinner?'

'Tommy, I'd love to. You've made my day, you really have.'

The Band on the Wall was a pub on Swan Street and it had a long history going back to the year dot. It used to have a fearsome reputation as a dive and there were stories that the owner, Eddie McKenna, was a crotchety old so-and-so whose temper could flare up if things were not to his liking but it was nothing more than a rumour.

The McKenna family had tried to change its name to the George and Dragon but without success because the market people would have none of it and the new name never took off. Which might go some way to explain why Eddie had a short fuse. The Band got its name because high up on the wall was a small stage that visiting musicians performed on. The pub also served simple meals and I thought this might be the ideal place to entertain Doris as the menu, I was told, was not too expensive. Now I was a porter with my own clientele I suppose I could now be considered well-off but not that well-off! So it was the Band or not at all.

I put on my new navy-blue suit which I had bought on the never-never from the newly opened Montague Burton's shop in town. I spruced myself up and met Doris at the corner of Shudehill and Swan Street and from there we strolled across to Number 25, the Band on the Wall. I was used to seeing Doris in her position behind the fruit stall and I'd never really noticed just how tall she was. Now away from the market I saw that she was at least six inches taller than me and I was five feet eleven. Furthermore, she was hefty with it. All the same, she looked quite pretty in the green dress she had on, the only trouble being that I had never seen her wearing anything else ever since I'd worked in the market. Maybe, I thought, taking the kindest view, it wasn't that she had only the one dress but rather that she liked the style so much she'd had multiple copies made up. We shook hands in greeting and I got the second shock of the evening. I'd never noticed before but she had callused hands the size of coke shovels and a grip like a boa constrictor. I managed to disguise my grimace but I made a mental note to ask Jimmy next day if he knew of a good hand masseur. Then I thought, what did I expect? After all, Doris worked in the market, lifting and lugging heavy crates of fruit and veg about the place. She could hardly be expected to have the soft, smooth skin of a lady of leisure.

'Good to see you, Doris. Sh-shall we go in?' I said.

'By all means, Tommy, let's go,' she replied, giving me a playful punch in the chest that would probably leave me with a nasty bruise on the morrow.

There was a small band consisting of a drummer and two piano accordionists playing a selection of the popular tunes of the day. We studied the menu and saw that there were three soups – lentil, mulligatawny, tomato – on offer as starters.

'Which one would you like, Doris?'

'I'd like to try all three.' She smiled. 'Then I won't be disappointed. Also some fresh rolls.'

I chose the lentil as it was the kind my mam used to make from the leftover weekend joint every Monday morning.

While waiting for the food, we ordered two pints of best bitter. It couldn't have been more than ten minutes to wait for the soup but during that time Doris had not only knocked back her pint but was beckoning to the waiter to bring two more.

'Not for me just yet, Doris,' I said. 'I've hardly drunk the froth off the top of mine.'

'That's all right, Tommy. You drink at your own pace. Me? I've learned to drink like a true market worker.'

Hardly had five minutes gone by when, giving a loud burp, she raised her hand to signal to the waiter to bring yet another pint. By this time, the soups had arrived and with loud slurping sounds she tucked in and demolished her three soups before I'd managed to finish my single broth.

We turned our attention to the main course and, from the restricted choices offered, chose battered cod, chips and peas.

Throughout, the little band played on and in my feverish imagination, Doris seemed to be belching in time to the melodies. After half an hour or so of performing, the musicians left their instruments to take a short break for a smoke. The interval didn't last long. It wasn't allowed to 'cos Eddie, the owner, took objection.

'Get bleeding well playing,' he bawled across the room, flinging a pint pot in their direction. 'I'm not paying you to sit around on your arses.'

My date with Doris was turning into a nightmare.

The main course arrived and Doris tucked into the chips and fish with the same gusto, burping and slurping and belching. It was noisier than elephant feeding time at Belle Vue Zoo. She could eat for England at the next Olympics, I thought.

'You may be wondering why I eat so quickly, Tommy,' she said, reading my thoughts. 'I'm used to sitting down at the table with my four brothers and it's always a case of each man for himself. You either grab what you can or go hungry.'

She was gobbling the food so fast, she dropped her fork in the sawdust on the floor and immediately stooped down to recover it.

'Leave it, Doris. I'll ask for a clean one,' I said, signalling to the waiter across the room.

'No need for that, Tommy,' she said, wiping the fork on the tablecloth since we didn't seem to be supplied with napkins. 'A bit of sawdust never did anyone any harm. It'll help soak up the beer, eh?'

Uppermost in my mind throughout the meal

365

was one question which repeated itself over and over again. 'How would you like Doris at your breakfast table for the next forty years?'

One look at her in the act of scooping the peas into the large yawning cavern that was her mouth and the question answered itself. We rounded off the meal with two coffees and any doubts I might have held up to that point were well and truly dispatched when she disposed of her fag by dropping it into the dregs of the coffee.

Eating finished, we went over to the saloon counter for a last drink and perched ourselves on the bar stools. I was on my second pint but Doris had reached her fifth, in addition to the couple of double gin-and-tonics she had downed in between.

'I was very nervous about asking you out tonight, Doris,' I said. 'I never thought you would say yes. A beautiful girl like you.'

'Enough of your blarney!' she exclaimed, giving me one of her friendly thumps that knocked me off my stool and on to my back on the floor. As I struggled to my feet, brushing off the sawdust, I knew I was going to need medical attention next day for a crushed hand, a bruised chest and possibly a spinal injury.

'Thanks for a thumping great evening, Doris,' I lied as I wished her goodnight. 'I've had a wonderful time.'

I avoided the possibility of another injury by not shaking her hand, substituting instead a quick peck on the cheek. I was lucky to get back to my room in one piece.

On Saturday afternoon as the team was getting changed for our match, I reported back to the gang in our cemetery shed.

'Come on, Tommy,' Charlie urged. 'The details! The details! The lowdown! How was it? What's she like? How did she strike you?'

'She's a belter.' I laughed. 'How did she strike me? Several times hard and with great accuracy.'

'But how far did she let you go?' Charlie persisted. 'What did she let you have?'

'Several black and blue bruises,' I said ruefully. 'Furthermore, she had the hands of a monster out of a horror comic.'

'Exactly how big would you say?' Jimmy asked. 'I bought my mother some gloves last Christmas, size seven. What size would Doris be, do you think?'

'I dunno,' I said. 'What size would an Irish navvy be? Say double your mam's, about fourteen.'

'Then for Christmas you could just buy her a couple of gunny sacks,' Alfie chuckled.

'Anyway,' I said, 'she's a good catch for someone because her dad owns a big fruit stall and all that. But for me she was a bit too pushy.'

Duggie's ears pricked up when he heard that.

'You know, I wouldn't mind giving her a tumble,' he said. 'I like a girl with a strong personality.'

'Then you won't be disappointed,' I said.

'With a girl like that, her father running a successful fruit business,' Duggie continued, 'we'd make a good match. With her four brothers working in the business as well and with our two stalls linked, why, we'd be one of the biggest concerns on Smithfield Market.'

'Doesn't sound much like a romance,' Jimmy laughed. 'More like a business arrangement.'

'If you want to go ahead and take Doris out, be my guest,' I said. 'She's all yours. But meanwhile I have the problem of giving her the old heave-ho. What do you fellahs recommend?'

'A clean break,' said Alfie decisively. 'Like pulling a bandage off a scab. Painful but quick.'

'No,' I said. 'I've known Doris for a long time, ever since our infant, school days and I don't want to hurt her. Things haven't really got started but I don't want her to think I'm ditching her because of her forceful personality I want a kinder, gentler way of giving her the elbow.'

'Not only that,' Charlie added with a malicious smile, 'she has four giant brothers who'll come for you if they think you've wounded their little sister.'

'The kindest way,' said Gordon, who was anxious to make a contribution and find an amicable solution, 'is to blame yourself. Just say something like, "It's not you, Doris. It's me. I'm not worthy of someone like you." That'll work.'

A week passed before I got the chance to speak to Doris.

As I passed her stall, I called out. 'We must talk, Doris. Any chance of us meeting this morning?'

'S'funny that, Tommy,' she replied, ''cos I've been wanting to speak to you. What about Fred's Café at nine this morning?'

At the morning break I ordered two cups of coffee and we sat down at a table. I was really nervous because I'd never ditched a girl before. Come to think of it, I'd never had a girl to ditch

368

in the first place. I was afraid I might make a complete mess of it and Doris would break down in tears and I wouldn't have been able to cope with that.

'I just wanted a few words with you, Doris,' I said gently, 'about our date last week.'

'What a coincidence,' she said quickly, 'because *I've* been hoping to have a few words with *you!* I'll come straight to the point, Tommy. I'm sorry but I don't think we should go out with each other any more. There's nothing wrong with you. No, it's me. I'm just not good enough for you.'

I hoped the relief didn't show on my face but I pretended that I hadn't expected to hear such bad news. 'I'm sorry to hear that, Doris. Was it something I did or said?'

'No, no, Tommy. Nothing like that. I'm a Smithfield girl, used to rough market ways, and having four big hulking brothers hasn't helped me in that regard either. Ever since I've known you in infant school, I've always found you gentle and kind. And now, you're such a gentleman I don't think it would work out between us. Might be best to call it a day before either of us gets too serious.'

We parted that morning and I went about the rest of the day whistling happily for I'd been let off the hook so easily. At the same time, I felt a bit miffed that she hadn't seemed more upset at losing a good catch such as me. But there you are. Later I learned that what had really happened was that Doris and Duggie's fathers had met privately and agreed over a pint that their children would make a good match. It was an arranged marriage of two market enterprises. I felt better when I heard this because it meant that Doris had not rejected me for personal reasons but because money and profit in the market had, as it always did, won the day.

Taking Doris out to the Band on the Wall put me off girls for some considerable time but not, I'm glad to say, for ever. The trouble was that my lifestyle didn't give me much opportunity to meet the opposite sex. I worked long hours from early morning till midday and after that I just wanted to go to bed. To sleep, I add hastily. The rest of my spare time was taken up with training and playing football with the gang. We'd built up a strong team and had been joined by a number of Collyhurst and Ancoats lads. So it is perhaps understandable that I didn't get much chance to meet any girls. My best chance, indeed my *only* chance, of meeting the opposite sex was through my work in the market, which was obviously very limited since Smithfield was, in the main, a man's world. But one day Duggie called me over as I was passing his father's stall.

'Hey up, Tommy. I think you've won a girl's heart. My sister, Mavis, told me that Sheila Primshaw who's a secretary in one of them market offices says she quite fancies you. She's a nice-looking girl and so it is quite an honour that she should be interested. She told Mavis that you reminded her of Billy Meredith. Why not give her a try?'

I'd seen this Sheila girl on the rare occasions when I'd had to visit her office on business and I'd always considered her a cut above an ordinary market worker-peasant like me. But how could any man resist it when he heard that a girl fancied him? Every man is conceited and an appeal to his vanity is bound to win him over. As for being like Billy Meredith, she couldn't have said anything more calculated to win my heart. Meredith, our Manchester City hero! Mind you, I couldn't quite see how she made out that I was in any way like him. For a start, I didn't have a moustache like him; his hair was dark and mine was sandy-coloured; his eyes were brown and mine blue. We were about the same height, being just under six feet, but that was about all we had in common. However, I was willing to be per- suaded otherwise. I took a closer look at my face in the mirror and had fresh thoughts. Maybe this Sheila Primshaw lady was right. Maybe I *did* have a look of the Welsh Wizard. For the rest of that day I felt ten feet tall.

I made it my business to find an excuse to introduce myself to this young lady, which wasn't all that easy since she worked as secretary for John Roseman and Company, Fruit Wholesalers, and her workplace was about thirty feet off the ground. Many market concerns had their offices built on stilts high above the market like this, lofty positions from which the occupants were able to look down on the workers below scurry- ing about the surrounding streets like neurotic ants.

Naturally my cronies couldn't resist making comments about her once they knew I might be interested in pursuing her.

'She must be from the blind school,' said Alfie,

'or she's at least short-sighted and can't see very well from that perch above the market.'

'I suppose she considers herself upper class, working in that office in the clouds,' Charlie observed.

'Well, superior anyway I replied. 'I've always wanted a girl I could look up to. As long as she doesn't look down on me as one of the peasants below.'

'It's a bit like Rapunzel in the fairy story,' Jimmy observed. 'You'll have to ask her to let down her hair if you want a date.'

One day I plucked up the courage and found the excuse I'd been looking for to climb the wooden stairs up to her lair. I was very nervous about approaching her and my anxiety got worse with each step I mounted. She was sitting behind her desk and looking very smart and demure when I finally reached the top. There was, however, a peculiar aroma about the office that I couldn't quite place.

'Good morning, sh-sh-'I began.

'Sheila Primshaw,' she said quickly, making a stab at what I was about to say. 'That's my name. Is that what you were going to say?'

'N-n-no, not that. My name's Tommy and what I wanted to know was sh-sh-should I take my cap off in your office? That's all.'

'No need, Tommy. We don't stand on ceremony up here. What was it you wanted?'

'I w-w-was-'

'Wondering if we had any orders for you? Is that it?'

'Y-y-yes, that's it. B-b-b-but I was w-w-wondering if you felt like going out with me some time.'

There, I'd got it out. I was as jumpy as a puppet on a string. I waited for the rejection.

'Mavis told me about you. Your name is Tommy, isn't it? And yes, I'd love to go out with you some time. Where would you suggest we go?'

'I-I was thinking about–'

'I hope you're not going to suggest that Band on the Wall dump. I heard on the market grape-vine that you took Doris Doonican there the other night. It's one remove from a tramps' soup kitchen. I wouldn't be seen dead in the place.'

'Then, wh-wh-wh -?'

'Where do I suggest?'

'Wh-what do you want to do, Sheila?'

'I'll go with you, Tommy, but it would have to be a decent restaurant in Market Street. Like Lockhart's.'

'Fine, Sh-Sh-Sheila. Then wh-wh-?' I was ter-rified in her presence.

'Where shall we meet? Is that what you were trying to say, Tommy?'

'N-n-no, Sheila. I was going to ask when can we meet. But where as well.'

'Let's make it Friday night at seven?'

'Right, Sh-Sh-Sheila. You're on.'

Bathed in sweat from the effort, I descended the staircase. Wow, I thought, that was an ordeal. But at least I've got a date with her.

On the following Friday, we met as arranged and I had to admit that, despite her bossy personality and tendency to talk over my stutter, she was exceptionally pretty and beautifully dressed in a smart two-piece costume. Duck-egg blue, she said it was. I felt proud that she had agreed to go out with me in public. Me, a lowly market hack. But what was that strange scent she was wearing? It smelled like a perfume blended with antiseptic. We shook hands in greeting and I noticed that she did not remove her gloves. At least, I said to myself, her hands look normal – a six or a seven, I should say.

'That's a lovely scent you have on, Sheila,' I said carefully.

'Oh, this? Do you like it? It's my own mixture of eau-de-Cologne and Listerine. I use it on my clothes and as a mouthwash. You can't be too careful nowadays with all these diseases about.'

We went inside and ordered a lovely meal starting with soup followed by a main course of chicken, English new potatoes, cabbage and butter beans. Before we began, Sheila opened her bag and unrolled a table napkin and took out her own set of cutlery. Also her own drinking glass.

'I don't trust the cutlery in these places. I've been reading recently in *Woman's Realm* about Louis Pasteur and how everything around us, everything we touch, is crawling with millions and millions of microbes. We've got to do everything in our power to fight them off.'

We went on to the next course and I noticed how delicately she ate everything, slicing up her food, including the beans, into tiny pieces about the size of a sixpence. If Doris had eaten too quickly, this lady ate painstakingly slowly and the meal lasted over two hours. Throughout, she drank only still mineral water, being unwilling to

take a chance on Corporation pop. We managed
to reach the end of the meal without falling dead
from some terrible disease.

'Wh-wh-what-'

'What about paying the bill and going home
now? Is that what you were going to say?'

'No. I was going to say what about a coffee or a
liqueur to finish off the meal?'

I might just as well have suggested prussic acid,
given her response.

'No, not for me, Tommy. That meal was quite
sufficient for me, thank you. Now, like you, I have
a very early start tomorrow and I think we should
call it a night.'

I walked her back to her home in Ridgeway,
Miles Platting. I wondered how she had sur-
vived living there because the district must have
had its share of germs and bacteria. I shook her
by the gloved hand once more and then im-
pulsively I bent forward to give her a peck on
the cheek.

'What do you think you're doing, Tommy?' she
gasped, as if I'd tried to rape her.

'I was going to kiss you goodnight, that's all.'

'I think we can forgo that tradition, Tommy.
After all, I have enough germs of my own to
contend with without taking yours on board too.'

A few days later I was reporting back, as was expected, to the gang.

'It was like a night out with someone who'd
escaped from Monsall isolation ward.'

Duggie said, 'Our Mavis told me to tell you that
Sheila quite likes you and she wouldn't mind

375

going out with you again.'

'I wouldn't dream of going out with her again unless I'd been sterilized, decontaminated and fumigated in advance,' I said. 'Not only that, because I stutter a little she thinks she has to finish my sentences for me. I wouldn't mind but she usually gets it wrong. Then there's her bloody name. I'd have too much of a problem just trying to pronounce it without stuttering: Sh-Sh-Sheila Primsh-sh-shaw!'

The gang laughed at the way I made fun of myself.

And that's how my second attempt to take a girl out ended. Enough was enough. I cleared my mind of the subject of the opposite sex and for the next few years, I concentrated on football and my job. Somehow, they seemed safer.

Chapter Thirty-Two

After my unlucky experiences at courtship, I settled into a dull but happy routine and the years flitted by almost unnoticed. During this time there were, however, two events in my calendar that stood out sufficiently to merit being described as 'red letter days'.

It was Manchester's proud boast that Smithfield Market was the equivalent any day of London's Covent Garden. Ours had been established as an open-air market, both wholesale and retail, since 1821 but, for a town like ours that was forever crowing that what Manchester thinks today, the rest of the world thinks tomorrow, being equivalent just wasn't good enough. So in the year 1853 to 1854, our huge six-acre fruit-and-vegetable bazaar had been framed and glazed. Now Mancunians could cock a snoot at London by claiming to have the biggest covered market in the world.

To celebrate the fiftieth anniversary of the opening of Manchester's 'crystal palace', the Corporation decided to run Olympic-style athletic competitions for the Smithfield workers. Specially struck medals to be inscribed and presented later with each of the three winners' names had been ordered. The meeting was arranged for a Wednesday in early November 1904, about six weeks before Christmas so as to avoid conflict with the pre-Christmas rush.

There were to be three main races round the perimeter of the market, a distance of about a thousand yards: a meat carcass-carrying competition; a speed-walking race carrying twenty-five baskets on the head; and finally a handcart dash with a full load. There were ten finalists for each of the events. In the meat carcass-carrying category, our particular champion was Alfie, while Charlie and Duggie were down for the basket-carrying contest; I was in for the handcart race. The streets around the market were cordoned off and the finishing line was outside the Market Hall in Goadsby Street where Alderman Herbert Bagshaw, Chairman of the Markets Committee, would be present to congratulate and shake the hands of the winners. Bert O'Neil and his constables were on duty to see that the crowds of excited marketeers thronging the streets did not get out of control and there was no hanky-panky of people trying to nobble any of the competitors.

Before the races began, the thirty competitors paraded like horses at the Derby in front of the market hall where punters could look them over and weigh up their chances. In the meat carcass event, Alfie was clear favourite because of his size and strength and the Smithfield bookies had chalked him up on their boards at 10 to 8; I was marked at 3 to 1; but the punters didn't fancy the chances of either Charlie or Duggie because of their small stature and they were given odds respectively of 10 to 1 and 20 to 1. In our gang, we had been looking forward to the big day for weeks once the date had been announced. We'd thought of doing special training for the games but then, with the exception of Charlie and Duggie, decided against it since we were all fighting fit because of our regular games of football and the physical nature of our jobs.

When the day came round, the only dark cloud on the horizon was the sight of Ginger Mc-Dermott and Mick Malone in the crowd 'cos the pair usually meant trouble. They had both applied to be competitors but had been turned down as the games were strictly for Smithfield workers only and they were hawkers on Tib Street. I hoped they weren't going to cause mischief for I knew from past experience that they could never accept rejection of any kind.

The first event began promptly at 9 a.m. when

Bert O'Neil blew his whistle and the meat porters were off, each humping on their shoulders a carcass of about 150 pounds, the weight of a fully grown man. No trouble for these hefty men who were noted for their beef and their brawn. The cheers and shouts of the watchers could be heard all round the district: 'Go on, Ned! You show 'em!' 'You can do it, Toby!' 'Leave 'em standing, Harry!' Our Alfie, however, was soon in the lead but as the field of competitors reached the corner of Oak Street and Copperas Street, Mick Malone stepped out of the throng and threw a rip-rap firework under the feet of the runners. One poor porter was sent flying in one direction while his hunk of meat went travelling in another. The competitor behind him fell over his body and landed on the deck. The men behind managed to avoid falling over the obstacles but at the cost of being slowed down by having to go round the hazards. The crowd in the vicinity of Mick roared in anger. 'You crazy little bastard, you might have caused serious injury!' yelled one. A constable was soon on the scene and Mick was led away.

Despite the confusion, it made no difference to the outcome for Alfie romped home an easy winner and breasted the tape with ten yards to spare.

The basket balancers were next. Not a competition I would have fancied taking part in as it required not only a fast walking pace but a fine sense of balance. The ten entrants set off in that peculiar mincing walk I'd never been able to imitate. I admired their skill but there were only two real experts in the race and they were rivals for first place. Charlie and Duggie! And no wonder, for they'd spent Sunday after Sunday practising and honing their skill. I'd have bet my life on Charlie but I was wrong because, just as they came round the bend into the final run, Charlie's tower of baskets became unstable and began to wobble. First he tottered, then he teetered, finally he staggered and, to the cheers and jeers of the crowd nearby, the whole lot came down and collapsed in a heap at his feet. Duggie, the 20 to 1 outsider, trotted home triumphantly.

It was the turn of the hand-carters next. When the whistle sounded, we leaped off like bats out of hell pulling our loads of about 340 pounds each. I didn't find it as easy as Alfie to take the lead 'cos I was up against seasoned market porters. I put everything I'd got into the race but a porter named Henry King was hot on my tail and I couldn't shake him off. The one big advantage I had over him was the difference in our ages. I was eighteen and he was around forty and when it came to fitness I had the edge. I put on an extra burst of speed and put a few more yards between us. I was conscious of voices urging me on. Uncle Brodie and Aunty Dorothy, beers in hand, were there on Copperas Street shouting encouragement for all they were worth.

'Come on, Tommy lad. You can do it! You can do it!' Aunty screamed.

'Imagine you're a young Clancy!' called Brodie.

Along Higher Oswald Street, I spotted Joe Brannan in the crowd. 'Show 'em what you can do, Tommy!' he yelled.

Those shouts of encouragement were all I needed to put me well ahead. Then, as we came to the straight along Goadsby Street, I saw him. Ginger McDermott. He had a malicious leer on his face.

'Come on, our Tommy!' he yelled. 'Now cop for this!'

He threw what I imagine was a thunder flash under my cart. There was a very loud bang and several spectators shrieked in panic.

'It's a bloody bomb!' yelled one.

'It's one of them bolshy anarchists!' shouted another.

The explosion gave me extra incentive to get away from the scene and so I kept pulling the cart for all I was worth until just ahead I saw in a blur the portly figure of Alderman Bagshaw and the finishing line. I put on one last effort and broke the tape with my chest. I'd won! Great cheers all round. I was champion Smithfield porter 1904. Worth more to me than winning the real Olympics which were being held at the very same time in America at St Louis, Missouri.

As for Ginger and Mick, they were led away to the cells and, since they were already on probation, were given a month in Strangeways. Will they never learn? I wondered.

Several weeks later we received our medals. We weren't required to attend at Buckingham Palace but only at Manchester Town Hall where we were not only presented with our awards by Mrs Bagshaw, but allowed to kiss her on her thickly-powdered, rouged cheek. The medals were quite something.

On mine it said: 'Smithfield Market Porter Champion. Handcart Dash. First Place. November 9th, 1904.'

The medal was accompanied by a certificate which read: 'This is to certify that Thomas Hopkins won first place in the Handcart Dash in the Smithfield Market Races on Wednesday November 9th, 1904. He is therefore declared as the Champion Market Porter 1904. Signed Alderman Herbert Bagshaw, Chairman of the Market Committee of Manchester Corporation.'

I wondered how my late Grandad Owen would have felt about that when he'd urged me all those years ago 'to go out and be the best at whatever you do'.

Our other two winners received similar awards. For them 1904 was a double celebration for they were keen followers of Manchester City which had won the FA Cup earlier that year when their team had beaten Bolton Wanderers 1-0, the winning goal having been scored by their beloved hero, Billy Meredith. They had been wildly happy at the result but disappointed that they'd been unable to afford the train fare to travel to London. Their personal success in the Smithfield Market Olympics made up for that a little.

My second red letter day occurred almost five years later in 1909 when Manchester United were in the FA Cup Final against Bristol City. Jimmy and I tried to organize a party to go down to the Crystal Palace stadium to support the team. We inquired about return train fares and found that they were much too expensive for many of the lads to go. The answer was a charabanc which could accommodate about fifteen to twenty passengers. The problem was that some of our Archangels team were avid Manchester City football supporters and no way would they consider going to London to support their rivals, the Red Devils. A job of persuasion was called for but it wasn't going to be easy.

'Come on,' I told Alfie and Charlie, the leading lights in the City camp. 'Just for once, forget your hostility. After all, City won the cup five years ago, so now it's the turn of our other Manchester team, surely. Think of the honour to our town. If United wins, it means that our city has won the FA Cup twice.'

'Nothing doing,' said Alfie. 'East is East and West is West. I wouldn't go to see United if they were playing at the end of our street.'

'Right, Alfie. Fair enough,' I said. 'Tell me, who was captain of City when they beat Bolton Wanderers in 1904?'

'Everyone knows that. It was Billy Meredith.'

'And who scored the winning goal that sealed the cup for the team then?'

'What is this? Some sort of general knowledge quiz? You know very well the answer again is Billy Meredith. He was both captain and scorer of the deciding goal.'

'And all of us on our Archangels team supported City on that occasion 'cos we were so proud of Meredith. And you know who's playing on Saturday for United, don't you? It's Billy

Meredith, now on United's team. So if you can't support the Red Devils, come and shout for Billy. We need you in order to afford the charabanc.'

That did the trick. We had seventeen names down for the chara.

Once it was all agreed, it took quite a bit of doing to arrange stand-ins for our market jobs because Saturday was always our busiest time. With a few bribes and lots of extravagant promises, however, we finally found enough substitutes to cover our work for the day. So, going to the Cup Final that year was a costly affair but it was only once in a blue moon, we thought.

'Don't forget to bring plenty of sandwiches for the trip,' I told the lads. 'We've arranged to have a few crates of beer on board, so we shouldn't be thirsty.'

There was a loud cheer at this piece of news.

'And one last thing,' I added. 'Don't forget to bring a big umbrella 'cos there's no roof on this bus. Let's hope it doesn't rain. It can also be very cold so bring a big overcoat or mac and a neck muffler as well.'

The twenty-seater motor coach with its uniformed, be-goggled driver picked us up outside the Harp and Shamrock pub on New Mount Street at 4 a.m. Many of our party did a fair amount of whingeing about the early hour.

'Call this early?' I exclaimed when they were all settled. 'For us market workers, this is late. I'm told that the trip can take about nine to ten hours and so if we're to reach London in good time for the kick-off, we had no choice. Anyroad, you can have a good nap on the way down.'

Few actually took advantage to have a snooze as we were too excited at going so far away from our natural haunts and seeing London for the first time. Not that we'd have much time for sightseeing since it was straight into the match and then home again afterwards.

'For those of you interested,' our driver announced, 'we'll be taking the A34 through Cheshire as far south as Cannock then on to the A5 for the rest of the way through Towcester, Stony Stratford, and St Albans. After that we'll be on the outskirts of London.'

Most of these places sounded foreign to our ears 'cos none of us had ever been this far afield before. He could just as well have announced that we'd be going through Timbuktu and Casablanca for all we knew about them.

'Do you think we're going to make it all the way to London in this charabanc?' Charlie asked the driver. 'I mean, they're made for outings to the seaside, to places like Blackpool, Southport, and New Brighton.'

Our driver seemed a bit miffed on hearing this belittling of his coach as he was proud of his chariot and what it could do. He was the talkative type, as most bus and taxi drivers are, and only too glad to put us 'young shavers' right about a few things.

'Don't you worry your head, young sir,' he chuckled. 'We'll make it all right and with time to spare. Why, lots of ladies drive cars nowadays; they're known as motorinas. Not only that, four years ago, a young lady named Dorothy Levitt drove from London to Liverpool and back all by herself in a De Dion Bouton. She was hailed as a public heroine. If she could do it, I'm sure we can manage it in this big wonderful charabanc of mine. Just remember, too, that this is the year that some young Frenchman named Louis Blériot is going to fly an aeroplane non-stop across the Channel. Have faith! I think I can safely say that we'll make it to Crystal Palace in dear old Lizzie here.'

'I'm glad this Blériot bloke is going to fly *non-stop* across the Channel,' Charlie laughed, 'because otherwise he'll land in the drink.'

'What exactly is a charabanc? Does anyone know?' asked Duggie.

Our driver was only too willing to supply the information. 'A charabanc,' he recited, as if reading it from a book, 'is short for the French *char-à-bancs*, which meant originally a carriage with wooden benches along the sides. The seats are a bit more comfortable nowadays.'

As far as Stony Stratford, our team of supporters sat quietly enjoying the beauty of the English countryside while Jimmy spent his time exchanging technical information with the driver about the combustion engine and the size and make of this particular motor. A subject, sad to say, to which none of us could contribute since we hadn't a clue what made the wheels of these horseless carriages go round.

'Is it difficult to drive one of these buses?' Jimmy asked.

'Not when you get used to all the levers. Sometimes I think you need to be an octopus to deal with them all at the same time. But what I would appreciate most when driving one of these things would be a big rear-view mirror and a speedo-meter as it's not always easy to keep within the speed limit. Also, at night it'd be helpful if we had brighter lights 'cos at the moment we have only these oil lamps and the motor horn to warn people we're coming. We've got to keep our eyes skinned in the fading light, I can tell you.'

'What if you hit an animal – a dog or a chicken?' Jimmy asked.

'Tough,' the driver replied.

Personally I was more concerned about the weather and I thanked the Lord that it remained dry and that we had no need for the umbrellas. At Stony Stratford we stopped for refreshments at the Bull Inn because we'd polished off our own provisions within the first hour of the journey. And while we were emptying our bladders, the driver took the opportunity to fill up his fuel cans with fresh supplies.

'This is one of the few places that we can replenish our petrol,' the driver said.

'How do you go on for fuel on a long journey like this?' Jimmy asked.

'Not easy. We sometimes have to buy it at chemist shops or even haberdashers, believe it or not. On a long journey like this, though, we have to carry our own supply in several two-gallon tin drums.'

As we were driving along, we suddenly spotted what looked like a boy scout waving a red AA flag. Our coach driver slowed down, gave him a cheery wave back and then continued on his way.

'What was all that about?' I asked.

The driver laughed. 'He's an Automobile Association Scout and he's been posted there to warn us about a police speed trap ahead. The bobbies hide in the bushes with a stopwatch, ready to pounce on any vehicle going over the regulated twenty miles an hour. It's one of the services the AA offer us drivers.'

After St Alban's, the sense of excitement and expectation became noticeably greater and the talk switched from the journey to the subject of football, both the players themselves and United's prospects.

'I hope you United lads haven't forgotten,' Alfie said, trying to stir it, 'that United lost against Bristol City one nil only two weeks ago in the league match.'

'Don't be so bloody miserable,' replied Charlie. 'It doesn't matter what happened two weeks ago. Today will be different, you'll see. The Reds are clear favourites 'cos they were league champions last year. Is there anything else you City supporters can find wrong? I'm sure if you rack your brains, you can find something.'

'There's another problem, Charlie,' Duggie said with a malicious grin. 'Both teams play in red shirts. So what are you going to do about that? That's got you.'

'If you'd read the *Manchester Evening News* this week,' Jimmy said, 'you'd know that Bristol are going to play in blue and United in white.'

'Not only that,' I added, 'the white shirts were specially designed by Billy Meredith himself. The shirt will have a red V-shape sash down the front and be made of heavyweight cotton.'

'Yeah, I read about that,' Alfie said. 'Billy runs a sports shop as a sideline and I'll bet he's making a small fortune in addition to his four pound a week at United. That's a lot better than when he was working in the coal mine as a pit pony driver on a pound a week.'

'And good luck to him,' added Charlie.

'Four pounds a week and the shop takings! There's money for you, isn't it!' Jimmy exclaimed in a corny Welsh accent.

'I love the way Billy always plays with a toothpick in his mouth,' I added. 'Just to show how easy it is to play brilliant football.'

'I read somewhere,' Charlie said, 'that he used to chew tobacco until the laundry women complained and refused to wash his shirts. Said they couldn't get the spit out. So he switched to toothpicks instead to help his concentration.'

'Eh, to change the subject,' Gordon said, 'I read that all eleven Bristol players are English while United has a mixed team of seven English, three Scottish, and one Welshman.'

'That's correct,' Jimmy said, 'but they're all British so what's it matter? Alex Bell, Jimmy Turnbull and Sandy Turnbull are Scottish, and then, of course, there's the Welsh Wizard himself, Billy Meredith. But the other seven, Harry Moger, George Stacey, Vince Hayes, Dick Duckworth, George Wall and Charlie Roberts, the captain, are all English through and through.'

It was nearly two o'clock when we arrived. We found our seats and settled down to wait for the three o'clock kick-off. The Crystal Palace stadium gradually filled up until it was packed to the

389

rafters. The sight of such a vast assembly of human beings in one place filled us with awe, even a vague fear. We learned later that there were over 71,000 spectators present.

'This is how I imagine the Valley of Josaphat will be,' said Gordon, his voice trembling in wonder as he looked round at the vast hordes of people standing and sitting in tiered ranks, 'when all the nations of the world that have ever lived on earth will be gathered together for the day of the Last Judgement.'

'Shut up, Gordon,' barked Charlie, 'or you'll have us all wetting our pants.'

The match began on time and Gordon had a point about the crowd, for the sounds that came from 71,000 throats all at the one time, moaning, groaning, sighing, yelling, bawling were enough to put the fear of God in the bravest of hearts.

It was a great match to watch and when Sandy Turnbull fired the ball past goalkeeper Harry Clay to give United the winning goal, you could have heard the roar that went up from the throng of United supporters all the way back in Manchester. The icing on the cake, which pleased the United lads and also our Blue companions, was when Billy Meredith was announced as Man of the Match for his outstanding performance at outside right. Even our reluctant City supporters had to admit it had been a stupendous match.

It took over an hour for us to get settled back on our coach. On the way back, it turned dusk and as our driver hadn't fancied driving in the gloom, the coach company had arranged for overnight

390

accommodation at the Old Sugar Loaf Inn in Dunstable in Buckinghamshire. Up bright and early on Sunday and after a breakfast of bacon butties and large mugs of tea, we were on the road again by 7 a.m. All the way back to Buxton, we sang the popular songs of the day.

'The Man Who Broke the Bank at Monte Carlo', 'Oh! Oh! Antonio!', 'Put Me Among the Girls', 'Down at the Old Bull and Bush', 'Comrades', 'Beer, Beer, Glorious Beer', and as we reached the outskirts of Manchester, 'Land of Hope and Glory'.

We reached Ancoats around three o'clock in the afternoon, having stopped once or twice for celebratory drinks at coaching inns along the route. What a day it had been! One that none of us would ever forget. Why, even our unwilling City supporters had to admit that it'd been truly the Reddest of Red Letter Days!

Chapter Thirty-Three

I had been a market porter for over five years and during that time had built up a good business of loyal customers. Most of my regular commissions were fairly easy, many of them half-hour jobs involving the simple carrying of greengrocers' orders out to their own transport parked on the edge of the market. For these I usually charged no more than half a crown. Others were more demanding, like the one to the fruit kiosk on Victoria Station, which involved lugging a heavy load of crates down the steep incline of Balloon Street and on to the smooth macadam of the station approach. There was always the danger that I would lose control down the hill and the crates of oranges and apples would break loose and roll away under their own steam down to the Victoria concourse. For this job I usually asked for a little more and I thought five shillings was a reasonable charge. In a good week, after paying one pound for the hire of the cart, I was left with around thirty-five shillings, a wage which put me, I suppose, in the high earnings category. My best job was still the daily commission to Ernie Ogden in Gaylor Street. Over the years, his orders had increased in size and complexity and so my charge had gone up accordingly until I was now collecting seven and six or eight shillings a day from him alone. This job took me up Oldham Road every day at around seven thirty.

As I crossed over Thompson Street, I used to pass a number of young women in clogs going in the other direction on their way to work in the mills and factories around the district. They usually travelled in little groups of three or four and were totally wrapped up in themselves, talking about their problems and affairs, sometimes enjoying a joke about some private matter. In one of these little groups there was a really attractive young lady who stood out from the rest and who had caught my eye a few weeks ago. She had auburn hair, rosy cheeks, blue eyes and, though she joined in the laughter, seemed a little quieter than her companions. I'd have loved to talk to her but if I'd tried to exchange greetings with her or any of her friends, I am sure I'd have become tongue-tied and my stammer would have appeared, so ruining everything. And if they'd laughed at my attempt to wish them good day, well, it didn't bear thinking about. I'd have been so petrified that it would have been the end of any further attempts at being sociable.

Sometimes, I felt that my pals in the Archangel gang had left me behind when it came to conquests with the opposite sex. We were all now in our early twenties and the others seemed to have found steady girlfriends. Duggie had married Doris a year ago and they were now running their own independent market stall: Dimson and Doonican; Jimmy was engaged to Angela Rocca; Alfie and Charlie had 'clicked' one night with a pair of girls they'd picked up on Oldham Street; Gordon hadn't shown any interest in girls and had even been talking about joining the priesthood. The way things were going, they'd all be settled in their own little grooves and I'd be left still looking for my ideal wife.

As for the young lady who'd attracted my attention on Oldham Road, I decided to bide my time until she didn't have all those workmates around her. My patience was eventually rewarded when one morning I found her walking alone. She seemed deep in thought as if she had something on her mind and I decided to put off approaching her as it didn't seem like the right time to butt into her thoughts. What if she snubbed me? That would have sent me scurrying back into my shell and no mistake. For the next few weeks, I must have passed her half a dozen times and given her a friendly nod but she was so preoccupied, she didn't seem to notice me at all. One morning, though, my chance came and, catching her once again without her friends, I decided to take my courage in both hands and speak to her.

I took a deep breath and gave her a cheery, 'Good morning. Sh-sh-should be a fine day today, I think.'

She smiled in my direction. 'Yes, I hope so,' she said quietly.

I continued on my way up Oldham Road, my heart thumping in my ribs. What a soppy thing for me to say! But there, I'd done it. Actually spoken to her and she'd answered me and recognized my existence. In many ways it had been quite a daring thing for her to do, replying the way she did, because women weren't supposed to speak to strange men on the street. Maybe my cart reassured her and she could see that I was a working man and not some crazy pervert. But that's by the by for, when she turned her head and smiled at me, my heart did a double somersault. Now, after all these years since Miss Corbett had drummed Robbie Burns's poems into our heads, I fully understood what the poet meant when he wrote:

I have heard the mavis singing
His love song to the morn
I have seen the dew-drop clinging
To the rose just newly born.
But a sweeter song has cheer'd me

394

At the ev'ning's gentle close
And I've seen an eye still brighter
Than the dew-drop on the rose.
'Twas thy voice, my gentle Mary
And thine artless, winning smile
That made this world an Eden
Bonnie Mary of Argyll.

I loved especially those bits about the gentle voice and the artless, winning smile. Anyroad, at least I'd made a start, not that I entertained much hope that such a lovely girl would look at me twice.

Pulling my barrow, I passed the same young lady every morning, sometimes alone and sometimes not, and fell into the habit of nodding and greeting her with the same rubbishy remarks about the weather. I really liked the look of her and, even though she said only the briefest of sentences in reply, the tender tone of her voice touched my heartstrings. Not that I could expect her to offer very much as an answer as my polite good mornings gave her little chance to say anything except to agree with my remarks about the elements.

'Turned out nice again' or 'Cold wind, today' or 'Looks like it might rain later'.

She always gave me that heart-melting smile and agreed with me but I really felt stupid that the best I could come up with were these observations about the climate. She must think I'm a walking barometer and work in the Manchester weather bureau or something, I told myself. The trouble was that I was too shy to say anything else. I would have loved to ask her out for a drink or for a meal but it just wasn't the done thing, and supposing she turned me down? I'd never recover from it. Anyroad, I'd be very surprised if a nice-looking lady like this didn't have a boyfriend already.

I mentioned my problem to Jimmy Dixon.

'Is she wearing clogs when you see her?'

'Yes, she is.'

'If she's on that part of Oldham Road at that particular time in the morning and wearing clogs, the chances are that she works at Westmacott's, the mineral water firm in Ancoats. You remember my fiancée, Angela Rocca, from St William's?'

'Are you trying to be funny, Jimmy? As if I could forget!'

He grinned. 'Of course, Tommy. I'd almost forgotten. You fancied her yourself when we were infants, didn't you?'

'That was a very long time ago, Jimmy.'

'Well, it so happens that Angela works at Westmacott's and I'll ask her if she can throw any light on this mysterious woman that Cupid seems to have picked out for you.'

A couple of days later he came back with the result of his inquiries.

'I was right,' he said. 'She does work at Westmacott's and her name is Kate Lally. What's more, she's a good friend of Angela's. And here's the icing on the cake, Tommy. She used to have a boyfriend but recently broke up with him.'

'You mean she's free?' I gasped.

'According to Angela, she is.'

'I'd love to ask her out on a date, Jimmy, but

396

I'm too nervous in case she tells me what I can do. What would a lovely girl like this Kate want with a lowly market porter like me?'

'Don't ask me!' Jimmy chuckled. 'But a faint heart never won a fair lady. So this is what I'm going to do. I've spoken to Angela about it and we're going to organize a night out at the theatre with Angela and myself; also a work friend of theirs called Hilda plus Kate's brother, Danny. You and Kate will make the party up to six. Are you on?'

'I'm on all right, Jimmy, but will this Kate Lally agree to go out with an unknown such as me? Why, I could be anybody!'

'That remains to be seen, Tommy, but we can only try to use our powers of persuasion. We won't say anything about you and then you can become her mystery man. Angela remembers you very well from the infants school, of course, and I'm sure that Kate will trust Angela's judgement. She knows that she wouldn't fix her up on a blind date with someone repulsive or someone who's just escaped from the asylum.'

And that's how things worked out. Jimmy and Angela booked a private box for the second house at the Grand Theatre for the following Friday night. I was a bit worried about the cost at first until Jimmy explained that it would be shared between the three men. The show, he told me, was a variety of acts, including singers, comedians, acrobats, jugglers and so on but the star was the famous Harry Lauder. I listened to Jimmy outlining the programme but hardly paid him much attention. I was far too worried about what Kate

Lally was going to say when she found out that her escort for the evening was to be the stuttering man who gave her the morning weather report. For the two nights before we were due to go out together, I hardly slept a wink. Then I worried some more in case I looked haggard through lack of sleep.

When the Friday evening came round, I first had a good wash-down with Pears soap, after which I honed my cutthroat on a leather strap and gave myself the closest shave I'd ever had. I examined my face carefully in the mirror, hoping against hope that I hadn't developed a pimple or two or nicked myself with the razor. I seemed to look all right but decided to make sure my face was smooth enough by giving myself a second shave. I must buy one of these new safety razors one of these days, I vowed. I'm sure they'll make a better job of it. And if I'm supposed to have a look of Billy Meredith, maybe I should grow a moustache like his.

I cleaned my teeth with Calvert's tooth powder, gargled with a breath-freshener, and brushed my hair carefully. Then it was on with my best white shirt, my starched collar, and the new tie I'd bought specially for this occasion. Lastly I put on my navy-blue Sunday suit and my best black shoes which I'd polished until they were gleaming. My old dad would have approved of them. Finally I was ready.

As I stood on Oldham Road waiting to board the electric tram to town, a shiver of joy suddenly ran down my spine. And I had the strangest feeling that tonight was going to be a major turning point in my life and all that had gone before had been no more than preparation for things to come.

Chapter Thirty-Four

The second house of the variety Jimmy had booked for was due to begin at eight fifteen and we'd agreed to meet outside the Grand on Peter Street half an hour before the show was to begin. This would allow us to have a chat and a drink in the theatre bar before the performance. I had never visited the Grand before as my only experience of the theatre had been Friday-night excursions to St James's music hall on Oxford Road to see and join in the melodramas. The Grand was considered to be a cut above a music hall like that, which was another reason for my nervousness. I found the terms used for this theatre's seating arrangements strange and hard to understand. Like the gallery (also called the gods) which I always thought was a place for shooting practice or for displaying art; there was the circle which wasn't a circle but was divided into the upper circle and the dress circle, the latter, I suppose, intended for toffs who were expected to turn up in dress suits. Finally there were the stalls, a really peculiar word for a theatre since we market people used it to describe the place where we kept our donkeys. Other terms were a complete mystery to me, for example the orchestra stalls where the musicians definitely did not sit, and one which I couldn't even pronounce, the *fauteuils*, let alone understand who it was meant for. And our little party was booked into the snootiest of them all – a private box. I hoped I was dressed right – I'd left my cloth cap behind as Jimmy had advised against it.

'Not quite right for a visit to the theatre,' he'd said.

I hoped, too, that I didn't put my foot in it by doing or saying the wrong thing. Living on my own in a bedsitter, I was likely to forget such niceties as remembering to stand up in the presence of a lady and opening the door for her. How I envied Jimmy as he always seemed so confident and at home in places like this. It wouldn't have done for me to arrive late on this first date and in my anxiety I overcompensated by getting there much too early. At half past seven I could be seen pacing up and down waiting for the others to arrive and if I'd been wearing the right uniform, I'd have been mistaken for the commissionaire who had been eyeing me suspiciously. At the appointed time, Angela and Jimmy arrived all dolled up to the nines and, to my eye, dressed as if they truly belonged to this scene of elegantly attired theatre-goers. Dark-haired, dark-eyed Angela was just as attractive as I recalled her being at St William's Infants School and I remembered why I had always fancied her so long ago.

'Glad you made it, Tommy,' Jimmy said cheerily. 'For a while you had me wondering whether you might do a runner.'

'I very nearly did, Jimmy,' I laughed.

'Good to see you again after all this time,' Angela said. 'Kate is really looking forward to meeting you.'

'I'm sure she is,' I grinned. 'She won't know if she's going to meet Jack the Ripper or the Hunchback of Notre Dame.'

'She should be so lucky,' Jimmy chuckled.

'My nerves have been shot to pieces waiting for this evening to come,' I said, feeling in my pocket for my cigarettes. To my dismay I found that in my rush to be on time, I'd forgotten to buy any.

'I badly need a smoke,' I said. 'Look, I'll just slip into the theatre kiosk to buy some. Shan't be five minutes. I'll also make myself useful by buying a couple of programmes.'

'Listen to Mr Moneybags,' Jimmy guffawed. 'Don't forget to come back.'

I was away for more than five minutes, however, as I found that cigarettes and programmes were available only in the theatre bar on the first floor. As I came down the stairs, I saw her and my heart skipped a beat. She was there with her brother Danny and another young, nice-looking lady in a hat that looked as if it could have been designed on a Smithfield Market fruit stall. But I only had eyes for Kate who looked even more lovely than when I'd greeted her on her way to work. She was dressed in a fur-collared coat and cream kid gloves with pearl buttons; at her neck she wore a cameo brooch and from her ears hung two beautiful drop earrings. She had applied a touch of lipstick and only a mere suggestion of face powder as she hardly needed it, given her fresh, country-girl complexion. She belonged in a fashion magazine and the sight of her confirmed what I already sensed deep down. I was in love with her. She was the girl I'd dreamed and talked about for so long.

I approached the group with the broadest smile I could muster, given the butterflies in my stomach. There were introductions all round and with Jimmy in charge of the presentations, there was no need for shyness as he never hesitated to say what was on his mind. After much handshaking and 'how-do-you-doing', Jimmy spoke to Danny's young lady, who'd given her name as Hilda.

'That's a beautiful hat you have on there. Makes you look taller and definitely becomes you. And I love those cherry things dangling on the top.'

Trust Jimmy to be blunt and hand out loaded, sarcastic compliments.

Hilda blushed with what I thought was pleasure but it couldn't have been for she excused herself and came back a few moments later minus the headgear. I heard her whisper later to Angela, 'If Jimmy liked it, there must be something wrong with it.'

While Hilda had been away, Kate and I had exchanged greetings.

'But I already know him,' she told the others. 'He's my weather man and I see him almost every morning on my way to work.'

'The real name of your weather man,' Jimmy chuckled, 'is Tommy Hopkins and he's been a good pal of mine ever since we were at school together.'

'I hope you don't feel let down to find I'm to be your escort for the evening,' I said to Kate.

'On the contrary' she smiled. 'I'm so relieved it's you. When Angela told me she'd arranged a blind date for me, I wasn't sure who I was going to get. I'm so pleased it's someone I know.'

'I should bloody well hope so,' said Jimmy, grinning at me. 'Once Tommy knew that Angela was a friend of yours, he's not stopped pestering for an introduction. Anyway, let's not stand outside here in the cold wasting good drinking time. Let's go in and have one at the bar.'

The saloon bar on the first floor was crowded when we got there but we managed to find a free table and we left the ladies to their conversation while we men pushed our way through the throng around the counter. Jimmy managed to catch the eye of the bartender and ordered the drinks: lager for us and port and lemon for the ladies.

'Well, what do you think, Tommy?'

'I'm really happy, Jimmy, and grateful to you for fixing things up. As for Kate, she's a smasher, the best-looking lady I've ever been out with.'

Danny overheard my remark. 'I'll tell my sister what you said when we get home.' He grinned. 'Like every other lady, she loves a compliment.'

'I can see you've got it bad, Tommy.' Jimmy laughed as he handed me the tray with the port-and-lemons. 'Now don't spill the ladies' drinks in your excitement.'

Before leaving the counter, I ordered and paid for the same round for the interval, the drinks to be left at a prearranged place in the bar.

The talk around our table flowed easily, thanks

403

to Jimmy acting as our master of ceremonies, encouraging us to forget our shyness and take part in the conversation.

'This is my first visit to the theatre,' Kate said, 'and being booked into our own private box makes me feel like Queen Alexandra. Should I wave to the people in the auditorium?'

'Maybe not advisable,' Jimmy said. 'Famous people have been known to get shot sometimes in their private boxes. Think of poor old Abraham Lincoln.'

'What about opera glasses or lorgnettes, Jimmy?' Angela asked. 'I've always fancied myself acting the part of a toff.'

'I think you'll find,' Jimmy chuckled, 'that you are so close to the stage, you won't need any opera glasses. It should be a really good show tonight. Not only do we have Harry Lauder, we have lots of top-class supporting acts.'

We downed our drinks and went into the main auditorium. We found that Jimmy had been absolutely right and we were taken aback at just how close we were to the stage.

'I don't know about *watching* the show,' I remarked. 'I think we're going to be in it!'

The fireproof safety curtain was down when we took our seats and so for the first ten minutes we spent the time reading the various advertisements on it telling us among other things about Bovril, Peek Frean's Biscuits, Boddington's Beer, Black Cat Cigarettes and of course Abdullah Turkish Cigarettes. When Hilda took a black cigarette out and inserted it into her long cigarette holder, I felt as if I was sharing the box with royalty.

The safety curtain slowly lifted, the musicians of the orchestra emerged one by one through the small door in front of the stage, switched on the little lights on their music stands, and began to tune up. The hum of conversation gradually died down and there was an atmosphere of expectation in the tobacco-filled air. There followed a roll of the drums and everyone automatically stood to attention for the national anthem.

The show opened with a variety of minor acts: performing dogs, a magician who closed his tricks by sawing a woman in half to the gasps of horror from all the ladies, our own included, a team of foreign-looking acrobats who built up a human pyramid with the top man practically in our box. I could have shaken his hand or patted him on the cheek. Next came a red-nosed comedian in a loud check suit who told a series of smutty jokes and finished with a vulgar song about how you can do a lot of things at the seaside that you can't do in the town:

Fancy seeing Mother with her legs all bare
Paddling in the fountains in Trafalgar Square

The use of the word 'bare' was enough to have the ladies in our group blushing in embarrassment.

Last of the introductory acts was a tenor with a wobbly voice singing about his silver-haired mother and his lost love who appeared to have walked out on him.

'With a voice like that,' Jimmy chuckled, 'I'm not surprised.'

At the interval we retired to the bar and were relieved to find that a tray with my name on it and our pre-ordered drinks were exactly where we had arranged. The generous tip I had given the bartender had been worth it.

The minor acts of the first half of the show were more than compensated for by the excellent performance of Harry Lauder with his funny stories about Scottish meanness and his superb rendering of many well-known Scottish ditties: 'Roamin' in the Gloamin', 'I Love a Lassie', 'Stop Your Tickling Jock' and 'Wee Deoch an Doris'.

Too soon, the evening came to an end.

'Well then, Kate,' I said as we were saying our goodnights outside the theatre, 'what did you think of it?'

'I loved every moment of it, Tommy, and I shall treasure this evening as long as I live. Thank you so much for escorting me and looking after me.' Then with a big smile on her face, she added, 'I shall expect your weather report as usual on Monday morning when you pass me on Oldham Road.'

'I loved it too,' I grinned, 'and, if I'm now part of your morning routine, I must make sure my weather forecast is accurate.'

'A most enjoyable evening,' declared Angela. 'We must do it again.'

'Leave it with Angela and me,' Jimmy told the party. 'We'll book for next Friday.'

'We'll look forward to that,' Hilda and Danny said together.

'And so will I,' Kate said, shaking Jimmy's

hand. 'When Angela first told me that you two had arranged this evening, I must admit I wasn't sure. But I've enjoyed it thoroughly, thanks to you both and Tommy's kind attention.'

'That'll be great,' I added warmly, 'but maybe next time, we'll book ordinary seats so that we are not part of the show.'

Everyone laughed and we parted company outside the theatre.

A little later, as I sat on the upper deck of the tram rattling its way up Oldham Road, I went over the events of the evening in my mind. The most wonderful I'd ever had and one that I'd never wanted to end. The details went round and round in my head: the genial company and the conversation that had flowed so easily and happily; the show itself with the variety of entertaining acts but especially the magnificent performance of Harry Lauder. And imprinted on my brain forever would be the sight of Kate standing there with her brother Danny as I came down the stairs from the theatre bar. To my eye, she'd been a vision of loveliness. Most of all there had been the sheer joy of her company for the last three hours.

What were my chances with her? I wondered. She'd sounded pretty keen when Angela had suggested fixing up another date with the same little group, so I must have made a good impression. Kate was my ideal but was I letting my hopes run away with me in even considering her as a possible life partner? Who did I think I was, imagining that such a beautiful girl would look at me twice? Just the same, when I looked back over my life and recalled the pain and the loss of so many people dear to me, I knew that Kate Lally was the one for me. She would be fresh hope, a new start, and a new life. And who knows, perhaps a family and a home of my own where I felt I truly belonged. How I longed for such a thing after being kicked around for most of my life from pillar to post.

Then a flood of negative thoughts filled my mind. What if she turned me down? I'd never get over it and that would be me finished. Wait a minute, I said to myself. Why do you always think about being given the push? Start thinking positively. What was it Jimmy had said to me: 'A faint heart never won a fair lady'? It was time I stopped these ideas of rejection before I'd even popped the question. A little voice told me to have courage. If Kate is the one, then don't let her get away. We have another date for next Friday and there's no reason why we shouldn't have lots more after that. I only know that I had a great time tonight and so did Kate. If we have enough great times like tonight, I'm going to go down on a bended knee and ask her to be my wife. As for me being rejected, that's a chance I'll just have to take.

I was suddenly awakened from my reverie by the tram conductor.

'Tickets, please,' he called. 'Come on, Rip Van Winkle, let's have your money.'

'Sorry, I was miles away thinking of something else,' I said, handing him my fare.

'Yeah, but is she worth it?' the conductor asked

with a cheeky grin.

'Oh, yes,' I replied in the same vein. 'Take it from me. She's worth it!'

Author's Note

If you would like to know what happens after Tommy's meeting with Kate, you will find that Kate herself has given a full account in *Kate's Story* which has been described as:

'A journey of hope and heartache which takes Kate from the hardships of the workhouse to the dubious comforts of a position in service to the rich; from the joys of marriage to a good man, to the sorrows and losses suffered during the Great War.

'Through it all, Kate fights against the odds with determination. Guided by her indomitable spirit and sense of humour, she discovers that it is possible to find contentment despite all that life can throw at her. Nostalgic and poignant, *Kate's Story* is a truly heart-warming read, rich in Billy Hopkins' trademarks of warmth, laughter and triumph over adversity.'

The publishers hope that this book has given you enjoyable reading. Large Print Books are especially designed to be as easy to see and hold as possible. If you wish a complete list of our books please ask at your local library or write directly to:

Magna Large Print Books
Magna House, Long Preston,
Skipton, North Yorkshire.
BD23 4ND

This Large Print Book for the partially sighted, who cannot read normal print, is published under the auspices of

THE ULVERSCROFT FOUNDATION